The Rock Music Imagination

For the Record: Lexington Studies in Rock and Popular Music

Series Editors:
Scott D. Calhoun, Cedarville University
Christopher Endrinal, Florida Gulf Coast University

For the Record: Lexington Studies in Rock and Popular Music features monographs and edited collections that examine topics relevant to the composition, consumption, and influence of the rock and popular music genres which have arisen starting in the twentieth century in all nations and cultures. In the series, scholars approach these genres from music studies, cultural studies, and sociological studies frameworks, and may incorporate theories and methods from literary, philosophical, performance, and religious studies, in order to examine the wider significance of particular artists, subgenres, fandoms, or other music-related phenomena. Books in the series use as a starting point the understanding that as both products of our larger culture and driving forces within that wider culture, rock and popular music are worthy of critical study.

Advisory Board

Joshua Duchan, Wayne State University; David Easley, Oklahoma City Univer-sity; Bryn Hughes, University of Miami; Greg McCandless, Full Sail University; Ann van der Mer-we, Miami University; Meg Wilhoite

Titles in the Series

The Rock Music Imagination, by Robert McParland
From Factory Girls to K-Pop Idol Girls: Cultural Politics of Developmentalism, Patriarchy, and Neoliberalism in South Korea's Popular Music Industry, by Gooyong Kim
Rock and Romanticism: Blake, Wordsworth, and Rock from Dylan to U2, edited by James Rovira
The Beatles, Sgt. Pepper, and the Summer of Love: Roll Up for the Mystery Tour! edited by Kenneth Womack and Katheryn Cox
U2 Above, Across, and Beyond: Interdisciplinary Assessments, edited by Scott D. Calhoun

The Rock Music Imagination

Robert McParland

LEXINGTON BOOKS
Lanham • Boulder • New York • London

Published by Lexington Books
An imprint of The Rowman & Littlefield Publishing Group, Inc.
4501 Forbes Boulevard, Suite 200, Lanham, Maryland 20706
www.rowman.com

6 Tinworth Street, London SE11 5AL

Copyright © 2019 by The Rowman & Littlefield Publishing Group, Inc.

All rights reserved. No part of this book may be reproduced in any form or by any electronic or mechanical means, including information storage and retrieval systems, without written permission from the publisher, except by a reviewer who may quote passages in a review.

British Library Cataloguing in Publication Information Available

Library of Congress Cataloging-in-Publication Data

ISBN: 978-1-4985-8852-2 (cloth)
ISBN: 978-1-4985-8853-9 (electronic)
ISBN: 978-1-4985-8854-6 (pbk.)

Contents

Acknowledgments		vii
Introduction: Themes in Classic Rock Music—Rebellion, Utopia, and Liberation		1
1	Listening to the Blues	15
2	The Imaginative Legacy of the Beats: Countercultural Utopia	41
3	Science Fiction Imagination and Fantasy in Progressive Rock	61
4	The End of the World as We Know It: Rock Music Dystopia	87
5	Rock Romanticism: Power Chords and the Visionary Company	115
6	Paperback Writers: Rock Music and Fiction	137
7	Human Rights, Community, and Global Rock	159
Selected Bibliography		187
Index		197
About the Author		209

Acknowledgments

This book is dedicated to music creators and listeners who continue to sustain hope in our world with imagination. Thank you to the musicians who have taken the time for conversation. Thanks also to Colin Helb, a fine teacher and musician, for his thoughtful reading, and to Thomas Kitts for coordinating rock music panels annually at the American Culture/Popular Culture Association conferences. I offer my gratitude to the folks at Lexington: Courtney Morales, who ushered this manuscript along, Lindsey Porambo, who acquired and encouraged it, and the editors of the "For the Record" series.

Introduction

Themes in Classic Rock Music—Rebellion, Utopia, and Liberation

Imagination is the source and spark of rock music. Rock music imagination expresses creativity and utopian dreams of transcendence amid hard realities and a quest for freedom. Some rock music listeners have remarked on rock's waning cultural influence but, in the words of Neil Young, rock can never die if it retains the imagination in which it was born. *The Rock Music Imagination* is about rock music dreams and rock music themes. It is an exploration of rock artists in their social and artistic contexts, particularly between 1964 and 1980, and of rock music in relation to literature: journalistic expression, fantastic imagination, and contemporary fiction about rock. As emotion, spectacle, sound, and imaginative expression, rock music brings us songs, stories, music journalism, and recordings. Loud, brash, extreme, rock welcomes a verbal medium that matches its colorful life and energy. So, this book considers the literature of rock. With flights of imagination and analysis of rock's cultural impact, rock music writing has quested after those "unities of imagination" that Greil Marcus sought in America. It seeks to discover how rock music touches our imaginative lives.[1]

Here we will look at themes that appear often in classic rock music: freedom and liberation, utopia/dystopia, community, rebellion, the outsider, the quest for transcendence, monstrosity, erotic/spiritual love, imaginative vision, and mystery. The "sixties" has a centrality in many discussions of rock music. *The Rock Music Imagination* embraces that pivotal point in rock music history, recognizing the imagination and creativity of blues and jazz artists, folk-rock and hard-rock musicians, female rock musicians, and progressive rock creators. It focuses on blues imagination, countercultural dreams of utopia, rock's critiques of society and images of dystopia, rock's inheritance from romanticism, science fiction and mythic imagination in progressive rock, and rock's global reach and potential to provide hope and humanitarian assistance. This study of rock music imagination recognizes that what we hear, the song-text, is mediated by how we imagine rock, or where rock takes our imagination. We encounter rock music in connection with images and writings about rock—journalistic, academic, fictional, or biographical. What we read about rock and how we talk about it affects our reception of it.

Expressions and descriptions of rock music tug us toward asking a central question: What is rock? The broadest definition of rock will embrace a multiplicity of styles and thousands of songs. Deep Purple pushes up the volume and crunches out the chords for "Smoke on the Water." Led Zeppelin plays "Kashmir" and it sounds rich with exoticism and incense. What is rock? Is it Metallica or Simon and Garfunkel? The Velvet Underground or Imagine Dragons? The Beatles ring out a sixth chord to end "She Loves You."[2] The Stones' "Jumpin' Jack Flash" rides on a blues riff. The Doors choose to have "Light My Fire" not resolve on the I (tonic) chord and conclude their song on V (the dominant). They give us two different stereo mixes of "Touch Me": so, listeners have the option to choose which version they like better. Bob Dylan's seemingly endless stanzas of "Desolation Row" go on for more than 11 minutes. The song proceeds in strophic structure, drawing us into this lengthy but powerful folk song. "For What It's Worth" by Stephen Stills is focused tightly into parts. There is no verse-chorus structure. There is no bridge. The contrast in this song is only within the effects and the vocals. Repetition drives the point home. Pete Townshend shifts textures, rhythm and meter, keys, and instruments all within the overture to *Tommy*, which emerges much like a symphonic piece. The Moody Blues employ an orchestral introduction and an orchestral ending on "Nights in White Satin," "Tuesday Afternoon," "Another Morning," and "The Sun Set/Twilight Time."[3] David Crosby's song "Déjà vu" seems to move across alternate states of consciousness as time shifts. The song is played in an alternate turning on guitar. And all of this is "rock"—at least in the broadest sense.

The term "rock" may be vague, encompassing a diversity of sounds, forms, and styles. It's the song that you play in your car. It is the thunderous blast that crackles across the stage lights at a concert. This study takes rock to be something meaningful, not mere distraction or only entertainment. Rock is a culture, a series of discourses. While rock is a mass marketed commodity there is in it also a sense of individuality, rebellion, and opposition. This text focuses on rock from 1964 to about 1980. That is, the "classic rock" referred to here is post-1950s and early 1960s rock and roll and pre-metal, alternative, grunge, hip-hop. It is in this music that romantic and blues traditions intersect and are the pivot on which rock swings.

Rock is anchored in the blues. It is an amalgam of Mississippi Delta blues and Chicago blues, country swing and Appalachian folk song, black spirituals and jazz, rhythm and blues and attitude. From traditional folk music it drew the strophic ballad form and verse-chorus pattern that repeats in so many songs. Rock inherited from the Tin Pan Alley pop song the AABA structure of two similar sections, a bridge that breaks away into new territory, and a final part that returns in some way to the original statement. Often the chorus of a pop song is introduced by a climb and may come to us with thickened harmonies. However, the bridge will take off in a different direction, or as alternative to the melody and harmony, or rhythmic patterns, of the verse and chorus. Rock draws upon these song forms and bends them in new patterns.

From the 1920s the Great American Songbook emerged with commercial, well-crafted songs by Cole Porter, George and Ira Gershwin, Harry Warren, Johnny Mercer, Richard Rodgers and Larry Hart, Jerome Kern and Oscar Hammerstein. West 28th Street at Broadway and 6th Avenue became Tin Pan Alley. Later professional songwriting came from offices in the Brill Building on Broadway at Forty-Ninth Street. The songs of Tin Pan Alley and Broadway became a foundation for the pop music industry and record business, as well as for radio, musical theatre, movies, and dancing and social gatherings throughout America. This songwriting was not the root of rock. The ballads and blues of southern blacks and whites was its source.[4] Rock and roll brought something new: the rhythm and blues and rockabilly that challenged the professional writers of musical theatre and popular songs. Rock employed polyrhythms, power chords, diatonic and pentatonic scales. Most obviously, it embraced new sound technologies and electrified the texture, tone, and presentation of songs.

Rock and roll expanded with the rise of radio and its call for three-minute songs. By the mid-1960s, some rock songs started to get longer. They were too long for AM radio airplay in their time. Brian Wilson's masterful production of "Good Vibrations" at 3:35 starts to get a bit long for radio airplay. However, it stays engaging through layered vocals, changing sections, and a variety of instrument choices that contribute to the song's texture. Crosby, Stills, and Nash's "Suite: Judy Blue Eyes" is a four-part song that goes on for seven minutes and twenty-two seconds. The song became a favorite on FM radio and as an album cut. The Grateful Dead's "Feedback" runs 8:52 and suggests an acid jam. (It is 7:49 on the CD remix.) Cream, Iron Butterfly, Santana, Led Zeppelin were also jam bands. Alvin Lee would take off on a guitar solo with Ten Years After and the song might end ten minutes after. Albums became increasingly important and songs incorporated effects. The Zombies "Time of the Season," for example, is enhanced by a studio mix, including breaths, harmonies, and rhythmic stops.[5] Frank Zappa made use of splicing techniques on *Plastic People*, joining together sections. The joining of parts or sections by The Beatles on *Sergeant Pepper, The White Album,* and *Abbey Road* involves sound on sound and the use of cross-fades. Attention turned from those 45s with the plastic adapter on the turntable to the LP with its cover-art and liner notes. Songs weaved together in concept albums. Rock became more complex and increasingly economically profitable.

Yet, there was also a desire for the straightforward, "authentic," determined little gem. Critic, collector, and musician Lenny Kaye documented grass-roots garage bands of the 1960s with the compilation *Nuggets* (1964–1968). These sounds were a precursor to later new wave/punk rock. That is, they were fairly raw and direct. These performances emerged before rock's complexifying prog-rock album era and before the near-total emphasis by record companies on unit sales. Rock, as a mass-cultural phenomena, moved into arenas in the 1970s with music acts like Elton John, Peter Frampton, Crosby, Stills, Nash and Young, and Fleetwood Mac. Bands like Boston, Foreigner, Bad Company, Van Halen, REO Speedwagon, and Bon Jovi landed on the charts: a pop-rock that prompted further punk rebellion. Billy Joel's *52nd Street* was the top album in 1979 for AOR radio. Rush criticized commercial radio playlists in "Spirit of the Radio" in 1980. In the mid-1980s another wave of independent punk-rock bands emerged, like Husker-Du, The Replacements, and Black Flag. With the rise of heavy metal and its increasing fan base in the 1980s, listeners tuned in to Iron Maiden, Scorpions, Judas Priest, AC/DC, Dio, Whitesnake, Ratt, Twisted Sister, and other bands.

There has long been the cliché of rock as music for the rebel. Rock and roll awakened disapproval. We might follow rock history as a dialectical movement of statement and response (thesis-antithesis). From the blues came the music of the British invasion bands. Some writers suggest that from a golden age of sincerity and authenticity rock music devolved into corporate cooptation that was recognized early on by Frank Zappa in "We're Only in It for the Money" (1968). It went from utopian dreams to dystopian perspectives. New wave/punk responded by rejecting cultural norms and embracing alienation and difference with defiance and irony. To be basic, dissonant, and even unpleasant was to be rebellious and engaged in a new language game.

IMAGINATION AND CREATIVITY

With imagination, rock music begins. The creative leap of the mind has been reported again and again in art and in science. Psychologist Frank Barron wrote: "The creative individual not only respects the irrational in himself but courts the most promising source of novelty in his own thought."[6] A lifelong researcher of creativity, Barron believed that artists are engaged in a search for ultimate meaning. Art historian James Elkins (2008) has offered the claim that "the border between intuition and calculation cannot be clearly defined."[7] Yet, one might say that creative rock musicians straddle along the borderline of the intuitive and the rational skills for making art. Some of this poetic confluence of the intuitive and rational may count as "literature."

Perhaps our rapid-paced and distraction-filled society keeps us from the dreamwork, affirmation, relaxation, and focus necessary for creative work. Songwriting musicians like David Crosby have spoken of how ideas may come when the mind is taken offline before sleep, in drowsiness or altered states. "I hear melodies in my head," Bono of U2 told an interviewer in 2005, "I have no idea where they come from."[8] Musicians interviewed by Jenny Boyd for her book *Musicians in Tune* (1995) spoke of a feeling that sometimes comes while creating music. They recognized that if one is open the song is "given" or may be "coming through" them. The experience has been one realized by composers. For example, what are we to make of composer Richard Wagner's comments that one dreary and desolate day in Spezia in Northern Italy he lay down to rest and began to hear music? Was it because he was well-studied and musically experienced and had spent much long effort in composition? Wagner reports that he heard a "rushing noise" like water and then an E flat major chord followed by a melody. This became the prelude to *Das Rheingold*. Considering inspiration and the musical talent of Mozart, the German literary genius Goethe reportedly said: "How can one say Mozart has *composed Don Juan*? Composition! As if it were a piece of cake or a biscuit. . . . It is a spiritual creation, in which the details, as well as the whole, are pervaded by one spirit, and by the breath of one life."[9] Creativity like this emerges from a state of readiness, one cultivated through many years of practice and involvement with music. The philosopher Henri Bergson once observed that, in his view, human knowledge involves, on the one hand, reason and empiricism and intuition on the other.[10] Psychologist William James writes: "Our normal waking consciousness, rational consciousness as we call it, is but one special type of consciousness, whilst all about it, parted from the filmiest of screens, there lies potential forms of consciousness entirely different."[11] Charles Tart describes normal consciousness is a "tool" for everyday purposes in the social and physical environment.[12] To speak of altered consciousness is to assume that this steady and stable state of our everyday consciousness is the norm, our "consensus state." Music stirs and lifts the listener to broader consciousness. The rock musician's creativity extends imagination to the listener for whom not only amusement, but a sense of wonder is a necessity.[13]

LITERARY IMAGINATION AND ROCK MUSIC

Literary imagination intersects with rock. Edgar Allan Poe is getting kicked in John Lennon's "I Am the Walrus," and he may also be found in songs by

Blondie, Lou Reed, or the Alan Parsons Project. In Bob Dylan's "Desolation Row," Ezra Pound and T.S. Eliot are in the captain's tower. Paul Simon refers to Emily Dickinson and Robert Frost in "The Dangling Conversation" and sets to music E.A. Robinson's story about a disconsolate man of wealth in "Richard Cory." David Bowie makes use of George Orwell's *1984* in *Diamond Dogs*. Rush recalls Coleridge's "Kublai Kahn" in their song "Xanadu" and Iron Maiden turns to his "Rime of the Ancient Mariner" on their *Powerslave* (1984) album. In "Re Joyce," Jefferson Airplane gestures toward Joyce's *Ulysses* and Molly Bloom's affair. Bruce Springsteen recalls John Steinbeck's *The Grapes of Wrath* in "The Ghost of Tom Joad." Kate Bush's "Wuthering Heights" (1978) is covered by Pat Benatar (1980). The title of Sting's second solo album *Nothing Like the Sun* is drawn from Shakespeare's sonnet. On "Don't Stand So Close to Me" (1980) The Police reference "that book by Nabokov." Kansas draws from Hermann Hesse's *Narcissus and Goldmund* and vaguely tells of two personalities that are of different orientations. Hesse's story points to the Apollonian-Dionysian dialectic that philosopher Friedrich Nietzsche saw in all art. Queen's Roger Taylor responds to Ralph Ellison's *Invisible Man* on power and powerlessness. Led Zeppelin's "Battle of Evermore" draws from Tolkein's *Lord of the Rings* and one of the final battles for Middle Earth. "Layla" was written when Eric Clapton connected his infatuation with Patti Boyd with Ganjavi Nizami's poem "The Story of Layla and Manjun." Manjun falls for Layla and sings to her. Layla's father declares that he will not marry her to a crazy man and Marjun goes off into the wilderness.

These are examples of what critic Stephen Paul Scher once called "literature *in* music." He distinguished this from "literature *and* music," in which a writer attempts to make use of musical figures and structures in poetry or in fiction. We can see this use of music in the fiction of James Joyce, Hermann Hesse, Thomas Mann, Marcel Proust, Aldous Huxley, and Anthony Burgess, as well as the jazz writing and "spontaneous prose" of Jack Kerouac. Poetry has long made use of musical devices. Indeed, music and poetry were once closely bound together in the ancient world and sounded in the epics of Homer. The troubadour traditions of medieval times are recalled in singer-songwriters, as well as in the poetry of Ezra Pound, or in John Keats's attention to vowel sounds, which he inscribed in his notebooks. The art song has set to music the poetry of dozens of poets, from Goethe and Heine to moderns like Wallace Stevens. (Franz Schubert created 650 lieder and Robert Schumann composed four song cycles and about 160 songs.) In American poetry, the verse of Walt Whitman and Emily Dickinson are each richly connected with music. T.S. Eliot's essay "Music and Poetry" investigates the connection, as does poet-pianist John Hollander in *The Untuning of the Sky* (1961), musicologist Lawrence Kramer in *Music and Poetry: The Nineteenth Century and After* (1986), and other critics.[14] Rock music lyricists make the same connection and rock songwriters like Bob Dylan, Bruce Springsteen, Joni Mitchell, or Leonard Cohen are increasingly entering textbooks and poetry anthologies.

Of course, a songwriter like Bob Dylan recognizes that while poetry and lyrics may share several qualities, they are also different. Poetry has its own internal logic. It may be condensed, pensive, oblique. It may be visual or typographical. Song lyrics must move in an intimate association with music. Yet, both song lyrics and poetry share in an oral tradition and express the poetic imagination. When you listen to a lyric or read a poem, you may ask who the speaker is and who is being addressed, where the setting and context is, and what the genre and presentation has to do with the way that song or poem makes a connection with you. When you listen to a rock song, which lines draw your attention? What moves you?[15]

The Rock Music Imagination proceeds in the following pattern:

THEMES IN CLASSIC ROCK MUSIC: REBELLION, UTOPIA, AND LIBERATION

This introduction sets forth themes that are present in rock music lyrics, music, and performance that will be explored in this book. These include rebellion, the search for community and utopia, and a quest for freedom or liberation from all constraints. With its roots in the blues, folk balladry, and country/rockabilly, rock and roll announced rebellion against convention in the 1950s and became associated with youth and counterculture during the tumultuous period of "the sixties." The communal dream of the mid to late 1960s and early to mid-1970s is reflected in rock music. This attention to freedom, community, pleasure, peace amidst war, social justice and reform, and a quest for transcendence was embodied in rock songs.

LISTENING TO THE BLUES

Rebellion and a quest for liberation from restraints is at the center of rock music. In one sense this could be related to the yearning for freedom of the blues singers. British Invasion bands (The Beatles, The Rolling Stones, The Who, The Kinks, The Yardbirds, The Animals, and others) drew heavily upon the work of blues players from Chicago, or the Mississippi Delta, who played with spirit and imagination. Their songs of hardship, struggle, aspiration, and Eros provided an inspiration and basis for the rock posture, musical structures, and sounds which followed. (And note that they were gutsy, imaginative artists in their own right, contributing sound and style.) The folk revival intersected with this, bringing with it an examination of social issues (Guthrie, Seeger, Dylan, Baez). When rock writers deal with the notion of "authenticity" in rock music, they tend to give attention to the roots of rock in blues, or to simple chord structures, like those of folk, which get transformed into power chords and underscore the assertion of straightforward messages. Rock's power is diluted when it becomes mere entertainment, a commercial symbol to sell product. It is strengthened, commercially and within the heart of the audience, when it asserts commitment and authenticity. Rock can both declare "Have a Good Time" and the goal of changing minds, perhaps even transforming culture. The creative sensibility and symbolic communication of rock are engaged against forms of repression. Rock seems to take on new life and relevance in times of stress and trouble.

THE IMAGINATIVE LEGACY OF THE BEATS: COUNTERCULTURAL UTOPIA

The imagination of the Beat Generation is a precursor to 1960s counterculture. We begin this chapter with Jack Kerouac's *On the Road* and begin to see a path that leads to a communal dream that appears in Woodstock. We may hear this dream of unity in the Youngbloods' anthem about everybody getting together to attempt to love one another. We see it in Jefferson Airplane's movement toward sci-fi dreams of community and the Grateful Dead's entourage and devoted fans. One may ask about the endurance of these ideals in Western culture. Then we will look at rock's engagement with themes of utopia and dystopia.

This chapter focuses upon the Woodstock generation and rock music of 1967–1974. There are a variety of works that illuminate this period, including Charles Reich's *The Greening of America,* Theodore Roszak's *The Making of a Counterculture* and *Where the Wasteland Ends,* and Todd Gitlin's *The Sixties.* The discussion here includes the San Francisco scene (with the Jefferson Airplane, the Grateful Dead, and other bands) and the Woodstock festival. The 1960s brought movements for social justice, women's rights, and ecological concern that coincided with this energetic phase of rock music. Utopian vision appears in the rock *zeitgeist* of the late 1960s and early 1970s.

SCIENCE FICTION IMAGINATION AND FANTASY IN PROGRESSIVE ROCK

Progressive rock, while derided by some rock critics, opened imaginatively up into fantastic concepts, spacey guitar and synthesizer soundscapes, and colorful album cover art and stage imagery. In this chapter we find bands that incorporated dazzling science fiction imagery and story lines into their musical creations. Whatever pretentiousness or bombast there was, progressive rock also explored musical complexity and creativity. This chapter overviews some of the imaginative creations from key bands from the late 1960s and early 1970s, like Emerson, Lake and Palmer, Yes, Genesis, and Jethro Tull. We then look on to the work of Rush and their interactions with the libertarian perspective of Ayn Rand and with science fiction.

THE END OF THE WORLD AS WE KNOW IT: ROCK MUSIC DYSTOPIA

Imagination twists toward an investigation of themes of dystopia in rock. This includes reference to elements of science fiction in rock. This section considers David Bowie, Rush, Iron Maiden, and others who have utilized science fiction motifs in their work, with reference to texts like George Orwell's *1984* and *Animal Farm*, Aldous Huxley's *Brave New World*, and Ray Bradbury's *Fahrenheit 451*, and stories by Isaac Asimov, Arthur C. Clarke, Ursula Le Guin, Robert Heinlein, Rod Serling (*Twilight Zone*), and others. Among the persistent cultural narratives is that the belief that there was a decline, a period of disillusionment of the countercultural utopian dream in the early to mid-1970s. Such a story line points to the loss of Jimi Hendrix and Janis Joplin, to Altamont, to Kent State, or to Watergate. Whether or not this perspective portrays public consciousness or not, it is clear that rock music was moving through a variety of trends and changes.

In the chapter on Dystopia reference to a wide variety of rock songs is used to explore dreams of social transformation and assertions of resistance to dehumanizing structures or factors of contemporary life. (We can, for example, hear Rush protest totalitarian forms on their album *2112*.) The chapter concerns rock and the utopian vision. It explores utopian themes expressed in rock songs and in utopian literature. This includes recognition of science fiction motifs we find in rock songs and performance and in science fiction texts such as: *Brave New World* (Iron Maiden, *Brave New World*), *1984* (David Bowie, *Diamond Dogs*), and *Animal Farm* (Pink Floyd, *Animals*) and other texts like Bradbury's *Fahrenheit 451* and Zamyatin's *We*. Rock confronts the modern world: its technology, its forms of anonymity or depersonalization, its need for harmony, creativity, and renewal.

ROCK ROMANTICISM: POWER CHORDS AND THE VISIONARY COMPANY

Impulses in rock music parallel several themes that we find in Romanticism: nostalgia and memory, rebellion and protest, innovation and the search for new forms, the Romantic ego, aspiration toward transcendence, the heroic journey and wandering, a malady of spirit, the outsider and alienation, monstrosity, and the quest for re-integration, a recognition of human emotion rather than overemphasis on Enlightenment reason, an opposition to instrumental reason, valuing imagination and mythopoeic thinking, experimentation with form, a concern with nature and earthiness, the natural, and authenticity, the songs of the people and "lyrical ballads," supernaturalism. These elements will be discussed with reference to rock songs and imagery, albums, and performance.

This exploration of rock imagination follows Perry Meisel's observations about what links rock romanticism and the blues tradition. Meisel sets up the image of the cowboy and the dandy in a synchronic model of crossing, the exploration of a chiasmus. We look across country and city, North and South, race and identities. One may add that rock romanticism and blues tradition each reformulated suffering and aspired to freedom. The black community developed an ironic voice in their search for a belated freedom. Romanticism seeks a higher, better world and compensates for its encounter with hard realities with dream and imagination. Black urbanity is a mode of "compensatory imagination" like Romanticism also is, observes Meisel. The crossings that are pursued here are country to city, South to North, black to white, British rock to America, and literature to music. Imagination is interiority that is externalized in artistic expression. This creative expression of rock imagination comes to us through intermediality (recordings, rock reviews and criticism, fiction, album art, magazines, blogs, performances). These various forms affect how we perceive and respond to rock music.

PAPERBACK WRITERS: ROCK MUSIC AND FICTION

Rock music writing is a form of cultural analysis that asserts that rock is a serious art form and a reflection of cultural values. The intersection of words, images, and music affects how we approach and respond to rock music. "Rock criticism recapitulates literary criticism's modes of reading," Perry Meisel observes.[16] It makes use of the close reading of New Criticism. It employs methods of new historicism, viewing texts within context. It recognizes that rock is passionate, mercurial, and obstinate.

This chapter looks at how fiction writers have approached this playful polyvalent discourse that upends expectations of social order. Rock music appeals across classes and boundaries and at times exercises the social disruptions that have been referred to as "carnival."[17] We may reflect on rock as a popular, non-elite, and participatory art, which we see in The Beatles' songs like "Sergeant Pepper" and "For the Benefit of Mr. Kite." The Beatles engage in parodic play, upending notions of high or low art and cutting across class and culture. John Lennon's "I Am the Walrus" breaks apart language, engaging in a free play of syntax and wordplay, like in Lewis

Carroll's "Jabberwocky." We may hear in Bob Dylan the wry wordplay of the jester, or we may see in Mick Jagger the flippant strut of the pugnacious dandy.

Rock music has exerted an influence on literary imagination and popular fiction. There are writers who listen to rock or jazz to jumpstart their creative process. (For example, Stephen King has said he listens to Metallica to get his writing going.) There are rock musicians who draw upon literature and film for ideas. (For example, David Bowie was an avid reader. Steve Harris of Iron Maiden watches films or reads horror and mystery fiction.) Obviously, novelists who have engaged rock music have listened closely to it as they have tried to fashion words to describe it and to tell stories about it.

Rock music journalism connected with the New Journalism of the 1960s. Subjectivity was a central quality of this creative commentary. In spirited style, these writers revived nonfiction writing. Writers like Tom Wolfe, Joan Didion, Norman Mailer, Truman Capote, Gay Talese, and Hunter S. Thompson carved out a path that was related to fiction writing. Rock journalism grew with *Crawdaddy* and *Rolling Stone* and with writers like Robert Christgau, the provocative and bratty insights of Lester Bangs, and Greil Marcus's search for "the unities of the American imagination." Alternatively, there has been academic analysis from baby-boom and Gen-X academics whose life-experiences have been touched by rock music and the postmodern context. In addition, there are many stories in which rock is central to the unfolding fictional plot. We will look at a sample of these novels. The various ways in which rock has been written about affects our perception and our experience of rock. The insights of journalist-rock critics, academics, musicologists, biographers, and fiction writers affect how rock's audience listens. Film, MTV, photography, and advertising have contributed considerably to our perceptions of rock. However, the written word continues to contribute to our encounter and participates in shaping reception.

HUMAN RIGHTS, COMMUNITY, AND GLOBAL ROCK

The concluding chapter looks at rock's place globally and at the role that the voice of women and men concerned with social justice play. This chapter argues that the dream of community, peace, civil rights, women's rights, and ecological concern, which emerged in "the sixties" are all related. Each has received expression in rock music. The efforts of Live Aid and other benefit concerts for famine relief and debt relief are highlighted. We hear the voice of Bruce Springsteen which came through in *The Rising*, following the 9/11 attack on New York's World Trade Center. Next discussed is the vision of U2 and how they have embraced a commitment to global concerns. U2's lyrics may be listened to from a secular angle as well as from a spiritually oriented one. Along with the expansion of rock across the globe, we see the rise of the female rock writer and performer since the 1980s. As we consider women in rock, we may reflect on possibilities for rock's future: ecofeminism, an ethics of care, and a *l'ecriture feminine* of creativity. Rock has not always fully embraced the significant voice of its female performers (most often in the role of singers, less frequently as instrumentalists). The voice of female rock performers should continue to join their male counterparts in the future. Finally, the chapter is also concerned with rock and human rights and causes like ecology/the environment. (There are more than 100 songs, across a wide variety of artists, that refer to ecological concerns.) Now in the first decades of the twenty-first century, rock and pop music have appeared in a wide variety of forms. Indeed, rock has become a highly commercialized medium. Rock can look squarely at the realities of the modern world and not lapse into nihilism. The voice of rock can register hope and can continue to express these ideals and "dream on."

While rock music has clearly become a highly commercialized popular art form, it continues to carry the themes of rebellion, desire for freedom, and hope for connection. It continues to sing out with social criticism and social aspirations. In addressing rock music themes and dreams, the intention of this book is to underscore the suggestion made in Steven Tyler's lyric for Aerosmith: that even when lines may come to our faces, or we recognize that we live among fools and sages, we can still hold to high ideals and dream on. Imagination—musical, lyrical, and visual—is central to this enterprise. *The Rock Music Imagination* focuses on themes, ideals, social criticism, and aspirations in rock music and affirms imagination and the lasting power of the human spirit.

NOTES

1. Greil Marcus, *Mystery Train: Images of America in Rock 'n Roll Music*. New York: E.P. Dutton, 1975, p. xii. It appears that there have been no book-length investigations of classic rock music's themes since James Franklin Harris's *Philosophy at 33 1/3 RPM* (Chicago: Open Court, 1993). While Harris's book does a fine job of introducing us to some of the overarching themes of the "sixties" generation with reference to rock music, it also leaves much out—and much that has occurred since then.

2. The vocals parallel the parts of the chord: McCartney on top at 8, John Lennon on 5, and George Harrison on 6. (Walter Everett, *The Foundations of Rock from Blue Suede Shoes to Suite: Judy Blue Eyes*, New York and Oxford: Oxford University Press, 2008, p. 343) Everett points out that throughout the song that 6 had been the root of a minor vi chord. Listen to "that can't be bad" (at 0:29 to 0.31).

3. See Everett, *The Foundations of Rock from Blue Suede Shoes to Suite: Judy Blue Eyes*. New York and Oxford: Oxford University Press, 2008, note p. 766.

4. Ben Yagoda, *The B Side: The Death of Tin Pan Alley and the Rebirth of the Great American Song*. New York: Penguin, 2015.

5. See Everett's brief comment in *The Foundations of Rock*, p. 614.

6. Frank Barron was cited by Willis Harman and Howard Rheingold in *Higher Creativity*. New York: Tarcher Perigree, 1984. See Frank Barron, *Creative Person, Creative Process*. New

York: Holt, Rinehart and Winston, 1969. For further reading on creativity also see Rollo May, *The Courage to Create*. New York: Random House, 1975; Brewster Ghiselin, *The Creative Process*. Berkeley: University of California Press, 1952, rpt. 1983.

7. James Elkins, *Six Stories from the End of Representation*. Palo Alto: Stanford University Press, 2008, pp. 99–100.

8. Michka Assayas, *Bono on Bono*. New York: Riverhead, 2005, p. 27.

9. Jenny Boyd and Holly George Warren, *Musicians in Tune: 75 Contemporary Musicians Discuss the Creative Process*. New York: Fireside, 1992. Wagner's experience is described in Harman and Rheingold, *Higher Creativity*. New York: Tarcher Perigree, 1984. Goethe, June 20, 1831, *Conversations of Goethe with Eckermann and Soret*. Trans, John Oxenford. London: G. Bell and Sons, 1874, p. 556.

10. Henri Bergson, "The Two Sources of Morality and Religion," *Creative Intuition*. New York: Henry Holt, 1917. See also Aldous Huxley, *The Perennial Philosophy*. New York: Harper, 1945. William James wrote: "Although so similar to states of feeling, mystical states seem to those who experience them to also be states of knowledge. They are states of insight into depths of truth unplumbed by the discursive intellect." Rudolph Otto writes: "According to our scale of values [we will consider the mystic's vision] either a strange fantasy or a glimpse into the eternal relationships of things." Rudolph Otto, *Mysticism East and West*. London: B. L. Bracey and R.C. Payne, 1957, p. 42.

11. William James, *The Varieties of Religious Experience*. (1902) Cambridge: Harvard University Press, 1985, p. 228.

12. Charles Tart, *Transpersonal Psychologies*. New York: Harper and Row, 1975, p. 3.

13. Nadine Hubbs, "Imagination in Pop and Rock Criticism," begins *Expression in Pop-Rock Music: A Collection of Analytical and Critical Essays*, edited by Walter Everett, with a consideration of the importance of imagination in C.G. Jung's thought. Walter Everett, *Expression in Pop-Rock Music: A Collection of Critical and Analytical Essays*. Ed. Walter Everett. Oxford University Press, rpt. London and New York: Routledge, 2007. This Nadine Hubbs describes as an activity of "going deeper into the imagery of something." (p. 3) Boyd and Warren, in *Musicians in Tune* present a Jungian approach to rock music creativity and interviews with rock musicians. This book has been reprinted as *It's Not Only Rock 'n Roll*, John Blake Publishing, 2013.

14. John Hollander, *The Untuning of the Sky: Idea of Music in English Poetry, 1500–1700*. New York: W.W. Norton, 1970. Lawrence Kramer, *Music and Poetry: The Nineteenth Century and After*. Berkeley: University of California Press, 1984.

15. To further examine the relationships of music and poetry, or popular song poetics, one might turn to Charlotte Pence's collection *The Poetics of American Song Lyrics* (2012), or to songwriter craft books like *Tunesmith: Inside the Art of Songwriting* by Jimmy Webb (Hyperion, 1999), *Songwriting: Essential Guide to Lyric Form and Structure* by Pat Pattison (Berklee, 1991), or Sheila Davis, *The Craft of Lyric Writing* (Writers Digest, 1984).

16. Perry Meisel, *The Cowboy and the Dandy: Crossing Over from Romanticism to Rock and Roll*. Oxford: Oxford University Press, 1999, p. 158.

17. "Carnival" is a term used by Russian literary critic Mikhail Bakhtin. His notion of many voices in the novel, or heteroglossia, may applied to some songs and albums. Bakhtin's notion of the carnivalesque is most fully articulated in his study *Rabelais and His World* (Cambridge: Harvard University Press, 1968). In *The Dialogical Imagination* we see traces of this idea in Bakhtin's "Discourses on the Novel," particularly in the figure of the fool (p. 404). *The Dialogical Imagination: Four Essays*. Ed. Michael Holquist and Caryl Emerson. University of Texas Press, 1981.

Chapter One

Listening to the Blues

A blues player looks out over a field into the distance at the sun melting through the evening sky. He shuffles his feet, lifts his guitar, and begins to play. He has blues imagination. Before long, the rhythm in his ears is the sound of the train heading North to the city. Chicago: city of big shoulders, meat packer to the world. Cargo trains hustling in and out. Blues blowing through the smoke. Dark wiry man like a question mark bent over his horn. Dude foot-tapping under a table, arm around his babe, gulping down a shot of booze with the rhythm in his throat.

Blues creativity is about transformation and rock is, in part, built upon appropriation or "borrowing" from blues tropes, riffs, and patterns. Blues is a creative genre in which the player is bound by structure but seeks breakthrough; it is twelve bars that compel one to seek variation and fluency, new synapses and pathways, innovations on pentatonic scales, slides, pulls and bends, changing rhythms, and inversions of chords. This is a music of creativity and moods: you've got the blues. The artist is open to ambiguity, pondering, and self-reflective rumination. He is that boy too young to be singing the blues, as Elton John sings in "Goodbye Yellow Brick Road." Yet, those blues that he feels are transformed into art.

In the 1950s, the blues tradition was in transition. The blues became electrified in Chicago, with performances in the southwest of the city. The blues players sang at Maxwell Street Market at Halsted and Maxwell, a bustling place of street vendors and shoppers. The blues were played at Pepper's Lounge, or at Zanzibar on the West Side, where Muddy Waters would relax between sets, glass of brandy in hand. Freddie King would drop by to listen. Muddy Waters (McKinley Morganfield) sang "Rollin' Stone" (1951), for which a band was named. On Chicago's South Side audiences heard Howlin' Wolf, Muddy Waters, Sonny Boy Williamson, Willie Dixon,

Junior Wells, and Otis Rush. They came to Chicago from the South, as part of a great migration north for jobs. Howlin' Wolf (Chester Arthur Burnett) traveled from Memphis in 1951–1952 to Chicago. Buddy Guy moved to Chicago in 1957. Ellas McDaniel (who became Bo Diddley) and Willie Dixon were from the Delta in Mississippi. Into the scene came Phil and Leonard Chess, immigrant Jews from Belarus, who ran the El Mocambo eatery, a place where prostitutes, pimps, and others congregated. El Mocambo became a jazz club in the evenings.[1] At the center of blues and early rock and roll recording was their company Chess Records at 2120 South Michigan Avenue. Started by Phil Chess (born Fisel Czyz in Belarus) and Leonard Chess (Lejzor Czyz) in 1950, the company introduced the electric blues to listeners far from Chicago. Chess produced Chuck Berry's "Johnny B. Goode," Muddy Waters's "Hootchie Cootchie Man," Bo Diddley's "Who Do You Love?" and Etta James's "At Last."[2]

In May 1955 "Ida May" by Chuck Berry became "Maybelline." The song was recorded with Chuck Berry on guitar, Willie Dixon on string bass, and piano by Johnnie Johnson. With this song Chuck Berry connected country and the blues, using his double-stop guitar leads. Of course, it was Chuck Berry's song and listeners may still cringe at the songwriting credit given to Alan Freed. The only reason that Allan Freed received songwriting credit on Chuck Berry's "Maybelline" was payola: pay for radio airplay. The copyright for Arc Music had to expire before Berry could get his song back.

In "Ripping Off Black Music" (*Harper's*, January 1973) writer Margo Jefferson argued that the uses of black music by white musicians and record companies had become "plunder." Of course, she could look back on years of race records, or further back to minstrel shows and blackface, as indicators of appropriation or racial abuse. In her article, Jefferson referred to her "dream" that the death of Jimi Hendrix was "the latest step in a plot designed to eliminate blacks from rock music so that it may be recorded in history as a creation of whites."[3] As Jack Hamilton points out in *Just Around Midnight* (Harvard UP, 2016), Margo Jefferson's dream "became true." As rock and roll became rock, blacks largely disappeared from much of rock music. The band Love from Los Angeles, Jimi Hendrix, and the appearance of Sly and the Family Stone at Woodstock were exceptions. As pop music split by genre the great musicians of color were R&B-soul-Motown artists. Any claim that black music "self-segregated" does not capture the whole story, observes Hamilton, who critically examines "how rock became white."[4] In this process, rock was shaped by its connection with the blues.

The transmission of the blues today comes to us from artifacts like recordings, live performances, rock transpositions of the blues, and writing about the blues. Blues literature affects how we listen to the blues and how we define it. We can read about the blues, spirituals, and jazz in the poems of Langston Hughes, the novels by Jean Toomer, Zora Neale Hurston, Nella

Larsen, and Ralph Ellison. Of course, stories also come from several locations where the blues came to life. Ian Inglis notes five prevalent blues city styles: Kansas City, New Orleans, Memphis, Chicago, New York. Rock appropriated from these places the blues structure and some of its themes, images, and symbols, including magic and superstition.

Critics have often pointed out that rock transposed the blues primarily through white musicians. There was a meeting of blues, gospel, and jazz and country. This mixture of black and white was music from the folk. As Theodore Gracyk puts it: "It is an art of the people made economically available to any and all listeners who can grasp it without any training or aesthetic specialization. It is extended across geography and can create imagined community."[5]

Literary critic Houston Baker has pointed to the centrality of the "blues matrix" for African American expression. If we go back to the music of the 1920s, we can listen to an extraordinary blend of blues and jazz. Carl Van Vechten, a white promoter of Harlem Renaissance writers, believed that black gospel spirituals and the blues were "the most important contribution American has yet made to the literature of music."[6] He wrote on black spirituals and admired their "unpretentious sincerity" and their "simple, spontaneous outpourings from the heart of an oppressed race."[7] Van Vechten insisted that blues and jazz songs should be recorded, so they would not be lost to posterity.[8] Yet, he lamented that now many were not being sung in dialect and he was concerned about a loss in authenticity because of this.[9]

John Lomax, who collected folk songs and folklore in Texas, had a particular interest in African American folklore. His musicology was often cited by American poet Carl Sandburg in his *American Songbag* (1927). Lomax brought his son Alan with him to work on field recordings of the blues in the 1930s, including the songs of Lead Belly. Alan Lomax had begun collecting "race records" and folk songs in the mid-1920s and by the 1930s he was publishing collections that began to preserve these traditions.[10]

In *The Souls of Black Folk* (1903) W.E.B. Du Bois wrote that "the problem of the twentieth century is the problem of the color line."[11] It was that color line that would have to be negotiated by the blues collectors (who might be regarded as paternalistic), by blues and jazz performers, and later by rock musicians. Minstrelsy, blackface by white performers, was enmeshed in this, as Eric Lott (1993), Perry Meisel, and others have pointed out.[12] Dozens of African American musicians participated in the development of "race records." Some of their names are familiar—Fats Waller, Otis Blackwell, Coleman Hawkins, Leslie Uggams—and some have faded in memory, like Bubber Miley, Savannah Churchill, and bluesman Gabriel Brown.

Popular interest in African American musical expression by white middle class music listeners can be traced back at least to the beginning of the twentieth century and ragtime, Dixieland, and swing jazz. For example, soon after the writer and critic Carl Van Vechten arrived in New York, Theodore Dreiser, editing the *Broadway Magazine*, gave Van Vechten an assignment to write on the opera *Salome*. Van Vechten became an assistant to the *New York Times* music critic Richard Aldrich in Fall 1906. However, Van Vechten soon moved toward his newfound interest in jazz and the blues. In the 1920s, into the early 1930s, the blues and jazz became a vigorous musical expression in New York City. Carl Van Vechten applauded jazz for its primitivism. But did white critics like Van Vecheten ever really understand black culture or jazz? Their search was for something authentic.

As Leon Coleman points out, Paul Robeson, Laurence Brown, and Jules Bledsoe sang at Van Vechten's apartment parties in New York. William Rose Benet, who heard them there, wrote in *The Saturday Review* that the more spirituals he heard the more moving he felt them to be.[13] Langston Hughes noted that the parties were reported on in the Negro newspapers.[14] Carl Van Vechten wrote a series of articles on the blues in *Vanity Fair*. In March 1926, he praised Bessie Smith. He reviewed seven collections of spirituals in the *New York Herald Tribune*: October 25, 1925, December 20, 1925, October 31, 1926. He encouraged black writers to make use of their folk heritage for self-awareness.

On Thanksgiving Day 1925, Van Vechten met Bessie Smith backstage at her concert in Newark, New Jersey. He and his companion at that show were the only white people in the audience. Langston Hughes wrote to Van Vechten the next January that he also had met Bessie Smith backstage in Baltimore. Hughes wrote: "She remembered you but didn't seem at all concerned as to whether articles were written about her or not. And her only comment on the art of the Blues was that it had put her 'in de money.'"[15] By that time Bessie Smith was famous for the hits "Baby, Won't You Please Come Home" (1923), "T'Aint Nobody's Business if I Do" (1923), "Careless Love Blues" (1925), and "The St. Louis Blues" (1925) (with Louis Armstrong playing the cornet).

Bessie Smith had begun her recording career with the line "Gee, but it's hard to love someone, when that someone don't love you." "Downhearted Blues" (February 15, 1923) was the first Bessie Smith recording to be released. It was number 1 for four weeks and sold 780,000 copies in six months. ("Downhearted Blues" was written by Alberta Hunter and Lovie Houston.) She was paid a flat fee of $125 per side. The hit record helped to salvage Columbia Records, which was going through some hard times. However, Smith was never paid any percentage of mechanical royalties. In contrast, blackface performer Al Jolson received seventy-five cents for every recording of a song released on the Brunswick label. He earned $70,385 for "There's a Rainbow Around My Shoulders" and "Sonny Boy," which sold 938,466 copies. When Bessie Smith began collaborating on writing songs, she did receive performance rights as a writer. Although, she did not earn royalties on her records, Bessie Smith made money with her live performances. As of 1925, she was earning about $2,000 a week, paying her musicians and troupe from her earnings. Porter Grainger, who had written for Smith, recognized that Van Vechten could be of much help to them. Smith only went to one of Van Vechten's parties to please Grainger. She felt thoroughly out of place, drank a lot, knocked down Van Vechten's wife, and got out of there.

Poet Langston Hughes called spirituals and the blues "Two great Negro gifts to American music."[16] His book *The Weary Blues*, dug deep into that tradition for a language that speaks the blues. In his poetry, Hughes engaged in blues phrasing, voicing, and structure and brought forth the oral appeal of the blues medium.[17] Langston Hughes wrote the lyrics for *Street Scene* (1947), a musical with book by Elmer Rice and music by Kurt Weill. His interactions with music continued throughout his poetry. Bebop sounds throughout *Montage of a Dream Deferred* (1951). Hughes' gospel musical plays in the 1950s brought gospel songs together with a loose plot. He wrote *Ask Your Mama: 12 Moods for Jazz* (1961). The rhythms, vocalizations, tempos, harmonic structures, and voicings that the poet Langston Hughes heard in the blues are those we hear transposed, modified, and electrified in rock music.

Another significant strand of rock music's origin is the ballad tradition which migrated from England, Ireland, and Scotland through the Appalachians and the American South. Preservation of this folk tradition was of concern to folksong collectors like John and Alan Lomax. In her book *Novel Sounds: Southern Fiction in the Age of Rock and Roll* (2018), Florence Dore offers reflections on "the southern literature of black vernacular music" and the ballads she calls "minstrel realism."[18] Dore does not develop a direct line of contact between rock and contemporary Southern literary fiction, but she does find an atmosphere of place and time in which they emerged. Dore makes the point that oral balladry of the South was a key source for rock and roll and had an impact on Southern literary fiction. She points out that these songs connect with the ancient ballad and oral traditions of medieval times. They also connect with African American vernacular traditions, although her study stays focused on the blend of white and black music of the South. She points out that Flannery O'Connor's "A Good Man is Hard to Find" (1953) refers to a Bessie Smith blues song and that Donald Davidson's *The Big Ballad Jamboree* emerged from the folk song "The Daemon Lover," an English ballad. In William Styron's *Set This House on Fire* (1960) a North Carolina resident listens to Lead Belly's recording from 1934 of "The Midnight Special." Robert Penn Warren and Carson McCullers, in *The Ballad of the Sad Café* (1951), also incorporate "vernacular ballads" in stories.

The blues became a voice of the African American community's quest for freedom and self-determination. Dore cites Ralph Ellison's observation in his review of Richard Wright's *Black Boy* (1945): "The blues is an impulse." She points out that we hear blues in Ellison's *Invisible Man* (1952) and James Baldwin recalls the gospel spiritual in *Go Tell It on the Mountain* (1953) and a drug-addicted musician's struggle and dreams in "Sonny's Blues" (1957). Such musical and literary expression would lift up black heritage and aesthetic tradition.

ROCK AND BLUES AUTHENTICITY

Rock and roll music emerged at a time when music created by African American musicians played a role in the American Civil Rights movement. Notably, there was Sonny Rollins' "Freedom Suite" (1958), Max Roach's "We Insist: Freedom New Suite," Art Blakey and the Jazz Messengers' "The Freedom Rider" (1961), John Coltrane's "Alabama," and Sam Cooke's "A Change is Gonna Come" (1964). Blues was an important contribution that by that time was coming back to America in the performances by white English rock and rollers.

Transatlantic contact by young British bands with American blues lifted rock bands into popularity in the mid-1960s. Several of these rock musicians responded while in their teens to African American culture and music. Chuck Berry, Little Richard, Fats Domino, and other black performers were central to this development. In Britain, Alex Korner created Blues Incorporated in 1961.[19] British musicians generally heard the blues on recordings. However, there were also some live performance tours. Muddy Waters appeared at the Leeds Triennial Music Festival in 1958. He turned up the amplifier and introduced slide and tremolo in his playing. His recording *The Best of Muddy Waters* appeared in London in 1958. He returned to Britain in 1962.

Meanwhile, Elvis Presley, Buddy Holly, Jerry Lee Lewis, and the Everly Brothers were also influential. The Hollies combined British pop, blues gospel, and country/folk chord patterns. Rhythm and blues and country met in The Beatles with the Mersey beat and vocal harmonies.[20] In the twentieth century, the blues legacy stretches from Robert Johnson to Howlin' Wolf and Muddy Waters to Elmore James, Albert Collins, and B.B. King. It is one of the singular roots of rock musicianship and it enters the entire musical world of guitarists like Eric Clapton, Jimmy Page, Johnny Winter, and many others.[21]

So, are the blues the basis of "authentic" rock? Blues-based rock has frequently been regarded as the most authentic form of rock, an unadulterated roots-rock that recalls rock's origins. Yet, to ascribe the word "authentic" to this is problematic. "Good music is the authentic expression of something—a person, an idea, a feeling, a shared experience, a Zeitgeist," wrote critic Simon Frith. He added, "Bad music is inauthentic." Philip Auslander writes of blues-rock: "the music is often defined in terms of an exclusionary concept of authenticity."²² Rock, building on the blues, was linked with rebellion. It protested against alienation and so asserted the authenticity of the self. If conventional society was alienated those who are not alienated in the conventional world were authentic. Authenticity is to be true, to be inclined toward real, true personal expression. Following this line of thinking, the use of the blues is authentic, and pop may be inauthentic. Even so, rock operates within commercial considerations. It does not necessarily subscribe to a view of art over commercialism.²³

In their book *Faking It: The Quest for Authenticity in Popular Music* (2007), Hugh Barker and Yuval Taylor seek to show "how the quest for authenticity has shaped the music we listen to."²⁴ Musicians, they claim, have the choice of whether to fake it or to stay real. They begin their book with the image of Kurt Cobain playing Lead Belly's "Where Did You Sleep Last Night?" The song draws upon the melody of "In the Pines," a truly mournful tale of a woman who loses her husband to a train accident and goes off to weep in the pines where the sun never shines. They point out that Cobain changed the first chord of each verse to a minor chord. He made the song even more depressing by slowing it down and lengthening it. In his version "black girl" became "my girl." The "authentic" adaptation by Lead Belly became an adaptation by Kurt Cobain.

BLUES STRUCTURE

The blues song establishes a home place (a key and tone) and proceeds to venture away from that place, moving through I, IV, V chords and returning home. In this sense a twelve-bar blues might be likened to a quest narrative. Each verse ventures out from the root chord. The strophic form of many rock lyrics is attached to the verse-chorus pattern, or to the A-A-B-A ballad form in which the bridge extends away. The Kinks "Everybody's Gonna Be Happy," for example, uses the strophic form. C7-G7 repeats in the verse. The chorus moves in major triads from Bb to F to A and then to D and C. Finally, it lands on G. The Animals' version of "The House of the Rising Sun" utilizes a repeating ballad form of four lines. While this is a traditional folk song in strophic form, tone, vocal delivery, and story line, the song is drenched in blues origins. Life has gone bad in New Orleans, the singer tells us, warning listeners that a life of sin and misery awaits those who follow a similar path.

The twelve-bar blues progression is a chromatic chord progression. It is usually based on I-IV-V chords, which can be played in any key. This blues pattern is immediately familiar to musicians who play blues-rock or jazz. The player incorporates variations in his or her playing. (I is the Tonic, IV is the subdominant, V is the Dominant) One may add sevenths and these often occur right before a chord change. The first line of a twelve-bar blues is four bars, as are the second and the third. (If the last bar falls on a dominant V chord, that bar can be a turnaround. The last measures will anticipate the turn.)

In a blues song the tone and energy of the music matches with lyrical content that draws upon experiences, often difficult ones. The blues, says Dennis McNally, is "the freedom sound, the call of those displaced from Mother Africa, the cry of the people who can't go home again." Blues were inspired "by the sound of the human voice."[25] This is a voice that presses toward expression, one that tells stories, dreams, hollers, and cries. It considers loss, turns pain into jest, asserts the self against the hard edges of the world.

The blues lyric comes to us in a strophe form, in which there are three lines. Lyrically, the first two lines repeat the same statement. The third line offers a variation: an extension of the statement, or a response to it. The twelve-bar blues may vary this pattern. The blues lyric usually tells a story, sighs a lament, or makes a wry comment on a situation. The lyric, in connection with the music, often expresses an emotion. The speaker may address a bittersweet relationship, jest or complain about it, or employ a double-entendre recalling the passion and visceral rock and roll of sex. The blues cries and moans and wails like a restless horn. It aches on the dissonant flat and purrs and springs back on a note in the voice that shimmers like a long, bent string.

The bluesman is prepared for changes in rhythm. Chuck Berry's "Johnny B. Goode" is built upon the blues but adds swing or shuffle rhythm, an up-tempo brightness, and a brief chorus, repeating the word "go." The chords move from B flat to E flat to F. The pickup note for "deep" is on B flat. There is a movement to E flat and "He" appears on F, ending the line on "bell" before we get to the repeating chorus. Chuck Berry plays the top strings of the chords, emphasizing those top two notes as he half-bars the chord, letting it ring out.

You can hear the blues in Elvis Presley hits like "Heartbreak Hotel," "All Shook Up," and "Hound Dog" which all drew upon the blues form. Elvis Presley's "Hound Dog" is a blues which makes use of the pentatonic scale. You can hear some blues in The Beatles too. The Beatles, while not primarily a blues-influenced band, played 1950s rock and roll. Rock songs often expand the twelve-bar blues structure. The riff for "Day Tripper" emerges from the blues. In "Day Tripper" the verse has two four bar phrases. This corresponds to blues structure. John Lennon repeats the first line of the lyric and he has "got a good reason" for this: it is a blues pattern to do so. The third line is chromatic (as you, like the vocalist, have probably "found out"). This moves into the guitar riff.

Listeners come to expect the chords that will follow in blues progressions, as Bryn Hughes, has pointed out in a dissertation. This harmonic expectation and variations from those expectations are one of the pleasures of listening. Hughes observes that "listeners are less accepting out of key successions when they are primed in classical style cues than when primed with blues-rock cues."[26] Music listeners depend upon normative patterns. Jimi Hendrix's "Hey Joe" is as an example that Hughes offers for us to consider. The song "provides the introduction to the creation of a musical environment," he says.[27] E is the tonal center. Blues inspired, this song descends through the minor pentatonic scale. The lyric poses a question seeking an answer. There are four measure phrases. The tonic chord of E matches the vocal line as it returns again. Here is an example of how rock's harmonic language established its "rules" within a context.

The twelve-bar blues tends to be stylistically consistent. It is present everywhere in rock. The expectation of the return is given in a twelve-bar blues in that twelfth bar. Hughes points out that experiments in listening show that "listeners prefer to hear harmonic events on strong beats . . . or in specific locations within a twelve-bar phrase."[28] You can't miss the pattern in Canned Heat's "Going Up the Country," Stevie Ray Vaughan's "Pride and Joy," or "Rock and Roll" by Led Zeppelin. It sounds from Chuck Berry's "Maybelline," riding on a G chord, and on "Blue and Lonesome" by the Rolling Stones.

THE LEGACY OF ROBERT JOHNSON

Central to the movement from the blues to rock is the figure of Robert Johnson (1936–1937), who recorded twenty-nine songs in San Antonio and Dallas, with twelve alternate takes. These appeared on the Vocalion label of the American Record Company. *King of the Delta Blues Singers* appeared on Columbia Records in 1961. The myth persisted that Robert Johnson met the devil at the crossroads and sold his soul to the devil for his guitar skills. Johnson sang songs like "Hellhound on my Trail," "Me and Devil Blues," "Preachin' Blues (Up Jumped the Devil)," and "Cross Road Blues," which all suggest dealings with the supernatural. In "Hellhound" the speaker faces lost love. His girl has forced him away with a magic potion. He feels the wind rising and the blues falling down like hail. In "Me and Devil Blues" he rejects superstition and yet blames the devil for what he is doing. It must be that old evil spirit. He would face that devil and assert to Satan, "I believe it's time to go." The supernaturalism recalls the stories of the conjure women of the deep South and the Legba legend, which focuses on a trickster figure among the West African gods. In these legends there is a psychic crossing. The blues stands at this crossroads: on thresholds between earth and heaven.

We hear references to this figure of good and evil in the songs of several blues players and vocalists, such as: Skip James, "Devil's Got My Woman"

(1931), Bessie Smith "Devil's Gonna Git You," (1928). Willie Dixon's "I Ain't Superstitious (But a Black Cat Crossed My Trail)" was sung by Howlin' Wolf. In this song the speaker denies superstition but reveals his superstitious anxiety. (We hear that kind of denial in 10 CC's "I'm Not in Love," for example.) Jeff Beck recorded the Willie Dixon/Howlin' Wolf song in 1968. Images of the female engaged in supernatural practices appear in Fleetwood Mac's "Rhiannon," ELO's "Evil Woman," and in "Black Magic Woman," covered by Santana. The Eagles describe a "Witchy Woman." In "Purple Haze," Jimi Hendrix sings about a woman who has put a spell on him. Enchantment continues to be important as Hendrix sings in "Gypsy Eyes" (1968) that he has been hypnotized.

BLUES INTO ROCK

British youth who were inclined toward music were listening to blues. The Rolling Stones were among them. Their transformation of the blues drew upon the productions of Chess Records and the Chicago blues.[29] Skiffle drew George Harrison's interest and he became aware of the blues, folk-country, and Lead Belly. He was in a skiffle group called The Rebels in 1957 and then was brought into the Quarrymen in 1958 through Paul McCartney, who was playing rock and roll with John Lennon. The skiffle fad opened the door for British youth who began seeking the original blues. Some of the "British invasion" bands included art school students who were naturally open to new ideas and forms, creativity and imagination. Blues for British youth was not commercial. It was something besides conservatism or conformity. The blues meant freedom and transgression. Eric Clapton personally related to the blues. He writes in his autobiography that he felt like his back was to the wall and "the only way to survive was with dignity, pride and courage."[30] He heard in the bluesmen one man with a guitar facing the world.

With the British Invasion bands Britain "enters into pop conversation," as Perry Meisel has observed.[31] The Spencer Davis Group from Birmingham, with Stevie Winwood, translated R&B into rock. The Beatles, from Liverpool, drew upon 1950s rock and roll of Chuck Berry, Little Richard, Elvis Presley, and others. In London, The Rolling Stones, The Kinks, The Who, The Yardbirds, and the Dave Clark Five emerged. From Manchester came the pop groups The Hollies and Herman's Hermits and the songs of Graham Gouldman. (Graham Nash would break with the commercial pop of The Hollies.) From Liverpool came acts like Gerry and the Pacemakers with vocalist Gerry Marsden. (Their music leaned toward jazzy pop and show tunes rather than rock and roll.) Cilla Black sang and worked at the Cavern Club, the site of early Beatles shows. The Searchers were a folk music group who scored a hit in 1964 with "Needles and Pins." Peter and Gordon were singing Beatles' ballads. Chad and Jeremy were something like Tin Pan Alley meets Pat Boone and the Everly Brothers. From John Mayall's Bluesbreakers came Eric Clapton, Peter Green (Fleetwood Mac), and Mick Taylor (Rolling Stones). Mike Bloomfield arrived on the scene in America. All of these guitarists affected how blues-rock was received.

THE ROLLING STONES

Several studies have underscored the debt that The Rolling Stones have to the blues and remark on their transformations of it. The Rolling Stones drew heavily upon the blues, transforming material from Howlin' Wolf, Willie Dixon, and other blues players. "Little Red Rooster" was a twelve-bar blues song that became a #1 hit in the United Kingdom. The Rolling Stones created new versions of songs like Robert Johnson's "Love in Vain." "(I Can't Get No) Satisfaction" emerges from a blues riff. So does "Honky Tonk Woman." The Stones' "Jumpin' Jack Flash" was born in a blues riff.[32]

In 1962 Mick Jagger and Keith Richards saw Blues Incorporated at the Ealing Club. They met Charlie Watts and Brian Jones. In July they played at the Marquee and they gradually became well-established on the London club scene in 1963. They recorded demos and they played at the Cavern Club in October. Andrew Oldham helped to shape the bad boy image of the Stones. Reception of the Stones was shaped by Ray Coleman's piece in *Melody Maker* (April 1963): "Would You Let Your Sister Go with a Rolling Stone?"[33] The rock press pointed to the Rolling Stones' connection with black music and to their rebellious stance as voices of cultural disruption. Jack Hamilton contends that the negative image press for the Rolling Stones "traffics in the language and imaging of racial threat." He writes that the Stones "relationship to black music and to race itself, is among the most complex and controversial of any white artists in the history of rock and roll."[34]

In 1964, The Rolling Stones released their first EP and then their first album (April 17 in United Kingdom and May 29 in United States). In June there was a television appearance in New York and a tour that began in San Bernardino. They recorded "It's All Over Now" at Chess Studios in Chicago. A second EP appeared in August and was followed by another album and an appearance in New York on the Ed Sullivan Show. The second Stones album was released in the United States January 15, 1965, with a third immediately following it. They had begun to catch the attention of the American audience that was so taken with The Beatles and other British bands. "The Last Time" was a single released in the United Kingdom February 26. When The Rolling Stones returned to the United States they recorded "Mercy, Mercy" at Chess. "(I Can't Get No) Satisfaction" was completed in Los Angeles at RCA Studios and was released June 6, 1965. The song caught fire and went to the top of the charts. The Rolling Stones concluded the year with "19th Nervous Breakdown" in December. The song was released early in 1966 and followed by "Paint It Black" and "Under My Thumb" in March.

Keith Richards has said that in 1966 he took some time away from the touring to return to listening to the blues.[35] He worked on the phrasing of Fred McDowell and Blind Willie McTell songs and on open E and D tunings. This led to his creating the music for "Jumpin' Jack Flash" and "Street Fighting Man." That period was a pivotal one for The Rolling Stones. It was a creative time. In 1967, they had released "Let's Spend the Night Together," with "Ruby Tuesday" on the B side. Their *Satanic Majesties Request* was recorded in Summer 1967. In September they split with manager Andrew Oldham. *Beggars Banquet* appeared at the top of 1968, with "Jumpin' Jack Flash" and "Street Fighting Man." They recorded "Sympathy for the Devil" between June 4 and 10. The song lyric takes us from crucifixion to the Russian Revolution to the Robert Kennedy assassination and connects us back to blues supernaturalism and a tradition of blues songs about the devil.[36] The *Let It Bleed* sessions began and continued through the end of the year. "Honky Tonk Woman" was written in December.[37] The year was perhaps more fateful: Brian Jones died and was found in a swimming pool on July 2. The Stones paid tribute to him at a Hyde Park concert July 5. Mick Jagger read two stanzas from Percy Bysshe Shelley's "Adonais."[38]

The Rolling Stones hit a creative peak from 1968 to 1972 in their *Exiles on Main Street* period. In *The True Adventures of The Rolling Stones*, Stanley Booth describes what it was like to accompany The Rolling Stones during this time. He adopts a narrative persona in which he seeks to be like Raymond Chandler's detective Philip Marlowe investigating a case. Booth witnessed The Rolling Stones firsthand in 1969–1970 and provides us with something like an oral history and diary through which we enter those times and gain access to the band. He tells us that he jotted his observations in small notebooks and then wrote longhand in larger notebooks before typing his recollections. Rock critic Greil Marcus wrote the foreword to this book. Since then, books on The Rolling Stones have tumbled out like dice from a gambler's hand.[39]

More recently, The Rolling Stones asked Donald Trump to discontinue his use of "You Can't Always Get What You Want." (This song was the B-side of "Honky Tonk Woman.") Despite that request, the president has continued to use the song at his rallies. The use seems peculiar. The song is countercultural. The lyrics assert that it is not possible to get what you want all of the time. Yet, you might obtain what you need. It is not clear what that might have meant to Donald Trump, or if he just liked the ascending boy's-choir vocal. It was an odd choice for a campaign rally. The use of a blanket music license was enough for his use of the song. However, "Jumpin' Jack

Flash" was the song that The Rolling Stones focused on during the days when Trump obtained his undergraduate degree from Wharton on May 20, 1968. They announced the song at a press conference on May 15 and released the song on May 24. In between, they viewed the film *2001* (May 18) and Brian Jones was arrested on a marijuana charge (May 21). That summer, Trump had officially joined the family real estate business. The recording of "You Can't Always Get What You Want" was begun by the Stones on November 16–17, 1968, at Olympia Studios during the *Let It Bleed* sessions. Surely, they never imagined that their song would be used fifty years later in political campaign rallies.

THE BEATLES

The Beatles engaged with blues explicitly in songs like "Yer Blues" and the riff-driven "Come Together." The Rolling Stones had a stronger, more direct, and more ongoing connection with the blues than The Beatles. However, The Beatles put variations on the blues to work in several of their songs ("Day Tripper," "You Can't Do That," "Bulldog," "Birthday," among them). John Lennon played "Ain't She Sweet," a 1920s song, in Hamburg. In Paul McCartney's household his father played Gershwin tunes on the family piano. They both listened to Chicago blues and reacted to the skiffle craze that attracted George Harrison. The Beatles brought together these styles along with Brill Building pop, as Ian Inglis points out. They drew upon Elvis Presley, whose "Hound Dog" (1956) derived from a 1953 blues song that was sung by Big Mama Thornton. The Beatles in Hamburg played songs popularized by Chuck Berry, Little Richard, Larry Williams, and Ray Charles. Among these songs were "Carol," "Memphis, Tennessee," "Rock and Roll Music," and "Too Much Monkey Business" by Chuck Berry, "Tuitti Fruitti" and "Good Golly Miss Molly" by Little Richard. They played "Kansas City," "Long Tall Sally," and "Everybody's Trying to Be My Baby." They played "Twist and Shout" by the Isley Brothers, "Money" by Barrett Strong, and "Chains" by Gerry Goffin and Carole King. The Beatles stretched the blues. The attitude of "I'll Cry Instead" is that of the blues set to a tune that feels almost country. John Lennon's "I'm a Loser" also emphasized a blues sentiment. "Can't Buy Me Love," for all its pop energy, comes to us in an adapted blues structure. "Lady Madonna" includes a walking bass run. "Get Back" develops that bass run movement further. "Get Back," which emerged from a jam with a riff, unfolds a playful narrative about JoJo and sweet Loretta in a variation on the blues. *Let It Be* also brought us "The One After 909" and "For You Blue," a country blues in D.

THE WHO

Performances by The Who generated that impact that makes rock exciting. Initially, as the High Numbers, The Who played R&B. Pete Townshend wrote songs built around power chords that expressed the view of an outsider. Pete Townshend's "I Can't Explain" resembles The Kinks' "You Really Got Me." The songs have a similar pattern of major chords that rock back and forth with staccato movement and pulse.[40] The Who's "Substitute" is somewhat similar, like a tight box in which four chords shift back and forth. In "Substitute" the speaker pretends to be someone he is not. Why not substitute me for him and coke for gin? "My Generation" moves back and forth between two power chords, which modulate up to two others. "My Generation" is angry, rebellious, alienated, and declares opposition to society that puts "us down." Roger Daltrey sang insistently of his determination and hope to die before he got old. He swung the microphone like a lariat. Townshend concluded stage performances of the song by employing feedback: putting his guitar up to his amplifier speakers and modulating the feedback from this. Keith Moon, not to be outdone, continued hard-hitting drums out to the end of the song at which he kicked and scattered his equipment. Driven by Keith Moon's passionate drumming and John Entwistle's intense bass playing, The Who were seemingly ever on edge, ready to break, or to break out. They were the social outsiders of "I'm a Boy," "Happy Jack," and "My Generation."

The post-war British industrial working class experienced increased leisure and consumerism. Mods adopted a social style and a freedom of hedonism.[41] The rise of subcultures signals "the breakdown of consensus in the post-war period" claims one critic.[42] Mod culture was a subcultural space for the "borderline rebel" involved in a form of refusal. Modernity affected identity and the search for authenticity. The impact of the modern city and technology prompted a way of life that asserted individuality and prompted symbolic gestures of dress. The second wave mods were rising at the time of The Who's *Quadrophenia*.

Mod subculture sought a cool separateness from conventional society that was signaled by clothes, scooters, and popping amphetamines. In "The Kids Are Alright" (1965) the speaker doesn't mind when his girl dances with other guys that he knows. They're alright and he can leave her with them. There is a togetherness, a unity. However, by the time of *Quadrophenia* Jimmy declares that mod culture has been superficial. In "Cut My Hair" he recognizes his effort to fit in. "Who Are You?" asks about identity. Has one individuality or is one engaged in conformity and fitting in?

Pete Townshend became a prolific and powerful songwriter. In 1967, he developed brilliant production for "I Can See for Miles." In 1968, he turned toward the teaching of Meher Baba, seeking wisdom. The next year, at Woodstock, The Who did not quite fit with the crowd. During their set Abbie

Hoffman stepped on stage to make an announcement and Townshend punched or kicked him away. The year 1969 brought the rock opera *Tommy* (1969). Townshend used suspended chords in "Pinball Wizard" and imagined a heroic boy suspended in blindness facing the world with an appeal: "See Me, Feel Me." He created a sensitive lyric of alienation in 1971's "Behind Blue Eyes," and dramatic musical passages in "We Won't Get Fooled Again." In "Baba O'Reilly," The Who pointed to a teenage wasteland and created a memorable keyboard part that was followed by a piercing scream. *Quadrophenia* (1973) was conceived as a rock opera like *Tommy*. The story line investigates and critiques the mods. In *Quadrophenia*, Jimmy asks his doctor (likely a psychiatrist) if he can see "the real me." Townshend, no doubt, had undertaken that quest for authentic identity. He followed on a path from the blues and *My Generation* to the mysticism of Meher Baba that underlay his work on *Quadrophenia*.

CREAM

Cream adapted the blues. Eric Clapton played guitar with John Mayall and the Bluesbreakers. In 1963–1964 other key blues bands included Blues Incorporated and Graham Bond and Cyril Davis All Stars. The British rock performers listened to the Americans Chuck Berry, Little Richard, Elvis Presley, Buddy Holly and blues players like Willie Dixon, Muddy Waters, Sonny Boy Williamson. Muddy Waters toured England in 1958. The Rolling Stones brought the American blues back to their American audience. The Kinks, The Yardbirds, and the Spencer Davis Group, The Who, Manfred Mann, Pretty Things, and Cream all drew upon the blues. Later listeners heard from Fleetwood Mac and Ten Years After with Alvin Lee, Free, and Led Zeppelin.

Cream drew upon the Mississippi Delta country blues and Chicago electric blues. Ginger Baker was in Alexis Korner's Blues Incorporated and Graham Bond Organization. Eric Clapton was a member of The Yardbirds (1963–1965), John Mayall's Bluesbreakers (1965–1966) and Cream (1966–1968). Cream produced *Fresh Cream* (1966), *Disraeli Gears* (1967), *Wheels of Fire* (1968, double album, one studio, one live). *Disraeli Gears* (Atco, 1967) included blues from Blind Joe Reynolds, "Outside Woman Blues." *Fresh Cream* (1966) had several blues songs: "Cat's Squirrel," (Mississippi blues), "I'm So Glad" (Nemiah Jones), "From Four Til Late" (Robert Johnston), "Rollin' and Tumblin'" (attributed to Muddy Waters), and "Spoonful" (Charlie Patton). Cream's album *Wheel of Fire* (1968) included "Sittin' on Top of the World" (recorded by Howlin' Wolf), "Crossroads" (Robert Johnson), "Train Time" (John Pugh), and "Born Under a Bad Sign" (Booker T. Jones and William Bell).

Eric Clapton recorded "Cross Road Blues" as "Crossroads." In "Crossroads" the word crossroad is on the downbeat at the top of the first verse and then on the second beat in the other verses. ("Crossroads" may use a tuning of EAEAC#A.) Clapton recorded the song live with Cream (on *Wheel of Fire*) and with Blind Faith (1969). He recorded it again with Derek and the Dominos (1970). Clapton focuses on a riff. He draws his riffs from the blues as motivic figures and repeats them, creating a riff pattern. There is also a riff in Jack Bruce's bassline in the verse, which connects with Ginger Baker's drumming. Cream's "Crossroad" expresses the twelve-bar blues with a two-bar answer. The shuffle pattern derives from Robert Johnson.[43] Clapton breaks out as a soloist. Of course, we look forward to his doing that. There is no alternate tuning in the Cream version. Cream picks up the tempo on the song and lifts it with amplification and rhythmic variation in the rhythm section. Cream makes the meter consistent throughout. The riffs serve to define this song.[44]

Cream's debut was on July 31, 1966, at Britain's National Jazz and Blues Festival. The band was managed by Robert Stigwood, who also managed The Bee Gees and later formed RSO Records. They appeared on the Reaktion label in Britain and on Atlantic Records in the United States. Ahmet Ertegun began to focus on featuring and promoting Eric Clapton. Ginger Baker had come from the Graham Bond Organization. Jack Bruce was virtuoso bass guitarist well-grounded in the blues. He played the bass as a lead instrument. (He would compose the memorable bass pattern of "Sunshine of Your Love," in which Clapton used octaves for his lead riff.) The sound of Cream was loud, propulsive rock and they soloed in tension with each other. Clapton used distortion and the wah-wah pedal, altering his guitar tone. Willie Dixon's "Spoonful" became a lengthy jam. "Toad" brought a Ginger Baker drum solo. "I Feel Free" was released as a single from Fresh Cream. The album *Disraeli Gears* brought out their rock sound further. Their compositions rested upon the blues. (Cream's "Strange Brew" with psychedelic lyrics uses Albert King's twelve-bar blues "Oh, Pretty Woman.") Tom Dowd and Felix Papalardi (who contributed to "Strange Brew") were involved with the production. Following his involvement with Cream, Papalardi founded Mountain with Leslie West.

The *Rolling Stone* magazine cover photo of Eric Clapton on May 1968 was taken by Linda Eastman. Clapton interviewed with Jann Wenner for that edition. Jon Landau was writing that "Clapton is master of the blues cliché."[45] November 26, 1968, at the Royal Albert Hall was the last Cream concert.

Clapton, of course, had a successful recording career with Derek and the Dominos and as a solo artist. "Let It Rain" and "Bottle of Red Wine" were written by Clapton with Bonnie Bramlett. "Let It Rain" begins by alternating the A and G chords. The verse moves from D to A minor to C-G and repeats

D-A minor-C-G-D. For the chorus, D provides the pick-up note and the harmony moves to A minor-C-G-D, descending with love raining "down on me" in the notes D, B, A. The bridge moves G-A-G-A to F# minor-A with E in the bass to a D sharp diminished chord and E minor and A repeat three times before Clapton's lead guitar breaks out into repeating A notes into sixteenth notes, descending to G, F sharp, E, D, then jumping to C, B, B, A, A and bent notes at the tenth fret and the fourteenth fret out to intense sixteenth notes up to the seventeenth fret. Of course, this tablature notation says little about the timbre of Clapton's guitar or his style. When he adapts the blues structure of J.J. Cale's "After Midnight" Clapton is riff-oriented. His line moves from A to C-C-A-G in the first two bars of the song, which is followed by a beat rest, and a triplet (G) in the third bar and F to E on down A-D-E, extending the D note on "about," and ending the phrase.

LED ZEPPELIN

Led Zeppelin's first four albums were clearly based in the blues. *Houses of the Holy* was the first Led Zeppelin album to deviate from this. Led Zeppelin's Jimmy Page plays blues riffs on "You Shook Me" and "I Can't Quit You Baby" (Willie Dixon). He played a version of "Dazed and Confused" with The Yardbirds, then beginning to lean psychedelic. "I Can't Quit You Baby" is a twelve-bar blues in which the last two measures lift. Led Zeppelin recorded this live. In contrast, "How Many More Times" is double-tracked and layered. "Communication Breakdown" draws upon the blues and gestures toward what will later become heavy metal.

Led Zeppelin I was a blues-based album. Led Zeppelin recorded two blues covers on that album. Led Zeppelin also covered Robert Johnson's "Traveling Riverside Blues." They covered Howlin' Wolf and other blues players: those wandering singer-songwriters of the Delta. "You Shook Me" and "I Can't Quit You Baby" were Chicago blues standards.

Jimmy Page brought his guitar work across many moods: heavy, driving blues, ethereal acoustic patterns, Celtic mysticism, mid-East, and Eastern sounds. His piercing lines and shimmering solos included some of the most memorable phrases in rock music: the powerful blast into "Whole Lotta Love," that ringing D suspended followed by the lyrical, aggressive solo at the end of "Stairway to Heaven." In Led Zeppelin's blues-based songs we encounter Robert Plant's lyrics that speak of darkness and light, illumination, and mystery. Musically and lyrically, some songs suggest a kind of passage and the hero's journey. "Stairway to Heaven" proceds from its pastoral opening to the energetic driven conclusion. (Robert Walser sees in this "contradictory sensibilities without reconciling them.") After "Stairway to

Heaven" we also hear the rollicking assertion of "Rock and Roll," with its blues rock in the key of A bounding along.

Led Zeppelin's "The Battle of Evermore," on *Led Zeppelin IV*, begins in a pattern of A minor to G and A minor to C, followed by the D chord and it stays with this harmonic pattern throughout. The vocal melody then jumps to A, an octave from the note on which the song began. The lyric begins with an interplay of light and dark; there is a queen of light and a prince of peace. There are agrarian images of hoes, plows, and apples, a rich and well cared for land that is spoiled by tyranny and war. The lyric tells us of a thunderous sound and waiting upon Avalon's angels: a mythic image of an ideal land. We are given imagery of a castle, a battle, bows and arrows flying, a dragon of darkness, magic runes, and a world that must be brought back into balance. "The Battle of Evermore" brings us one of Robert Plant's most developed mythical narratives.

FLEETWOOD MAC

Mick Fleetwood played drums and John McVie played bass for John Mayall and the Bluesbreakers. This became the core rhythm section of Fleetwood Mac. Producers Mike Vernon and engineer Gus Dudgeon began to work with new guitarist Peter Green on the Bluesbreakers' third album (the second in the recording studio). *A Hard Road* (1967) was an album titled after an Otis Rush song. This was a blues-based band. "The Stumble" was an instrumental from Freddie King. "Dust My Blues" came from Elmore James. Green listened to B.B. King and other blues players. In Green's instrumental, "The Supernatural" (on side two) he used reverb on his guitar lines, a lead approach that evolved from blues playing.

Fleetwood Mac toured Britain in 1967. They released their debut album on February 28, 1968. Peter Green's blues-rock was complemented by and contrasted with the style of Jeremy Spencer, who brought into the band's sound slide guitar, up-tempo blues, and Elmore James blues influences. Green and Spencer wrote most of the songs and drew upon traditional blues. There were covers of songs from Howlin' Wolf ("No Place to Go"), Sonny Boy Williamson ("Got to Move"), Elmore James ("Shake Your Moneymaker") and Robert Johnson ("Hellhound on My Trail").[46] Fleetwood Mac arrived in the United States in May 1968 in San Francisco, where they associated with The Grateful Dead. Guitarist Danny Kirwan joined the band for their second album, *English Rose*, and was featured on his song "Jigsaw Puzzle." Kirwan also contributed "One Sunny Day" and "Without You," Spencer's songs were "Evening Boogie" and "I've Lost My Baby." Side Two opened with Peter Green's song "Black Magic Woman," which would later be turned into a memorable hit by Santana. The side closed with Green's song and guitar solo on "Albatross." *Mr. Wonderful* (1968) included the Elmore James blues song "Dust My Broom."

Then Play On was Fleetwood Mac's next album. By this time, Peter Green was evidently becoming increasingly affected by drugs and, according to some accounts, the onset of schizophrenia. During the band's series of shows in Germany, he appeared to be unraveling. A local group apparently lured Green into a drug-laced coterie that manager Dennis Keane later likened to a cult. Green, who was already indicating an interest in leaving the band, was gone by Spring of 1970. For the subsequent recording *Kiln House*, Christine McVie made an important contribution. In 1971, *Future Games* emerged as Danny Kirwan took a lead role in creating the band's soft-rock sound and Bob Welch took Spencer's spot. *Penguin* followed with Christine McVie and Welch contributing songs and with Bob Weston and Dave Walker as members of Fleetwood Mac. *Bare Trees* (1972) was the final album with Danny Kirwan. It included Bob Welch's "Sentimental Lady." *Mystery to Me* (1973) included Bob Welch's "Hypnotized." *Heroes are Hard to Find* (1974) included Christine McVie's song "Come a Little Closer." It paved the way toward the inclusion of Stevie Nicks and Lindsey Buckingham in Fleetwood Mac.

In the mid-1970s Fleetwood Mac broke into superstar pop status with a string of singles and their platinum-selling *Fleetwood Mac* (1975) and *Rumours* (1976). The 1975 album brought hits with "Say You Love Me," "Rhiannon," and "Over My Head." On *Rumours* nearly every song was a pop hit. The album was recorded in Sausalito, California, on a twenty-four-track with recording sessions fueled by cocaine use. The three vocals of Christine McVie, Stevie Nicks, and Lindsey Buckingham intersect in harmonies. The Fender Rhodes and Hammond B3 organ join guitars and bass guitar and percussion that sometimes includes maracas and congas. Lindsey Buckingham's distinctive guitar stylings add new features to the record. Nicks' "Dreams," Buckingham's "You Can Go Your Own Way," the collective collaboration "The Chain," and Christine McVie's "Don't Stop," "You Make Loving Fun," "Songbird," and "Oh, Daddy" all received extensive airplay. Fleetwood Mac aimed at "pop" and achieved it in extraordinary fashion. This was a recording in which the singing of troubled lyrics of separation met with bright music that sounds happy and harmonious. *Tusk* (1979), a double album, gave Fleetwood Mac the space to experiment with new wave/punk and creating a new sound.

JIMI HENDRIX

Of course, in considering the creative transpositions of the blues into rock one has to recognize the imaginative power of Jimi Hendrix and how it shone through his innovative guitar playing. His guitar styling was rooted deeply in the blues. The Jimi Hendrix Experience featured Hendrix with drummer Mitch Mitchell and Noel Redding, a guitarist who played bass. Hendrix wrote and played "Red House," a slow blues, in 1966. Their first album included "Hey, Joe," "Purple Haze," "Foxy Lady," and "The Wind Cries Mary." The third track on side two, "Third Stone from the Sun," had a melody that used octaves and included Hendrix's use of feedback. The Jimi Hendrix Experience played at the Monterey Pop Festival in 1967 and Hendrix set a Stratocaster on fire. The band then played six nights at the Fillmore West. The band moved toward psychedelic rock and Hendrix developed a variety of guitar sounds. On Hendrix transforming the blues, Paul Gilroy wrote that he was "electrifying them, blending and bending them into different kind of protest and affirmation."[47] He called Hendrix a gypsy who expressed a "utopian quality." Hendrix looked to the future, to the not-yet. He expressed a hope that still speaks to us.[48]

Fundamentally, the guitar wizardry of Hendrix is blues based. Jimi Hendrix's "Hey, Joe" is CGDAE in a repeating pattern. The listener to this song makes choices. What will come next? What are the most likely next tones, given the tonal center and pitch and movement of the melody? The listener has a sense of the key, the tonic or root, and phrases are anticipated. These could confirm the tonic or resist it and contrast with it.

Hendrix utilizes several effects on "Purple Haze," including the wah-wah pedal, tremolo, reverb, echo, and phase shifter. A pattern of G-G-G-F-F-G builds the song. His vocal drifts through blues figures and his lead breaks are metrical and include distortion and slides. In "Love or Confusion" there is vocal spontaneity, accents on the off-beat, a vocal rising on the word "love" and falling on "confusion," and the effect of noise, as Sheila Whitely recognizes.[49]

Hendrix's absorption of jazz is discussed by Charles Schaar Murray in his chapter "Hear My Trane a Comin" in *Crosstown Traffic*. The unfolding of improvisation in "Third Stone from the Sun" is jazzlike, he concludes. (Jazz players—non-fusion ones, he reminds us—tend to aim for a clean sound.) Hendrix, of course, employs sonic effects from the electronics of his guitar, pedals, and amplifier. For example, at Woodstock he transformed "The Star-Spangled Banner" into an anti-war anthem with electronic feedback and distortion that suggested shrieks and explosions.

BLUES, JAZZ, AND JOHN COLTRANE

The blues expresses resistance to inequality, alienation, segregation, poverty, and dislocation. Jazz and rock emerged from blues roots and share similar attitudes of creative resistance. In *Ascension: John Coltrane and His Quest* (1995), Eric Nisenson points out that "jazz has usually reflected its times, although it was often created as inherently music of rebellion against a reactionary and inhumane status quo."[50] John Coltrane played and lived his music.[51] This embodiment of the music rings with a notion of authenticity. These are the qualities also esteemed in rock music.

Eric Clapton has acknowledged the influence of Coltrane's sound. Jimi Hendrix and Frank Zappa also listened to Coltrane. The Byrds "Eight Miles High" draws upon Coltrane's "India." Jerry Garcia of the Grateful Dead once commented on the flow of Coltrane and "making statements that to my ears sound like paragraphs."[52] Rock musicians have listened to Coltrane's modal harmony, his use of repetition, and his lyricism. Nisenson points out that the improvisation of many San Francisco groups was modally based and some of this might be attributed to their listening to Coltrane's *A Love Supreme* and to Eastern influences.[53] (Coltrane himself became increasingly interested in Eastern meditative practice.) Coltrane's *Giant Steps* was also influential. Nisenson adds: "The reason for Coltrane's continuing popularity is clear: his sound . . . it was this sound that would end up haunting both listeners and musicians, even if many of them believed he was going off the deep end."[54]

The influence of John Coltrane appears in the innovative intersections of jazz with rock. For example, Lifetime was a fusion group with drummer Tony Williams, who had an impact on Miles Davis' fusion music. The band included John McLaughlin on guitar and Larry Young on organ, both of whom were influenced by Coltrane.[55] Much of the music was modal with tempo and metrical changes. McLaughlin followed the teaching of Sri Chinmoy and he created the Mahavishnu Orchestra (based on his Hindu name).

In Coltrane's *My Favorite Things,* (1960) the Gershwin tune "Summertime" has a passage that musicologist Lawrence Kramer indicates possesses the quality of a narrative. "It contains an extended passage suggestive of the process of dwelling on and then crossing a threshold that is characteristic of both heroic quest narrative and coming-of-age story."[56] Kramer's describes Coltrane's "Summertime" by observing that "The music starts abruptly with an unprepared tenor sax solo." Coltrane is "giving out George Gershwin's famous melody at what might be called the vanishing point. The listener seems to break in during a process of melodic transformation that has already begun, is already well-advanced, and in the very next moment will carry the melody beyond recognition."[57]

Coltrane takes Gershwin's tune to darker, more dissonant places. Musicologist K.J. McElrath hears a slow-moving harmonic progression that suggests blues. Walt Weiskopf points out an implied major thirds cycle in Coltrane's solo break (E minor-G7-Cmajor-Eb7-Abmajor-B7-Eminor). David Demsey recognizes a "preoccupation with . . . chromatic third relations" and observes that Coltrane references Indian ragas.[58] What they all witness is innovation. Kramer comments that "Gershwin's combination of pentatonicism and blues inflection evokes an image of idyllic rural contentment and black simplicity." In contrast, "Coltrane's rapid and complex version of the melody superimposes a second image of urban turmoil and black sophistication."[59] Coltrane disassembles Gershwin's melody and then reshapes it. "The process can be described in terms of narrativity," observes Kramer, "almost, indeed, in the elegiac terms of a descent to a kind of underworld and return to life."[60] This is the journey of Odysseus, Aeneas, Jesus descending into hell on the third day, carving out a path to redemption.

Coltrane's saxophone is here "the personification of a suffering, heroic, questing subjectivity."[61] While Coltrane's sax pushes away from the melody, the piano maintains the interval of a third and develops its figures around it, as Kramer points out. A low double-bass solo comes from Steve Davis that Kramer suggests "is thick, almost inarticulate" and in which "the overall effect is a kind of blind groping."[62] In Coltrane's version of "Summertime" the conclusion is described as "an aggressive appropriation has been replaced by a kind of cultural and emotional dialogue." It is "a significant moment of self-overcoming and self-creation."[63]

"My Favorite Things" remakes the Rodgers and Hammerstein song.[64] Each of Coltrane's passages that evoke "the burden of a long tradition of Negro spirituals suggests both irony and revaluation."[65] Nisenson observes that there is Stravinsky-inspired polytonality and lyrical phrasing in "My Favorite Things" which gives it what he calls "an indigo hue."[66] It may be useful to note that jazz inverts chords and has moving chord substitutions. (Sometimes the cadence will lead to the root by perfect intervals of fourths.) One might run a twelve-bar minor harmonic pattern, as in Coltrane's "Equinox." Coltrane pushes harmony and improvises inventive melody lines. It is this imaginative recasting of familiar tunes that caught the attention of rock musicians like Clapton and Hendrix, who listened to Coltrane's variations on melodies and drew inspiration from that spirit for their guitar playing.

In Spring 1966, Coltrane brought his listeners who were familiar with his work back to his signature tunes to establish ground from which he could leap toward "new, unexplored terrain," Nisenson suggests.[67] The year 1966 also included a Coltrane tour of Japan. He played one gig after this at the Village Theater, which would soon be named the Fillmore East. He pulled back from public performance. He continued to record, including tracks that would be assembled for *Interstellar Space*. "Coltrane increasingly took on the role of shaman," observes Nisenson.[68] His playing suggested voyages, journeys, expanded consciousness.

Coltrane's influence was far reaching and even appears in curious anecdotes. David Crosby, whose music is jazz influenced, listened often to Coltrane. He tells the story in his autobiography of a serendipitous moment. One day when he was traveling with musicians listening to John Coltrane's music, they had to pause at railroad tracks to wait for what turned out to be a coal train.

NOTES

1. In 1994, the University of Illinois-Chicago expanded into what had been the Maxwell Street Market area. Gene and Harry Goodman, the brothers of Benny Goodman, set up a publishing partnership with Leonard and Phil Chess that they called Arc Music. The Goodmans arranged for international rights and Chess-owned songs that were covered by non-Chess artists.

2. The building at 2120 South Michigan has been preserved as the Willie Dixon Blues Heaven Foundation.

3. Margo Jefferson, "Ripping off Black Music," *Harper's* (January 1973).

4. Jack Hamilton, *Just Around Midnight*. Cambridge: Harvard University Press, 2016. See Hamilton's introduction.

5. Theodore Gracyk, *Rhythm and Noise: An Aesthetics of Rock*. Durham: Duke University Press, 1996, p. 20. See also Gracyk, *On Music: Thinking in Action*. London: Routledge, 2018.

6. Houston Baker, *Blues, Ideology, and Afro-American Literature: A Vernacular Theory*. Chicago: University of Chicago Press, 1984; Carl Van Vechten, "Folk Songs of the American Negro," *New York Herald Tribune Books*. October 25, 1928, p. 52.

7. Carl Van Vechten, "Folk Songs of the American Negro," p. 63.

8. Carl Van Vechten, "Folk Songs of the American Negro," p. 52.

9. Carl Van Vechten, "All God's Chillun' Got Songs," *The Nation* 62 (August 1925): 24, 63.

10. Lead Belly sang at the Modern Language Association Convention in Philadelphia in 1934. The musicology of John and Alan Lomax encouraged the creativity of Woody Guthrie, Pete Seeger, and others and stimulated the folk revival. Blues-folk in Greenwich Village in New York included the music of Dave Van Ronk, Ramblin' Jack Elliott, and Eric von Schmidt. Blues players fell under the influence of Reverend Gary Davis. A folk music scene developed in the folk clubs at Bleeker and MacDougal, The Bitter End, The Gaslight, or down the road at Gerde's Folk City. Bob Dylan was given a copy of *Robert Johnson: King of the Delta Blues* by John Hammond. A new generation of blues players emerged in different areas of the United States, with Stefan Grossman, Danny Kalb, David Bromberg, Ry Cooder, John Hammond, Jr., John Fahey, Roy Book Binder, Jorma Kaukonen.

11. W.E.B. Du Bois, *The Souls of Black Folk* (1903), rpt. New York: Dover 1994, p. v.

12. Eric Lott, *Love and Theft: Black Face Minstrelsy and the American Working Class*. Oxford and New York: Oxford University Press, 1993, rpt. 2013; Perry Meisel, *The Myth of Popular Culture: From Dante to Dylan*. New York: John Wiley, 2009, p. 129.

13. Leon Coleman, *Langston Hughes as Dramatist*. University of Oregon Press, 1984, p. 99. William Rose Benet, "Cursive and Discursive," *Saturday Review II*, January 26, 1926, pp. 505–7. See also Leon Coleman, *Carl Van Vechten and the Harlem Renaissance: A Critical Assessment*. London and New York: Routledge, 1998.

14. Langston Hughes, *The Big Sea*. New York: Alfred A. Knopf, 1940, p. 251. References to "the blues" appear throughout Langston Hughes's writing. Movement and kinetic energy unfold in Langston Hughes' poetry, as in R&B, jazz, or hip-hop. Jazz is largely rooted in the blues and jazz culture enters Hughes's work in many places. "Montage of Dream Deferred" has jazz flowing through it, as does "Ask Your Mama" is a performance piece heavily influenced by jazz. There is "Beale Street," "Cabaret," "Cabaret Girl Dies on Welfare Island," "Jazz as Communication," "Jazz Band in a Parisian café," "Jazzonia," "Jazz Girl," "Lady in a Cabaret," "The New Cabaret Girl," "Nude Young Dancer," "BeBop Boys," "Jazz, Jive, and Jam." We hear the blues floating through the children's poem "The Blues," the short story "The Blues" in *Simple's Uncle Sam*, and the short story "The Blues I'm Playin'." Hughes has given us lyrics to the song "Blues at the Waldorf," composed by David Martin, and to the song "Blues Montage," composed by Leonard Geoffrey Feather. Along with "The Weary Blues," there are poems titled "Blues at Dawn," "Blues Fantasy," "Blues in Stereo," and "Blues in a Box." Indeed, blues lie at the heart and center of Hughes's expression as a poet. He makes use of lyric forms, ballad stanzas, blues and jazz rhythms in poems like "Reasons Why." He uses call and answer form in poems and gives us blues culture as a subject of poems like "Cabaret" and "Young Singer." Among his poems are "Barefoot Blues," "Bound No'th Blues," "Crowing Hen Blues," "Down

and Out," "Fortune teller Blues," "Hard Luck," "Homesick Blues," "Juice Joint: Northern City," "Little Green Tree Blues," "Maker of the Blues," "Mid-winter Blues," "Po Boy Blues," "Red Roses," "Six-Bit Blues," "Red Clay Blues," and "Young Gal Blues." His poem "Curious" is one stanza arranged in six lines of a blues lyric.

15. Langston Hughes, Letter to Van Vechten in Johnson Collection, Yale University Beinecke Rare Book Library.

16. Langston Hughes, "Songs Called the Blues," *Phylon* Vol. 2, No. 2 (1941): 143–45.

17. Hughes, "Songs Called the Blues." Hughes wrote: "Let the blare of Negro jazz bands and the bellowing voice of Bessie Smith singing the blues penetrate the closed ears of the colored near intellectuals until they listen and perhaps understand" (Langston Hughes, "The Negro Artist and the Racial Mountain," *The Nation* [June 23, 1926]).

18. Florence Dore, *Novel Sounds: Southern Fiction in the Age of Rock and Roll*. New York: Columbia University Press, 2018. See the introduction, pp. i–v.

19. This unit would include Charlie Watts, Ginger Baker, and occasionally include performances by John Mayall, Jimmy Page, Keith Richards, and Brian Jones.

20. Perry Meisel considers the early "low" blues-country Beatles and later "high" art Beatles as they break through the high-low art dichotomy, p. 146.

21. In Chicago, Mike Bloomfield went to the blues clubs and developed his blues guitar playing. He later met Paul Butterfield, who created the Butterfield Blues Band.

22. Simon Frith, *Performing Rites: On the Value of Popular Music*. Cambridge: Harvard University Press, 1996, p. 260; Philip Auslander, *Liveness: Performance in a Mediatized Culture*. London: Routledge, 1999, rpt. 2008, pp. 69–70.

23. Simon Frith, meanwhile, raised the question of whether the technologies rock uses are authentic. It is these technologies that "made the rock concept of authenticity possible in the first place." Simon Frith, "Art Versus Technology: The Strange Case of Popular Music," (263–79) *Media, Culture and Society* Vol. 8 (July 1986): 269.

24. Hugh Barker and Yuval Taylor, *Faking It: The Quest for Authenticity in Popular Music*. New York: W.W. Norton, 2007.

25. Dennis McNally, *On Highway 61: Blues, Race, and the Evolution of Cultural Freedom*. Berkeley and New York: Counterpoint, 2014, p. 235.

26. Bryn Hughes, "Harmonic Expectation in 12 Bar Blues Progressions," dissertation at Florida State University in 2011, pp. xiv, xvii.

27. Ibid.

28. Hughes, "Harmonic Expectation in 12 Bar Blues Progressions," p. 4.

29. Helmut Staubmann, *The Rolling Stones: Sociological Perspectives*. Lanham: Lexington, 2013, p. 9.

30. Eric Clapton, *Clapton: The Autobiography*. New York: Broadway Books, 2007.

31. Perry Meisel, *The Myth of Popular Culture: From Dante to Dylan*. New York: John Wiley and Sons, 2009, p. xii.

32. Barry J. Faulk contends that *Exiles on Main Street* "marked a crossroads of rock for rock's sake." (Ch.3) The Rolling Stones' classic blues compilation *Confessin' the Blues* was released as a 42 track two disc set on November 9, 2018, with cover art by Ronnie Wood.

33. Helmut Staubmann points out that a mutual interest in the blues brought the members of the Rolling Stones together. *The Rolling Stones: Sociological Perspectives*. Ed. Helmut Staubmann. Lanham: Lexington Books, 2013, p. 38.

34. Jack Hamilton, *Just Around Midnight*. Cambridge: Harvard University Press, 2016.

35. www.timeisonourside.com

36. Mick Jagger declares rebellion in "Street Fighting Man." Hamilton sees these songs as filled with a "fascination with violence." He notes that the "transgressive images and the content of their music grew more and more intertwined."

37. In 1969, bluesman Ry Cooder played on "Love In Vain" and "Sister Morphine."

38. Upon death, in Shelley's panpsychist view, one's consciousness joins all.

39. Stanley Booth, *The True Adventures of the Rolling Stones*. Chicago: Chicago Review Books, 1984.

40. "I Can't Explain" may be played with F-Eb-Bb-C chords.

41. Catherine Villanueva Gardner, "The Who and My Generation: Philosophical Recollections of a Former Second Wave Mod," *The Who and Philosophy*. Ed. Rocco J. Gennaro and Casey Harison. Lanham: Lexington, 2016, p. 4.

42. Gardner, p. 17.

43. The 8th notes rhythm syncopating the 4ths of the 8th notes, the G-A leading to the next 8th notes.

44. Cream recorded "I'm So Glad" by Skip James. Skip James and Son House brought their Delta blues to the Newport Folk Festival in 1966. Son House became lost to alcohol and Skip James died October 3, 1969. Cream was interested in Buddy Guy's "Hoodoo Blues."

45. Quoted in John Milward, *Crossroads: How the Blues Shaped Rock n'Roll*. Boston: Northeastern Press, 2013, p. 101. *Live Cream, Live Cream II* were compilations that appeared later. *Goodbye* included "Badge" by George Harrison and Eric Clapton.

46. Christine McVie did not appear on this first Fleetwood Mac album.

47. Paul Gilroy, "Bold as Love: Jimi's Afrocyberdelia and the Challenge of the Not-Yet," *Critical Quarterly* (December 2004): 26.

48. Gilroy, pp. 26–27.

49. Sheila Whiteley, *The Space Between the Notes: Rock and the Counterculture*. London and New York: Routledge, 1992, p. 22.

50. Eric Nisenson, *Ascension: John Coltrane and His Quest*. New York: Da Capo, 1995, p. 257.

51. Nisenson, *Ascension*, p. 261.

52. Cited by Nisenson, *Ascension*, p. 230.

53. Nisenson, *Ascension*, p. 233.

54. Nisenson, *Ascension*, p. 206.

55. Nisenson, *Ascension*, p. 239. Nisenson is critical, saying that Ian Hammer's synthesizer essentially created guitar sounds that matched McLaughlin's guitar sound and lacked different colors. There was jazz playing without a rock sensibility in the use of the "dynamics of electronic instruments" (p. 241). He points more affirmatively to McLaughlin's later work on *Love, Devotion, Surrender* with Carlos Santana. He observes that "The first and longest track is a reworking of the first section of *A Love Supreme*" (p. 241). He proceeds to consider the fusion work of Chick Corea, Herbie Hancock, and of Weather Report (pp. 242–46).

56. Lawrence Kramer, *Musical Meaning: Toward a Critical History*. Berkeley: University of California Press, 2002, p. 245.

57. Kramer, p. 247.

58. K.J. McElrath, (jazzstandards.com); Walt Weiskopf and Ramon Rider, *Coltrane: A Player's Guide to His Harmony*. New Albany, IN: J. Aebersaid, 1991, p. 23; David Demsey, *John Coltrane Plays Giant Steps*. Milwaukee: Hal Leonard, 1996, p. 145.

59. Kramer, p. 247.

60. Kramer, p. 249–50.

61. Kramer, p. 250.

62. Ibid.

63. Kramer, p. 251.

64. Kramer writes: "it seeks to make the archaic (Phrygian) modality of the first half of Rodger's tune the basis of something more than a nostalgic Schlagober" (p. 252).

65. Kramer, p. 253.

66. Nisenson, p. 208. These songs ("My Favorite Things," "Naima," and others.) also appeared in a live album, *Coltrane Live at the Village Vanguard Again*.

67. Nisenson, p. 207.

68. Ibid.

Chapter Two

The Imaginative Legacy of the Beats

Countercultural Utopia

Rock between the 1960s and the 1980s was the soundtrack of a generation. Mixing with Motown and radio pop songs, rock was a culture text: a shared point of reference. David Gates wrote in *Newsweek* (2006): "Not even the Jazz Age took popular music as seriously as people of my generation did.... For many of us, rock and roll wasn't just music; it was a cause, a cult, a movement. It divided parents and children, it taught its devotees styles, attitudes, ideologies and behaviors.... It gave strength and comfort to the alienated and misunderstood. Its basic stance was rebellion."[1] Joseph A. Kotarba defines rock as "a primary source of everyday meaning for the first generation raised on it."[2] He begins his book with the image of an audience of baby-boom-aged fans at a Tom Petty and the Heartbreakers concert and notes Simon Frith's observation that rock has been "fundamental" to the experience of growing up after World War II. Adults hold onto rock music, making sense of the world through it, Kotarba claims.[3] On the other hand, is this merely a form of nostalgia for what Bruce Springsteen calls the "glory days" of one's youth? How does rock music intersect with identity, experience, values, and one's worldview?

The baby boom generation arose amid the soundtrack of rock and the waves of the counterculture. Amid rock's extension throughout culture in 1967, arose the dream that counterculture could be emancipatory. Rock music "dove"-tailed with hopes for peace and the rise of the anti-war movement. It connected with a call for women's rights, ecological awareness, and dreams of transcendence and social transformation. Rock connected with utopian visions of brotherhood. America had witnessed many such visions. During the time of *Looking Backward* (1887) by Edward Bellamy, there were dozens of utopian dreams. Even so, there was nothing quite like the counterculture of the 1960s.[4]

In his notable book *The Making of the Counterculture* (1970), Theodore Roszak observed the interest among youth to "investigate the non-intellective consciousness." He pointed to a growing interest in Eastern approaches to consciousness which he asserted "calls radically into question the validity of the scientific worldview, the supremacy of cerebral cognition, the value of technological prowess."[5] An Eastern worldview allows a place for silence. The "Western intellect is inclined to treat silence as if it were a mere zero: a loss for words indicating the absence of meaning."[6] Roszak writes a chapter on "Journey to the East and Points Beyond." He "calls into question the anthropocentric arrogance with which our society has gone about mechanizing and brutalizing the environment in the name of progress."[7] An illusion of separation is related to exploitation of the earth.

A counterculture arose to address these ideas and critique contemporary Western culture. Hippie was derived from "hip," or "tuned in." Life was best lived in freedom and openness. Woodstock typified this dream of community, "a sense of cultural identity."[8] The crowd was like a living organism, an audience with tribal identity. It flourished in Haight-Ashbury, near San Francisco State College, and in gatherings in Golden State Park, like the "Be-In" there on January 14, 1967. The spirit was alive at the Fillmore, in the psychedelic music at the Avalon Ballroom, at the Monterey Pop Festival (June 16–18, 1967), and in the Summer of Love. It expanded and found roots in many places across the United States and in Europe. *Time* magazine featured a story on July 7, 1967, titled "The Hippies: Philosophy of a Subculture." That philosophy was conveyed simply: Do your own thing. Tune in, turn on, drop out. Blow your mind. Reject straight society. There were precursors to this. Some of the attitude, the rebellion, the re-tuning of life may be traced to the Beat Generation.

THE BEAT GENERATION

In Jack Kerouac's *On the Road* we read: "I looked out the window at the buzzing night street of Mission; I wanted to get going and hear the great jazz of Frisco—and remember, this was only my second night in town."[9] The San Francisco experience of Kerouac's fiction is filled with a jazz aesthetic in which words unfold like music, seemingly improvised, swinging and rolling, popping and hissing and buzzing with intensity. Sal Paradise, the narrator, goes to "a sawdust saloon with a small bandstand on which the fellows huddled with their hats on."[10] We are invited into sound and images of the club: "The behatted tenorman was blowing at the peak of a wonderfully satisfactory free idea."[11] Sal Paradise describes the scene and the sound, "a mad crowd" that was "rocking and roaring."[12] We roll down to sounds "Baugh" and "Beep" and "up to EEEEE!" There is a vocalist singing like "in scorn, Billie Holiday's lip sneer."[13] We read: "Dean was in a trance. The tenorman's eyes were fixed straight on him; held a madman who not only understood but cared and wanted to understand more and much more, and they began dueling for that."[14]

Music was sustenance for the Beats just as it was to youthful dreams in the Jazz Age. When John Clellan Holmes differentiated the Beat Generation from the Lost Generation of the 1920s, he wrote that the Beat Generation took the ruins for granted. "They were brought up in these ruins and no longer notice them," he wrote. "The wild boys of today are not lost, often scoffing, always intent faces elude the word and it would sound phony to them."[15]

In 1951, at 454 West 20th Street in New York, Jack Kerouac again wrote a version of *On the Road* on a 120-foot scroll. After a divorce, he moved in with Lucien Carr and Allen Ginsberg. In 1955, he met poets Lawrence Ferlinghetti, Gary Snyder, Kenneth Rexroth, Michael McClure, and Philip Whalen. On September 5, 1957, *On the Road* was published. In *On the Road*, Sal Paradise, arriving in San Francisco, realizes that he is 3,000 miles away from his aunt's house in Paterson, New Jersey. "I wandered out like a haggard ghost, and there she was, Frisco—long, bleak streets with trolley wires all shrouded in fog."[16] We meet Dean Moriarty and hear that "He was Beat—the root, the soul of Beatific."[17] We travel and see America. *On the Road* concludes with Sal sitting on a river-pier looking out at the sky over New Jersey, thinking out to America, where he can "sense all that raw land that rolls in one unbelievable, huge bulge over to the West Coast, and all that road going, all the people dreaming in the immensity of it."[18]

Kerouac never stayed for long in San Francisco. He was a wanderer. However, he wrote candidly in his journal: "San Francisco is so homelike to me; and I would live there someday."[19] In his notebook, Jack Kerouac writes of a "haunted moment" in San Francisco in 1949. He calls this a "Dickensian Vision on Market Street." The San Francisco nights were "filled with moral pangs and dark moral worries and decisions."[20] He passed what he refers to as a hash-house beyond Van Ness and saw a sign for Fish and Chips. There he saw "a pink faced anxious English woman (an English womany as any in a film)." The woman standing there gazed at him. Kerouac writes: "Something went through me, a definite feeling that in another life this poor, dear woman had been my mother and that I, like a Dickens' footpad, was returning after many years in the shadows of the gallows."[21] From Market Street he walked to Carolyn Robinson Cassady's apartment on Liberty Street, recalling Lowell, Massachusetts. He writes that only there and here "can there be such steep, star-pack't night."[22]

In 1955, New York dismantled the Third Avenue El-train line that passed through the Bowery. A bit of light at last shone in on the dives, as the Five Spot opened its doors for the jazz crowd in 1956. The club's Cooper Square address was a one-minute walk north from the future location of CBGBs. On the way you'd pass by where composer Bela Bartok once lived at 350 Bowery at the corner of Great Jones Street in the 1940s. Down Skid Row the other way was number fifteen where composer Stephen Foster hummed his last notes.

In 1956, Allen Ginsberg's "Howl" was published by Lawrence Ferlinghetti's City Lights Books.[23] Kerouac started *Desolation Angels*. He visited William S. Burroughs upon sailing to Tangier, where he helped to type *Naked Lunch*. (With Allen Ginsberg, he met Timothy Leary in 1961.) He wrote *Big Sur* while in Orlando, drinking heavily. In 1966, he went to his mother's home in Hyannis, Massachusetts, but his mother had a stroke and was paralyzed. Kerouac, who drank far too much for his own good, was beaten outside a bar in September 1969. He later collapsed at home from cirrhosis of the liver.

When Ken Kesey's novel *One Flew Over the Cuckoo's Nest* (1962) became a film, the film critic Pauline Kael wrote in *The New Yorker* that "it preceded the university turmoil, Vietnam, drugs, the counterculture. Yet, it contained the prophetic essence of that whole period of revolutionary politics going psychedelic." The story is set in an Oregon mental hospital. (Kesey had participated in an Army study of mind-altering drugs in 1960.) The novel positions individuality against conformity and rejects behaviorism, institutional practices, and assumptions about rationality.

In 1964, Kesey and associates, who called themselves the Merry Pranksters, took a cross-country bus trip to the World's Fair in New York and back to California. Among them was Neal Cassady, who Kerouac based his character Dean Moriarty on. Cassady had been arrested on a marijuana charge in 1958 and was released from San Quentin in 1960. At the Kesey ranch, the "acid tests" began with Kool Aid laced with LSD. (Author Tom Wolfe turned this episode into his book *Electric Kool-Aid Acid Test* [1968].) In 1966, Kesey was charged with marijuana possession and fled to Mexico.[24] From the Merry Pranksters, Hugh Romney (Wavy Gravy) went on to start Hog Farm at Taos, as a utopian experiment. He was one of many who dreamed of communal possibilities and the simple merits of going back to the land.

UTOPIAN DREAMS

Rock music connected with utopian dreams and communitarian experiments. In some respects, the visions and hopes of countercultural utopians corresponded with an American quest for community and democracy that goes back to the foundations of the United States of America. This quest for freedom, community, or utopia was prevalent in the nineteenth century with communities like New Harmony, Oneida Community, the Shakers, and Fourierist experiments. In the 1880s, the period of Edward Bellamy's *Looking Backward*, there were many dozens of utopian experiments.[25] Hippie communes in the 1960s and early 1970s emphasized social sharing. Stephen Gaskin in San Francisco had a class of up to 1500 students and went on a speaking tour. In 1967 Gaskin left San Francisco and settled with others on 1,700 acres at The Farm in Tennessee. The community was spiritually based. At Strawberry Fields a stockbroker Gridley Wright set up a community on forty acres in Decker Canyon near Malibu. Timothy Leary visited. It prospered for about five months and it did not last. A study by poet Judson Jerome estimates that about 750,000 people lived in as many as 10,000 communities between the mid-1960s and the mid-1970s. Many of these communal experiences were short-lived. There was the Rainbow Family of Living Light, Renaissance Community, the Family/Children of God, and dozens of others that sought to recreate society on a "small is beautiful" scale.[26]

By the late 1960s, rock had become a cultural discourse that offered "insight into the tensions between representations of utopian imagination with the often-hard realities of experience of work," wrote Carl Rhodes in *Outside the Gates of Eden: Utopia and Work in Rock Music, Group and Organization Management* (February 2007). The cultural theorist Herbert Marcuse, observing America's youth, wrote: "What I am really interested in is this togetherness between the band and the audience, and the togetherness of the audience. In other words, I am interested in the relation between rock music and political radicalism."[27] Other thinkers have been interested in the communal aspect of audiences when they are engaged in rock concerts. In *Traces of the Spirit* (1998), Robin Sylvan sees the rock concert as a religious ritual experience. Deena Weinstein has pointed to comparative mythologist Mircea Eliade's hierophanies. Ian Inglis, in *Performance and Popular Music*, writes of "the profound, even spiritual response to the experience of . . . participation in live musical performances."[28]

Another aspect of the quest for freedom or spiritual experience was experimentation with substances, which were viewed as paths to expanded consciousness. LSD was legal in the United States until October 6, 1966. Of course, not many people were acquainted with the drug until after this date.[29] For some LSD was an experience of learning about self in the universe. Timothy and Richard Alpert (Ram Dass) advocated this. The International Foundation for Internal Freedom began at Newton, Massachusetts, and then went to Millbrook, New York. It shut down during 1967.

Rock was closely connected with the impulse toward freedom. "[T]o the utopian impulse of sixties rock this was a music of liberation and transcendence of untrammeled authenticity, of passion, truth, and love," Marianne DeKoven writes.[30] "That there was the possibility of a utopian alternative ... was always the implied alternative to 'Maggie's Farm' or 'Desolation Row.'" She recognizes the movement of women toward "modes of agency" and assertion of their rights. "Although sixties rock was dominated by men there were some visible extremely successful women," she says. She claims that the key folk-rock voices were "characterized by a deep, passionate, visionary sincerity; clarity of purity; a directness of emotion."[31] That passion and vision were alive before commercialism and excess swallowed it up. The authors of *Music and Your Mind: Listening with a New Consciousness* view the sixties as "a period of introspection, motivated by disillusionment with establishment values in government, religion, and culture."[32] They call this a "Pandora's box" and argue that this fell into consumerism as well as into non-drug approaches to altered states of consciousness.

Of course, some mainstays of this period were both creatively and economically successful. They survived drug culture and sustained a concern with social justice. One example of this is Crosby, Stills, Nash, and Young. Recently, Graham Nash has created new work like *This Path Tonight*, while documenting CSN and his own career. Stills has toured with Judy Collins. Crosby has revived his songwriting amid collaborations and has been amazingly prolific, generating four albums across about five or so years. Young, who has arguably been the most commercially successful and influential occasional member of CSN&Y, has raised funds for autism research, assisted with Farm Aid, and argued the rights of Native Americans of Canada. Crosby, who has written on musicians engaged with social justice causes, recalls Woodstock on a recent album. To conclude *Here if You Listen* (2018), Crosby revisited Joni Mitchell's "Woodstock" in collaboration with Becca Stevens, Michelle Willis, and producer Michael League. Crosby's album arrived as a somewhat improvisational studio creation developed by all of them. Amid richly clustered, tumbling vocals we hear Crosby's musings on the mysteries of life and death. At other times it seems as if Crosby, coming full circle, has settled back into the jazz-alternate tunings and vocal improvisations of his first solo album. He sounds creative and happy with his recent collaborators. Of course, some of his first collaborators, after he concluded his days with The Byrds, were the members of the Jefferson Airplane and the Grateful Dead. These days if one turns on PBS it's déjà vu: There they are, the Grateful Dead, their younger selves in their raggedy glory gigging for viewer donations with the ghost of Jerry Garcia, "Truckin'" again.

Jefferson Airplane and the Grateful Dead

In the 1960s, rock music coalesced with countercultural ideas, lifestyle choices, and personal expression. Record albums increased in visibility around 1965–1966 with recordings like The Beatles' *Rubber Soul*, The Beach Boys' *Pet Sounds*, Frank Zappa's *Freak Out*, and Bob Dylan's *Blonde on Blonde*. In 1967, as counterculture spread across the United States, The Beatles' *Sergeant Pepper's Lonely-Hearts Club Band* stirred responses of wonder and a flurry of musical activity. The year 1967 brought Jimi Hendrix's *Are You Experienced?* and Jefferson Airplane's *Surrealistic Pillow*. This period saw the gradual rise of FM radio and the appearance of rock music publications. In 1966, *Crawdaddy* emerged as Paul Williams mimeographed copies and Jon Landau and Richard Meltzer began writing for that magazine. Jann Wenner started *Rolling Stone* in November 1967, with an image of John Lennon on the cover in combat gear and a feature article on the Monterey Pop Festival within its pages.

In San Francisco, bands like the Jefferson Airplane and the Grateful Dead were right in the middle of this scene. Marty Balin, Grace Slick, Paul Kantner, Jorma Kaukonen, Spencer Dryden, and Jack Casady had formed a band that would shake things up. The Jefferson Airplane made their debut at the Matrix in August 1965 and signed with RCA that November. They played at the Fillmore in 1966 with songs that appeared on their debut album *Jefferson Airplane Takes Off* (August 1966). They drew upon folk music and the blues and their music unified youthful audiences into a subculture in the San Francisco Haight-Ashbury scene. In 1966–1967, there was no distinction between audience and band members. The Grateful Dead, the Jefferson Airplane, Quicksilver Messenger Service, Big Brother and the Holding Company. And other bands were closely connected with their listeners.

Jefferson Airplane was the first San Francisco band to sign with a major record label. They produced their next album *Surrealistic Pillow* (1967), which included the hit singles "Somebody to Love" and "White Rabbit," with its hallucinogenic references to *Alice in Wonderland*. Grace Slick sang "Somebody to Love," a song in Dorian mode, which rose to number five on the charts, and "White Rabbit," which reached number eight. Their drug-culture song recalling Alice in Wonderland broke onto the charts and increased their visibility across the United States and in Britain. The Jefferson Airplane and the Grateful Dead both became involved with hallucinogens and the quest for alternate lifestyles that brought the counterculture into contact with psychedelic rock.

Between 1966 and 1970, the Jefferson Airplane and other San Francisco bands entered psychedelic music in explorations of human consciousness. When the Grateful Dead got onstage, what they wanted, according to Jerry Garcia, was "to be transformed from ordinary players into extraordinary ones, like forces of a larger consciousness."[33] Drummer Mickey Hart has written that the Grateful Dead's music was "intuitive," a "collective journey."[34] Hart has addressed the band's sense of the spiritual in and about music. He has remarked on Mircea Eliade and Joseph Campbell and their mythical sense. Joseph Campbell compared the ritual aspect of a Grateful Dead concert to a Dionysian festival. In her study on the Grateful Dead, Nancy Reid concluded that the Grateful Dead generated "controlled trances": "These shifts in consciousness may be experienced as metaphoric deaths or journeys to a mythic world," she wrote.[35]

Music and substances aided a shift in consciousness that brought the musicians to presence, to being there within the music. The Grateful Dead and the Jefferson Airplane recognized that they were involved in a rock ritual in which their audiences were entranced. Music and communal ritual suggested shamanic rites, seeking ecstasy, playing music with spontaneous openness, and being in the moment. Mickey Hart has mentioned that he read in Mircea Eliade that shamanic songs recall a primal "lost language" and "animal powers."[36]

The Grateful Dead began in 1965 as the Warlocks and they became the Grateful Dead in December of that year. The Grateful Dead drew upon the blues, R&B, country, and what they called "jug band music."[37] They would play more than 2,000 shows across thirty years. Their music combined bluegrass, the blues, improvisation as in jazz, jamming, psychedelic exploration, and free-form spontaneity. They connected with their audience in a communal orientation. They explored the music and entrainment in a dialogue or conversation with each other and their audience. The Grateful Dead focused on being in the moment, in the flow, or as Phil Lesh put it: when "you're just there."[38] Jerry Garcia came from a background in folk music, playing banjo, guitar, steel pedal guitar. Bob Weir also had a folk background but was also drawn toward electric rock. Bill Kreutzmann was deeply involved with blues and R&B and Ron McKernan (Pigpen) was also engaged with the blues. Phil Lesh had studied music and was familiar with atonal composition and orchestral music like that of Schoenberg, Stravinsky, and Webern. Lesh investigated bassline possibilities as Hart explored Native American shamanistic music, Tibetan ritual, West African rhythms, Brazilian percussion, and classical Indian influences channeled by Alla Rakha and Ravi Shankar.

In *The Grateful Dead and the Art of Rock Improvisation* (2013), David Malvinni focuses on the Grateful Dead's song "Dark Star" and relates the song to acid tests and a cosmic frame.[39] He notes that the Dead performed the song mostly between 1968 and 1974, the height of the Sixties era, and that *Deadlist* says the band played the song 213 times. The free-flowing style of the band suggests a quest for connection and transcendence. Jerry Garcia in an interview with Charles Reich in *Rolling Stone* commented: "there's a lot of universe available, and there's a whole lot of experience available over here." The band is a "signpost" pointing to this cosmic reality. "Dark Song" is less a song than "a playing experience." The song "reflects the metaphysical world in which the Dead live."[40]

In his liner notes for Creedence Clearwater Revival, music critic Ralph Gleason referred to San Francisco as a center of rock music that was "a revolutionary force." Gleason was right about the rock music creativity of San Francisco, although CCR was undercut in this review which appeared on the back of their own album cover. In the San Francisco scene, area musicians turned to the blues rock that was popularized by the British invasion bands like The Rolling Stones, The Who, The Kinks, and The Animals. Jefferson Airplane's guitarist Jorma Kaukonen would transform the finger picking blues of Reverend Gary Davis. He listened to Buddy Guy, to Sonny Boy Williamson, Mississippi Fred McDowell, Lightnin' Hopkins, and Robert Johnson, as he picked up an electric guitar. John Cipollina of Quicksilver Messenger Service, Sam Andrew of Big Brother and the Holding Company, Peter Lewis of Moby Grape, and Country Joe Mc Donald listened to blues players and developed their substance-fueled guitar playing. The Fillmore West, the Avalon, and clubs like The Matrix were filled with the pulse of blues-rock and the emerging creativity of these bands.

Meanwhile, British psychedelic bands like Pink Floyd, Procol Harum, The Moody Blues, and The Nice created a basis for progressive rock between 1966 and 1970. Blues and folk based groups like Jefferson Airplane and the Grateful Dead would continue to foster one brand of hippie consciousness and music, while the emergence of British progressive rock would follow with Emerson, Lake and Palmer, Yes, Genesis, Gentle Giant, Renaissance, and Jethro Tull between 1970 and 1975.[41] The work of Jefferson Airplane and the Grateful Dead is part of this psychedelic phase. They exemplify the musical quest for freedom and transcendence that was vitally present in sixties counterculture.

Jefferson Airplane, in their hallucinogenic, creative outpourings on *Surrealistic Pillow* seem to be the Dionysian band *par excellence*. Greek mythology speaks of Dionysus, the wine god, as a force of creativity, destruction, and renewal. In the Greek drama *Antigone*, the Chorus of senators lift their hands and voices in appeal to Dionysus for healing and transformation for the city of Thebes. Rock music has been linked with the Dionysian by some of its fiercest critics, from Allan Bloom in *The Closing of the American Mind* (1986) to Robert Pattison's *The Triumph of Vulgarity*. Yet, this creative impulse toward breaking free and remaking the world is also one of rock music's strengths. The Dionysian consciousness expresses itself in radical novelty, a willingness to risk ecstasy and chaos. The ancient Greek drama *The Bacchae* by Euripedes warned against having emotion overcome reason. The chorus in *Antigone* indeed appeals to Dionysus as the patron of Thebes but also counsels against humans who dare to exceed the boundaries of moderation. Rock is immoderate: it seeks highs of ecstasy and wonder and it plays with illusion.

Transcendence was a dream of the sixties that was closely connected with rock music. The late 1960s brought a turbulent period of countercultural resistance to the Vietnam War characterized by student protests, calls for change in the social imagination, and drug-induced quests for transcendence. The "sixties," a period that several sociologists suggest extends from about 1965 through the early 1970s, was a time of idealism and sociopolitical restlessness. For some listeners, rock music became associated with drugs, sex, spiritualism, or a quest for higher consciousness. With this idealism arose progressive movements in civil rights, feminism, environmentalism, justice and equality, and opposition to war. In *The Making of the Counterculture*, Theodore Roszak viewed counterculture as a loose collection of people who felt disaffiliated. Timothy Leary believed that spiritual development could come from LSD and consciousness-raising. Todd Gitlin, observing America through a sociological lens, observed that the counterculture sought pluralism and pursued issues with political resonance and a sense of community free from the mainstream. The Jefferson Airplane joined The Doors, bringing their music and ideals overseas with them on a European tour in 1968.

Rock music supported an ethos of rebellion, declared a negation of convention, and sought an alternative to "the system." From folk rock came apocalyptic songs like "Eve of Destruction" and the protest of "For What It's Worth." At Woodstock, Jimi Hendrix's guitar wailed in feedback that suggested percussive bombing in Vietnam. Rock counterculture listeners sought freedom of consciousness and lifestyle. Others wished to change the world. They became involved in civil rights, women's rights, or in social and political concerns. Some rock fans simply enjoyed the music. Some audience members were more interested in listening to music and getting high than in fostering the transformation of society. They protested what they felt to be repressive and then participated in hedonism and expressive indulgence. Indeed, some individuals likely wanted to step out of the society altogether. Others stayed on in their communities, spending time with family and friends, working their jobs, or attending school. America persisted through the years of the Nixon administration and Watergate, years that saw Woodstock, Altamont, the rise of progressive rock, folk-pop singer-songwriters. These were years of change for the Jefferson Airplane, as they morphed into the commercially successful Jefferson Starship.

The Jefferson Starship evolved from the Jefferson Airplane in the early 1970s. Former band members Jorma Kaukonen and Jack Casady created music grounded in the blues as Hot Tuna. Grace Slick and guitarist Paul Kantner joined forces and sang about a group of people escaping earth in a hijacked starship. They produced *Blows Against the Empire* (1971), an album nominated for a Hugo Award. Kantner and Slick created what they called the "Planet Rock and Roll Orchestra." The *Sunfighter* (1971) album followed and Jefferson Starship appeared in 1974. "Miracles" on the *Red Octopus* album was a huge single, reaching number one on the *Billboard* charts. The band's *Earth* (1978) album offered another of their biggest hits, "Count on Me," a single with richly layered vocals. A *Creem* review called Jefferson Starship's music "faceless, expert, and bland."[42] The review suggested that a quality of "seriousness" that could be found in the lyrics of Bob Dylan, Elvis Costello, Michael Stipe of REM, Peter Gabriel, and some Neil Young songs was lacking.[43]

The years during which some of the members of the Jefferson Airplane reinvented themselves as Jefferson Starship were a time of soul-searching for some who passed through San Francisco. Some seekers turned East, quite seriously exploring meditation and spirituality. They pursued alternatives in Eastern religions and theosophy and followed the encouragement of figures like Ram Das (Richard Alpert) to "be here now." Alan Watts offered thoughts on how to link Eastern thought and Western psychology and Harvey Cox observed the movement toward Eastern spirituality in *Turning East*. Rock musicians like George Harrison, Pete Townshend, and John McLaughlin turned East for Enlightenment. For others, sitars were exotic and talk of chakras was trendy. Esotericism and new age approaches could be co-opted by capitalist entrepreneurs as marketing strategies. Hallucinogenic drugs were tools for a spiritual quest for some people and recreational escape for others. Questioning of authority came with questioning the reliance on technocratic culture and a desire for communal relationship rather than atomization. Many individuals sought peace but had to deal with an unsuspected undertow of violence present in the counterculture and the wider society. Myth or mythopoetic awareness offered a narrative that was different from conventional daily life in Britain, or in America. Some psychedelic bands, or progressive bands, seized upon these alternatives.

In another development, rock moved increasingly toward the theatrical. Rock had long been associated with performance: transgressive expressions of shake, rattle, and roll like Little Richard's antics, Jerry Lee Lewis's wildness at the piano, or Elvis's gyrating pelvis. The makeup and stage performances of David Bowie and Alice Cooper and dozens of progressive and heavy metal bands are theatrical play and expressions of imagination, Eros, and breaking out of "straight" society. They challenge inherited modes of perception and seek a non-repressive social order. Play, spontaneity, and fantasy challenge conventional boundaries of order with a kaleidoscopic variety, a sensuous immediacy in which improvisation is allowed to happen. Such creative rock bands claim artistic as well as commercial goals. They oscillate between work and play, thinking and feeling, fantasy and realism, concept and imagination. For them, rock connects with personality; rock lives within musical structures and ventures to break out musically, sometimes theatrically, wandering into strangeness or tempest and passion. Rock bands defy order.

Science Fiction Dreams and *Blows Against the Empire*

Science fiction imagination marked the transition of the Jefferson Airplane to Jefferson Starship. As band members were drifting away toward other concerns and Jefferson Airplane was dissolving, Paul Kantner turned toward science fiction concepts. Kantner had grown up reading science fiction and *Blows Against the Empire* (1970) would be his science fiction concept album. As a teenager, Kantner read of C.S. Lewis's *Prelandra* and *Out of the Silent Planet*. He read novels by Robert Heinlein, like *Methuselah's Children*, which serves as a basis for the story line of his album. The development of *Blows Against the Empire* was concurrent with Grace Slick's pregnancy and the birth of their child, China Kantner. Thus, the idea of new birth intersects on this album with dreams of a countercultural utopia. They will free their child from government restrictions and realize a life of freedom. Imagining spaceships, Kantner wrote "Let's Go Together." Kantner's acoustic guitar and his banjo playing on his cover of Rosalie Sorrel's "Baby Tree" contributed to the folk music inspired edge of the album. Grace Slick's piano playing served as one of the musical centers for the recording. The shimmering multitracked vocals on her own composition, "Sunrise," took the album to the higher dimension toward which it aspired. The overall theme was one of countercultural idealism typified by a breaking away from the constraints of earth.

Paul Kantner's work on his record began after the departure of drummer Spencer Dryden from Jefferson Airplane. Kantner's album was recorded at Pacific High Recording Studios and at Wally Heider's recording studio in San Francisco. Phil Sawyer was the recording engineer for the *Blows Against the Empire* project. They brought Jack Casady and Joey Covington into the sessions, along with Jorma Kaukonen and Peter Kaukonen, at a time when they were involved with their band Hot Tuna. Also contributing to the recording were members of the Grateful Dead, Jerry Garcia and Mickey Hart, David Freiberg of Quicksilver Messenger Service, and David Crosby and Graham Nash, who often recorded at Wally Heider's studio. Graham Nash, in his autobiography *Wild Tales*, recalls that David Crosby was involved with the Jefferson Airplane and with Grateful Dead members in a group they called the Planet Earth Rock and Roll Orchestra.[44]

There is a free-flowing jam quality to this record that corresponds with the freedom sought by the musical collective that was assembled to create the record. (A similar attitude seems to pervade "Music is Love," the first song on David Crosby's solo album, which includes a hippie collective sing-along in drifting, improvised harmonies.) The story line for *Blows Against the*

Empire says that this group of individuals seeks to break free from the oppression of Uncle Samuel, or present-day America. "Mau Mau (Amerikon)" begins the album with Kantner's vocal out front and a raggedy proto-grunge sound. The lyric encourages celebration and play and life. "The Baby Tree" rings out on banjo and brings us to an imaginary island where the babies grow on trees and fall to earth into the loving arms of happy couples. With "Let's Go Together" the collective joins together in an energetic ensemble that sounds like a live performance. Acoustic guitars generate an energy that supports chorus vocals. Kantner's singing is joined by this chorus and Grace Slick's voice, holding out notes, cuts through above them. In "A Child is Coming" the group gathers before dawn, tripping on acid, wondering at the possibilities of the break of dawn and a new day. Kantner introduces the image of a park in which he claims he will be a diplomat. The guitar chords driven song has bright lead guitar lines and Slick's vocal, rising in the background, echoes the lines sung by Kantner. David Crosby's vocal joins with other vocalists on this song and on "Have You Seen the Stars Tonite" on Side Two of the album.[45]

"Sunrise" opens side two and Grace Slick sings both vocal parts, overdubbed. "Sunrise" blends into the story of "Hijack," in which the group seizes a transport to the orbiting starship and then ventures off into space. They leave orbit in "Home" and we then hear "Have You Seen the Stars Tonite." Kantner's twelve-string guitar plays octaves and fifths in an alternate tuning in open C. Background vocals are overdubbed and processed. There are sound effects suggesting engines and a starship in flight. There is an inserted audio piece from a 1953 *War of Worlds* film in which a woman cries out, seeking to get free, and a ray gun fires. In "X-M" the ship's engines are prepared and the mutiny is fought for control of the spaceship. The idealists succeed in their effort. The ship is propelled around the sun and beyond the solar system.

Kantner presents the spaceship as a vehicle for community. It appears as something like a house in which a group of like-minded people can travel in search of a new way of life. This spaceship is one of a self-contained society that has developed its own perspective. Kantner dreamed this spaceship community could break from the larger society and could find renewal. Robert Heinlein's *Methusalah's Children* provided the basis for this countercultural vision. (Kantner asked for permission from Heinlein for the use of his images and Heinlein readily agreed.) The spaceship society that Kantner presented led directly to the Jefferson Starship. They are the spaceship family.

Robert A. Heinlein's story "Universe" provides the theme that a spaceship might carry people forth on a multigenerational mission into space. *Orphans in the Sky* (1963) collected this story with its sequel. In this story Hugh Hoyland and his companion live on a spaceship, an interstellar world in motion, on which many generations have lived and died. A mutant shows him the night sky and its stars and planets beyond the spaceship: a universe he has never seen. The story pulls together the pieces of a back story that recalls that there was a mission to a star that was expected to last for sixty years. There was a mutiny and there was a destructive time that wiped out the memory of the mission. Robert A. Heinlein's *Methuselah's Children* (1958), which was central for Kantner's vision, shows the departure of a group of families to space so that they can escape the persecutions they experience on earth. From this, Kantner drew the theme that a family-like group of companions might escape the sociocultural limitations of 1960s America and dream of creating new possibilities. Science fiction meets with utopian dreams in transformations like this one. They appear to have a relationship with a sense of cultural dislocation or technological change, as Larry McCaffrey has observed. A song, a story, or a recording like *Blows Against the Empire* may reflect a reaction against "the fears and assumptions of the period in which it was written," writer Neil Gaiman has pointed out.[46] The song-concepts confront the world with a utopian dream of transformation.

Blows Against the Empire was nominated for a Hugo Award: the only record to have ever been so recognized. However, no award was given that year. *Blows Against the Empire* (RCA Victor LSP-4448) was the first recording to make use of the Jefferson Starship name. The record was a silver LP with Russian art on the album cover and a collage inside. The record reached number twenty on the *Billboard* album charts.

The image of "leaving" is captured on the song "Wooden Ships," by David Crosby, Stephen Stills, and Paul Kantner, which appeared on *Volunteers* (1969). The song was recorded again for *Crosby, Stills and Nash* (1969) and *So Far* (1974). "Wooden Ships" is apocalyptic. After a nuclear war the wooden ships seek shelter. This group intends to sail away to freedom—not on a spaceship this time. They are leaving and are not needed by the culture they will escape from. What rings out clearly is an affirmation drenched in beautiful vocal harmonies.

Jefferson Starship was more mainstream commercial than Jefferson Airplane. The transformation of Jefferson Airplane into Jefferson Starship was a gradual process. Vocalist Marty Balin had left Jefferson Airplane. He would return later to Jefferson Starship and record the hit "Miracles" on *Red Octopus*. Jorma Kaukonen and Jack Cassady formed Hot Tuna. Jefferson Starship took off on the *Billboard* charts in 1975. *Red Octopus*, with the hit single "Miracles," became a platinum album, selling thousands of copies. Kantner remained at the band's center in subsequent years.

The Jefferson Starship enlisted the iconic image of the spaceship. In rock music iconography, the spaceship may be a symbol for launching and taking off, departure from convention and norms, or the aspirations of a band. (Consider the rocket images on album covers for Boston or ELO.) The Jefferson Starship imagined possibilities like that. They were a band in the spirit of late sixties revolution, yearning for social transformation. The starship idea suggested something cosmic, or the hope of transcendence. It was this romantic and utopian hope that was at the center of countercultural dreams of escaping a technocratic modern world and creating a better world of peace and harmony beyond it.

NOSTALGIA

"The sixties" are remembered nostalgically by some as a time of hope that faded into a time of disappointment and loss. Folksinger Don McLean's "American Pie" begins in memory and nostalgia. The song traces the rise of rock music and of personal and social idealism and the decline of "sixties" hope. Optimism and hope fill the first words of the song. If he has a chance, says the speaker, with his music, he could set the world dancing. Yet, soon comes the chill and the newspaper on the doorstep stuns the speaker into immobility. He recalls "the day the music died." The smile is gone when we get to the girl who sang the blues, or to the man at the sacred store. The music will no longer play. There is a sense of loss. Perhaps this is a song about the loss of innocence. Yet, something plays here—as if in resistance to the lament in the lyric. The G-C-D chord pattern steadily picks up energy, as the imagery spills forth all those symbols of late fifties rock and roll and sixties pop. The pundits variously interpret the jester as Dylan, the king as Elvis, and the quartet as the Beatles. The Rolling Stones linger behind the lyric as Jack flash uncomfortably settles down on a candlestick. We're eight miles high with the Byrds. The coat may have been borrowed from James Dean but that's our voice. The voice that comes from us—from community—is the one that collectively sings the chorus here: *"we"* are singing the chorus. In folk song sing-along tradition, it is our voice; with McLean's voice, this collective voice moves together into the memorable chorus.

This suggests that we imagine history collaboratively, constantly redefining it. McLean's song and our interpretations of it are both involved in this kind of redefinition. The past becomes part of our collective identity in the present. Fred Davis, in 1977, wrote in the *Journal of Popular Culture*: "clearly if one can speak of a collective identity crisis, of a radical discontinuity in people's sense of who and what they are, the late sixties and early seventies came about as close to realizing that condition as can be imagined." McLean's song positions a kind of community of song against this disintegration. They may sing of everything being lost and going to hell, but in doing so affirm solidarity and promise.[47]

Don McLean's "American Pie" is a kind of memorializing: a representational form that propagates and perpetuates memory while speaking of kinship and of community. McLean is the storyteller for a community much like

Homer was for the Greeks, conveying here a musical "epic" of seven or more minutes. "McLean has brought us soundly and safely back from his nostalgic reverie," wrote Tom Nolan in *Rolling Stone* in his review of *Homeless Brother* in January 1975. But wasn't the nostalgic reverie the point of *American Pie*?

ROCK REISSUES AND GREATEST HITS ALBUMS

Rock records have become cultural texts. They are repositories of cultural history. Indeed, how rock musicians are understood in the present has something to do with how they are remembered. If we regard recordings as cultural artifacts, with each re-packaging of an album there is a transposition and its "cultural status is reconstructed" observes Andrew J. Bottomley. The new construct "decodes a text's past and recodes it for the present," he writes. These reissues are "a cornerstone of the commercial recording industry."[48] Yesterday's songs are embedded in cultural memory.

Historian Bernard Bailyn has said of memory, "It's relation to the past is an embrace . . . ultimately emotional, not intellectual." "Nations don't remember. Groups of people do," Jay Winter says. "The remembered past is a much larger category than the recorded past," observed John Lucacs in 1968.[49] Andy Bennett observes: "Rock originally defined by an aesthetic dating back to the mid-1960s is now being culturally and historically repositioned through the application of heritage rock discourses." Rock from the mid-1960s, he says, "espoused its own performative, cultural and aesthetic discourses."[50]

The Beatles provide a glimpse at this tendency toward memory and nostalgia. Memory studies give us a lens through which we can investigate the cultural impact of The Beatles upon the generation of listeners who first experienced them and those who encountered them later. The Beatles act as a catalyst for remembering the 1960s. In his introduction to *Realms of Memory*, Pierre Nora tells us that "history is needed when people no longer live in memory but recall the past through the assistance of documents that help to recall it."[51] Narrative and memory are closely bound together in this way in several of The Beatles' lyrics. Much of their music, like life itself, is focused on process, transforming time into form. Their songs anticipate the future ("When I'm 64") or look backward (the "When I was younger" of "Help"). Memory is a theme that begins to appear on the albums *Rubber Soul* (released December 3, 1965, in the United Kingdom and December 6 in the United States) and *Revolver* (released August 5, 1966) with the songs "Eleanor Rigby," "Here, There and Everywhere," and others filled with the spirit of memorialization.

In "Yesterday" (1965), the singer's recollection looks sadly into the past, recognizing the suddenness of change. "Yesterday" poses the theme that memory involves a recollection of loss. In "You Won't See Me" on the *Rubber Soul* album we hear about the loss of a time "that was so hard to find." The song underscores the "benign use of nostalgia" that Gary Burns finds in The Beatles' work during this period.[52] On *Rubber Soul* in the romantic reverie of "Michelle" the song's speaker summons up the French language as he declares his love for Michelle. Even so, he appears to sense a kind of passing of their love. The lyrics that address the French girlfriend seek a language of the heart, "words that go together well." The music contributes a wistful mood.

London became "a point of departure" in The Beatles' work after 1966, according to Annette Hames and Ian Inglis; it was a point "from which to elaborate on other, non-localized themes—of nostalgia, consciousness, and history." The Beatles had left Liverpool and its working-class environs behind. This, observes Kenneth Womack, "accounts for the band's understandable sense of emotional dislocation."[53] The need to relocate their lives amid the swirling world of Beatlemania pulled them toward memory. What had begun with *Please Please Me* (1963), their first album, was now accentuated by change. "In My Life" brings together music and lyrics that evoke a wistful longing for the past. With "In My Life," John Lennon explores memory explicitly. While some places and people remain vivid, others recede and disappear. "Memories lose their meaning," Lennon sings, although he knows that he will often pause in recollection of the people and places that have made up his life. "Sergeant Pepper" also begins by looking backward: "It was twenty years ago today."

Jaime Weinman writes in *MacLeans* of the demise of rock nostalgia. She asks, will rock become "a charming relic"? Weinman claims that in 2016 there were "warning signs that the marker for rock and roll sentimentality is not what it used to be." HBO's *Vinyl* (created by Martin Scorcese with input from Mick Jagger), Cameron Crowe's *Roadies* on the Showtime channel, and FX's *Sex Drugs and Rock and Roll* with Dennis Leary were cancelled. "Why is there less appetite for stories about rock?" the writer asks. Is it that those stories are by now all too familiar? Is it due to a generation gap? Does rock now have less appeal to young audiences who are attuned to the pervasive force of hip-hop? Has not rock become just one of many options?[54]

Are aging rock bands only "pale ghosts of their youthful selves," or are they adding something to the cultural moment now, fifty years after Woodstock? Critics like John Strausbough lament a loss of vitality of the rock music infused by the baby boom generation. The generation started out as world-changers and the bands lapsed into nostalgic tours. He cites James Miller's observation that "rock is all about being young or pretending to be young."[55] He goes on to say that rock ought not to be played by "fifty-five-year-old men with triple chins wearing bad wighats, pretending still to be excited about playing songs they wrote thirty or thirty-five years ago and have played thousands of times since." This critic insists that "rock is not family entertainment." He refers to The Rolling Stones as "the most obvious, perhaps depressing examples of a once great rock band that kept playing years and years after they had gotten too old."[56] Yet, this critic does not make clear why they ought not to play concerts and appear on public television broadcasts if people still want to hear them. Presumably he believes (perhaps rightly) that they have lost their vitality and are simply cashing in on their notoriety and rock music legacy. Rather than retiring gracefully and collecting royalties and social security checks, bands return for the summer season nostalgia tour. "Every year ancient rock bands rise from their graves and rule the nights again."[57]

NOTES

1. David Gates, "A Fan's Notes, The Boomer Files," *Newsweek* Vol. 148, Is. 3 (July 17, 2006).
2. Joseph A. Kotarba, *Baby Boomer Rock n' Roll Fans*. Lanham: Scarecrow, 2013, p. 3.
3. Kotarba, pp. 2–3.
4. Of course, there was in the 1960s also conservative culture in America and in Britain and the developing global reach of rock.
5. Theodore Roszak, *The Making of the Counterculture*. London: Faber and Faber, 1970, p. 82. For other books that examine the countercultural sixties, see: William L. O'Neill, *Coming Apart* (1971), Allen J. Matusow, *The Unraveling of America* (1984), Todd Gitlin, *The Sixties, Days of Rage*, (1987), Terry H. Anderson, *The Movement of the Sixties* (1995), Peter Braunstein and Michael William Doyle, *Imagine Nation: The American Counterculture of the 1960s and 70s* (2002), Mark Hamilton Lytle, *America's Uncivil Wars* (2006), Irwin Unger, *The Sixties* (2011), Michael J. Kramer, *The Republic of Rock Music: Music and Citizenship in Sixties Counterculture* (2013). See also the journal *The Sixties*.
6. Roszak, pp. 82–83.
7. Roszak, p. 137.
8. Timothy Miller, *The 60s Communes: Hippies and Beyond*. Syracuse: Syracuse University Press, 1999, p. 82.
9. Jack Kerouac, *On the Road. Road Novels, 1957–1960*. New York: The Library of America, 2007, p. 174.
10. Kerouac, *On the Road*, pp. 176–77.
11. Kerouac, *On the Road*, p. 177.
12. Ibid.
13. Kerouac, *On the Road*, p.178.
14. Ibid.
15. John Clellan Holmes, *New York Times Magazine* (November 16, 1952).
16. Kerouac, *On the Road*, p. 53
17. Kerouac, *On the Road*, p. 175.
18. Kerouac, *On the Road*, p.180.
19. Jack Kerouac, Journal p. 784. Jack Kerouac "Journals 1949–50" part published in *Windblown World*. Ed. Douglas Brinkley. New York: Penguin, 2004. The notebook records journeys through the United States. This also appears in Jack Kerouac, *Road Novels, 1957–1960*. Ed. Douglas Brinkley. New York: Library of America, 2007.
20. Kerouac, Journal, *Road Novels, 1957–1960*. p. 782.
21. Kerouac, Journal, *Road Novels, 1957–1960*. p. 783.

22. Ibid.
23. Lawrence Ferlinghetti turned 100 in 2019. At 99, he produced an experimental novel, *Little Boy*. New York: Penguin-Random House, 2019.
24. Kesey next wrote *Sometimes a Great Nation*. His last works were *Sailor Song* (1992) and *Last Go Round* (1994).
25. Charles Rooney, in *Dreams and Visions: A Study of American Utopias, 1865–1917* (Praeger, 1985) identifies more than 100 works dealing with utopian fiction.
26. See E. F. Schumaker, *Small is Beautiful: Economics as if People Mattered*. New York: Harper, 1973.
27. Herbert Marcuse, *Marxism, Revolution and Utopia: Collected Papers of Herbert Marcuse*. Ed. Douglas Kellner and Clayton Pierce. London and New York: Routledge 2014, p. 348.
28. Ian Inglis, *Performance and Popular Music*. Aldershot: Ashgate, 2006, p. xiv.
29. The painted school bus and 1964 road trip of Ken Kesey and the acid test would later be captured in Tom Wolfe's writing *Electric Kool Aid Acid Test*. New York: Macmillan, 1968.
30. Marianne DeKoven, *Utopia Limited: The Sixties and the Emergence of the Postmodern*. Durham: Duke University Press, 2004, p. 119.
31. Ibid.
32. Helen Bonny and High Savary, *Music and Your Mind: Listening with a New Consciousness*. New York: Harper and Row, 1970, rpt. 1990, p. 9.
33. Nancy Reist, "Clinging to the Edge of Magic: The Shamanic Aspects of the Grateful Dead," *Perspectives on the Grateful Dead: Critical Writing*. Ed. Robert G. Weiner. Westport: Greenwood, 1999, p. 183–84. The Grateful Dead was Jerry Garcia, Bill Kreutzman, Bob Weir, Phil Lesh, and Ron McKernan and they played more than 100 shows across 1966–1967. Drummer Mickey Hart sat in with The Grateful Dead in September 1967 and became part of the band. Tom Constantin also played keyboards with them in 1968.
34. Mickey Hart, *Drumming at the Edge of Magic: A Journey into the Spirit of Percussion*. Acid Test, 1998, p. 216.
35. Reist, p. 185.
36. Hart, p. 169.
37. David Malvinni, *The Grateful Dead and the Art of Rock Improvisation*. Lanham: Scarecrow, 2013, p. 36.
38. Phil Lesh interview with David Gans, *Conversations with the Dead: The Grateful Dead Interview Book*. New York: Da Capo, 2002, p. 110. Also see *Relix* 2002 interview with Phil Lesh. See interview with David Gans on KPFA April 1997.
39. David Malvinni, p. 73. All of chapter three in his book is devoted to "Dark Star," which appears as representative of the band's cosmic reference.
40. Jerry Garcia was interviewed by Charles Reich and Jann Wenner, "Garcia: Signpost," *Rolling Stone* pp. 35, 58. Malvinni observes that Phil Lesh drew upon Charles Ives' 4th Symphony ideas for tone clusters, unmetered barring, and free polyphony. p. 83.
41. "What united the Bay area bands was their need to assimilate traditional American folk musics, particularly the blues, into rock" (Robot A. Hull, "Sound and Visions: Psychedelia," p. 286. Originally published in *Creem* [January 1981], the essay is reprinted in *Fifty Years of Rock Journalism*. Ed. Barney Hoskins. New York: Bloomsbury, 2003).
42. *Creem* 1974 (p. 71). Variations on this theme have been provided by Coleman, 1992 (p. 447), Considine, 1992 (p. 663), and Evans, 1992 (p. 364), who are cited in "Rolling Stone Album Lists" by Steve Jones *Pop Music in Press*. Philadelphia: Temple University Press, 2002. M. Coleman's reviews are on Barry Manilow, The Carpenters, Journey, and Neil Diamond. Steve Jones, *Pop Music and the Press*. Philadelphia: Temple University Press, 2002.
43. See Simon Frith, *Sound Effects: Youth, Leisure and the Politics of Rock and Roll*. Ann Arbor: University of Michigan Press and London: Constable, 1983, p. 163.
44. Graham Nash, *Wild Tales*. New York: Crown Archetype, 2013, p. 199.
45. Nash, p. 199.
46. Neil Gaiman, Foreword to Samuel R. Delaney, *Einstein Intersection*. Middletown: Wesleyan University Press, 1998, vii.
47. Fred Davis, "Nostalgia, Identity and the Current Nostalgia Wave," (pp. 414–24.) *Journal of Popular Culture* Vol. 11, No. 2 (1977): 421.

48. Andrew J. Bottomley, "Play It Again: Rock Music Reissues and the Production of the Past for the Present," *Popular Music and Society* Vol. 39, No. 2 (2016): 151–74.

49. John Lukacs, *Historical Consciousness or Remembered Past*. New York: Schocken Books, 1985. David W. Blight at Yale University has explored history and memory to look at "how societies remember their common myths, to explore public collective historical consciousness." He is the author of *Race and Reunion, The Civil War in American Memory*. University of Massachusetts Press, 2001. See also Jay Winter. "Film and the Matrix of Memory," *American Historical Review* Vol. 106, No. 3 (June 2001).

50. Andy Bennett, "Heritage Rock: Rock Music Representation and Heritage Discourse," *Poetics* Vol. 37 (2009): 474–89. Bennett, in *Remembering Woodstock* (2017), and David Shumway in "Rock n' Roll Soundtracks and the Production of Nostalgia" (*Cinema Journal* Vol. 38, No. 2 [Winter 1999]) reflect on the looking back of rock audiences of the baby boom generation. They both recognize contribution made by film to nostalgia. Shumway points to Claudia Gorbman's observation that the use of popular music in films has changed the relationship between music and image, p. 36. Claudia Gorbman, *Unheard Melodies: Narrative Film Music*. Bloomington: Indiana University Press, 1987.

51. Pierre Nora, *Realms of Memory*. New York: Columbia University Press, 1996–1998. Introduction i–v.

52. Gary Burns, "Refab Four: Beatles for Sale in the Age of Music Video," *The Beatles Popular Music and Society*. Ed. Ian Inglis New York: St. Martin's Press, 2000, p. 186.

53. Kenneth Womack, "The Beatles as Modernists," (p. 227) *Music and Literary Modernism*. Ed. Robert McParland. Cambridge Scholars Press, 2009.

54. Jaime Weinman, "The Demise of Rock 'n Roll Nostalgia," *Macleans* (October 2016).

55. John Strausbough, *Rock 'Til You Drop: The Decline from Rebellion to Nostalgia*. London: Verso, 2001, p. 2.

56. Strausbough, p. 3.

57. Strausbough, p.13.

Chapter Three

Science Fiction Imagination and Fantasy in Progressive Rock

Progressive rock sought to re-enchant the world with fantasy. This was romantic imagination pushed toward the fantastic. The progressive rock of the late 1960s and early 1970s has been linked with the counterculture, psychedelic music, and references to classical music. It may also be associated with the spirit of Romanticism. There were countercultural connections with progressive rock music's attention to myth, imagination, and grandiose visions. Some listeners were intrigued by these ideas and others found the fantasies and classical music references of progressive rock bands pretentious. Yet, critics have recognized in the audience for progressive rock a connection with the countercultural rejection of impersonal bureaucracy. Countercultural fascination with epic subject matter and mythopoeic fantasy are linked with some strands of science fiction and with romanticism.[1]

During the first wave of psychedelic rock in the mid to late 1960s the imagination of British bands brought innovations. In that era, Pink Floyd employed an array of keyboards, guitars, and sound effects. Procol Harum's single "A Whiter Shade of Pale," in 1967, introduced the Hammond organ sound which added an aura of cathedral-like mystery. A second wave of progressive rock began to emerge with King Crimson, playing in minor keys, with acoustic and electric guitars and Mellotron, while making use of medieval images. Genesis, Yes, Emerson, Lake, and Palmer, Jethro Tull, and Gentle Giant were part of this phase.[2] Progressive rock was imaginative and drew upon fantasy literature. Science fiction approaches and mythological elements appeared in the creative work of the bands. Often progressive rock's images and lyrics appear with references to mythology, science fiction, and fantasy.

Progressive rock is adventurous. Music leaves the "home" place of the tonic and moves on in an adventure to new harmonic areas. A dystopian or utopian narrative often accompanies these musical excursions. (One questions "civilization" in dystopian narrative, and one imagines a wonderful future in the utopian narrative.) The fictional adventure begins with a call and one journeys forth to some exotic and dangerous place to encounter challenges that test one's mettle. The hero crosses a border of common civilization into a land of savagery or mystery. One enters the twilight zone.

The monomyth of the hero's journey features heroic masculinity in the fantastic adventure tale. (Iron Maiden's "Aces High," the haunted "Rime of the Ancient Mariner.") British progressive rock has inherited the legacy of the British adventure tale. Within British progressive rock adventures are the fantasies of heroism. The hero seeks beyond the prosaic and travels into the extraordinary. There are explorations by land, air, and sea in imperial narrative that open the boundaries of adventure toward discovery of new realms. This is an impulse that underlay some of the creation and formation of science fiction and the horror story. It is a journey into an unknown future or back to the mysteries of ancient lost civilizations in remote, almost inaccessible places. This is an imperial romance, the scientific romance that may reveal what lies hidden. The tale generates a mythical figure of masculine prowess in which one is facing the challenge of battle or of a new world. In Joseph Campbell's model of the hero's journey, the vigorous and righteous hero ventures outward to this world to face the ordeal and will return (*nostos*) with a boon to bestow on the society.

Early on, progressive rock was associated with psychedelic rock. Psychedelic music encouraged synesthesia: the connection of sounds and textures and colors of tone. The relationship of progressive rock with classical music is evident in its "continuous use of tone and instrumental virtuosity" observes Edward Macan.[3] The instrumental lines, harmonic schemes, and metrical changes in progressive rock appeal to musical virtuosity. A sense of ritual is attached to the music and surrealism, light shows, and a "psychedelic zeitgeist" sometimes accompanies the music.[4]

To investigate the imaginative reach of psychedelic and progressive rock is somewhat atypical of rock studies. As Kevin M. Moist points out in "Global Psychedelia and Counterculture" in *Rock Studies* there is a "distance . . . from the usual beaten paths of popular music research."[5] However much a stretch an exploration of psychedelic rock may be, it illustrates an important phase in the history of rock. Psychedelic rock and progressive rock display what Michael J. Kramer called "hybrid and syncretic" tendencies.[6] The "psychedelic imaginary" is inscribed with intermediality, synesthesia, suggestions of space and expansiveness, and countercultural values. The utopian dreams embodied in concept albums suggest the achievement of transcendence, *as if* the countercultural audience had already arrived at utopia.

Psychedelic rock was alive and well in San Francisco with the Jefferson Airplane's *Surrealistic Pillow* and the Grateful Dead's extended concert jams. The Dead drew upon the blues, R&B, country, and what they called "jug band music."[7] Jerry Garcia in an interview with Charles Reich in *Rolling Stone* commented: "there's a lot of universe available, and there's a whole lot of experience available over here." The band is a "signpost" pointing to this cosmic reality. The song "Dark Star," he said, is less a song than "a playing experience."[8]

Cosmic reflection is deeply intertwined with the creativity of psychedelic bands like the Grateful Dead and progressive bands like Yes. When psychedelia emerged in the late 1960s, it brought key changes and time signature changes, modal melodies, surreal lyrics, and extended instrumental solos. It also brought imaginative uses of mythical imagery. The music accompanied a culture, in San Francisco and elsewhere, that embraced marijuana, peyote, mescaline, and LSD. This intersected with notions of mind expansion emerging from the thought of figures like Timothy Leary, Alan Watts, Aldous Huxley, and Eastern sages like Yogananda. In America, psychedelia emerged in the music of the Jefferson Airplane, the Jimi Hendrix Experience, The Doors, and Santana. Yet, it was mostly in the creativity of British bands that psychedelia met with the first wave of progressive rock. Psychedelia included the sounds of Pink Floyd, the Yardbirds, Traffic, and Soft Machine, and influenced bands like The Moody Blues. LSD experience led to light shows by Pink Floyd, which added props, dry ice, and a falling waterfall for "Set Controls for the Heart of the Sun." Extramusical props entered concerts by ELP, Pink Floyd, or Yes. On the ELP world tour of 1973 Keith Emerson's keyboards appeared as a massive array of technology. When Carl Palmer played his solos, his drums were synchronized with laser lights. Genesis and Yes used fog machines and laser lights. Science fiction met with technology in space music and the synthesizers of musicians like Gary Numan.

In progressive rock we hear the use of multitracking, reverb, echo, feedback, and ornate melody lines.[9] Progressive rock juxtaposes acoustic and electronic sections within instrumentals or songs. This may signal a compositional framework in which the pastoral and the organic are set alongside the technological, the artificial, and the innovative. This form sets side by side the ancient or mythical and the modern or technical, as in Emerson, Lake, and Palmer's *Brain Salad Surgery*.

While it enchanted many listeners, progressive rock irritated others. There was antagonism from the rock music press.[10] However, such a perspective may rest upon the preferences of a few major rock critics for blues-based rock and stripped down three chord songs played with attitude. Progressive rock seemed meretricious when set alongside the blues tradition, which relied upon guitars, bass, drums, and sometimes an organ or a harmonica backing a focused, grungy, sometimes seedy vocalist. Claims of the authenticity in blues-rock by Dave Marsh, Simon Frith, and others have become matters of record. These critics contrasted blues-based rock with progressive rock, which they dubbed inauthentic. To some synthesizers (from minimoog, circa 1971) at the center of progressive rock may have seemed excessive. (Keith Emerson used them as a lead instrument. Gary Numan in 1979 aimed for a sense of space. Depeche Mode used synthesizers in the 1980s for a pop sound. By then the DX7 keyboard had become a big deal.) For the rock bands who invested themselves in roots guitar-driven rock synthesizers were an affront. They preferred to project a gritty work ethic and a sound you could imagine came from the garage on a dirty city block or the back room in a concrete warehouse. Music was a no-nonsense release from a grimy, dystopian world.

When progressive rock first emerged, Kalefah Sanneh observes, the dominant narrative of rock claimed that "pretention was the enemy."[11] Sanneh recalls Lester Bangs' disdain and Robert Christgau's derision toward progressive rock. However, Sanneh recognizes that progressive rock continues to interest listeners and concludes that rock history is "cyclical." Sanneh notes that rock critic Bill Martin views progressive rock as "emancipatory and utopian." Indeed, Martin supports the view that progressive rock was an extension of 1960s counterculture and cites The Beach Boys' *Pet Sounds* and The Beatles' *Sergeant Pepper's Lonely-Hearts Club Band* as pivotal albums that encouraged experimentation with musical arrangements and the concept album.[12]

Prog-rock drew upon classical music, emphasized musicianship and musical virtuosity, and made use of fantasy literary genres. Bach, Ravel, Mussorgsky, and Brahms entered progressive rock and quotation from classical music brought it into new territory. Keyboardists drew upon Bach, Liszt, and Chopin and borrowed techniques from Bartok, Ravel, and Debussy. Audiences became familiar with Matthew Fisher's Hammond organ solo on Procol Harum's "Whiter Shade of Pale" (1967). Harpsichord entered the Moody Blues' *In Search of the Lost Chord* (1968) and Procol Harum's *In Held Twas I* (1968). In the early 1970s, Keith Emerson sent his Hammond organ sound through a Marshall amplifier. He made use of J.S. Bach's Tocatta and Fugue in D minor for his organ solo in "Rondo." (The Rondo form is a basic form of classical music. The Rondo has multiple sections. One of these sections, often the first, carries the tonic key. This tonic key section is contrasted with other sections, or episodes. (For example, ABACA.) There may be further complexities in this scheme. These sections introduce other tonal colors and themes.) Keith Emerson and Greg Lake repeatedly drew upon classical composers. "The Barbarian" is from Bela Bartok's *Allegro Barbaro* (1911) and "Knife Edge" is from Leos Janacek's *Sinfonetta* (1926). *Pictures at an Exhibition* takes its title from Modest Mussorgsky (1874) and a solo piano piece orchestrated by Maurice Ravel. On *Brain Salad Surgery* (1973), "Tocatta" was an arrangement from the fourth movement of Alberto Ginastera's Piano Concerto number one. ELP turned to Aaron Copland's *Fanfare for the Common Man* on Works, Volume 1 and "Hoedown" from Copland's *Rodeo* (1942) on *Trilogy*. Ravel's *Bolero* (1928) lay behind "Abaddon's Bolero."

King Crimson, opening for The Rolling Stones in Hyde Park in 1969, played "Mars the Bringer of War" by composer Gustav Holst. They produced *In the Wake of Poseidon* (1970) with the twelve minute "The Devil's Triangle," which drew directly from Gustav Holst's *The Planets* (Opus 32). That composer's work related the seven movements of his composition to the planets. "Mars, the Bringer of War," an intense rhythmic ostinato in 5/4 time, is the first of these movements. Many other references to classical repertoire were soon to follow. Rick Wakeman, on Yes's *Fragile*, played a solo from Brahms' 4th Symphony (Opus 98, 1885). Meanwhile, Steve Howe's introduction to "Roundabout" was clearly based in classical guitar. Bach's contrapuntal compositions were frequently employed by prog rock groups. Jethro Tull's "Bouree" on *Stand Up* (1969) used the 5th movement of Bach's Lute Suite in E minor (also later used by Led Zeppelin and Alter Bridge) and Genesis' "Horizons" by Steve Hackett on *Foxtrot* (1972) used the Prelude from Bach's first cello suite. On *Nursery Cryme* Hackett taps on his guitar and draws out an idea from Bach.[13]

The incorporation of classical music offered bands an opportunity for virtuosity and musical expression. The Moody Blues connected their recording of *Days of Future Passed* with the London symphony orchestra in 1968. ELO's cover of Chuck Berry's "Roll Over Beethoven" offered the advice that Tchaikovsky should be told the news of rock and roll's presence on the scene.

VISUAL IMAGINATION

Fantastic visual images were created for progressive rock LP records. This imaginative cover art work drew upon surrealism and often incorporated science fiction and fantasy scenes. For example, Emerson Lake and Palmer covers for *Tarkus* and *Brain Salad Surgery* reflect a society affected by something mechanistic or robotic. William Neal's cover for *Tarkus* and H.R. Giger's cover for *Brain Salad Surgery* made use of science fiction imagery. ELP's theme is human self-awareness and consciousness versus dehumanizing technology.

In listening to these albums, the audience was invited to entertain an imaginative concept presented through the artwork. The romantic visual imagination participated in illustrating the concepts behind record albums, contributed to stage shows, and assisted in the marketing of recordings. Music is just music the purists have said since the nineteenth century. However, rock music has been interpreted through the imagery of lifestyle fashions, album cover art, photography and film, band logos, MTV, and advertising. In the meeting of psychedelic and progressive rock there appeared elaborate visual designs that suggested expansiveness, wonder, and otherworldliness. Listeners were treated to imaginative visions of fantastic landscapes.

There was a period of vivid rock music art before the vinyl album cover shrunk down to a CD and film-screens shrunk down to phones. Psychedelia, glam, and progressive rock created intermedial relationships between rock music, the visual arts, and the performing arts. This iconography expressed a band or artist's vision and affected how audiences imagined and defined the music. There were the vibrant colors and imaginative designs of Roger Dean (for Yes), Hugh Syme for Rush (beginning with *Caress of Steel*), H.G. Giger (for ELP), Dave Hardy's space art (for Hawkwind) and others.

Of course, several rock artists have emerged from art schools, or have developed an interest in painting or drawing. David Bowie notably worked across art forms, painting, creating costumes and characters, envisioning theatrical expression. The transitions in the music of The Beatles was accompanied by a movement from their suits to colors and the buoyant films *A Hard Day's Night* and *Help!* to the animation of *Yellow Submarine*. One may remember the band through the sketched image on the cover of *Revolver*, Peter Max's designs, the brilliant caricatures on the cover of *Sergeant Pepper's Lonely-Hearts Club Band*, John Van Hamersveld's *Magical Mystery Tour* cover, or the image of The Beatles crossing Abbey Road. John Lennon drew pencil sketches and married the concept artist Yoko Ono. Paul McCartney visited art museums, enjoyed film, married Linda Eastman, a photographer, and later took up painting after 1983. And who is to say that Ringo's interest in hair-styling wasn't artistic?

Look across rock music and one can see Jerry Garcia's pastel paintings and neckties, Janis Joplin's sketches, the painting of Joni Mitchell, Dan Fogelberg, John Mellencamp, Cat Stevens, and Ronnie Wood. There is the photography of Graham Nash, the sketches and watercolors of Bob Dylan, the art of Kim Gordon of Sonic Youth, David Byrne, Patti Smith, and post-Jefferson Starship Grace Slick. The creativity of Freddie Mercury, Pete Townshend, Brian Eno, Keith Richards, Roger Waters, and Pink Floyd were amplified as they cultivated visual and musical talents while in art school. From Andy Warhol and the Velvet Underground to Patti Smith's connection with Robert Mapplethorpe and from David Bowie's art-bending across different planets to Anthony Benedetto (Tony Bennett) paintings, the correlations between visual artistry and musical expression are striking.

Progressive rock bands showed a marked preference for extended instrumentals and for myth and science fiction concepts. Rock critics like Lester Bangs, Robert Christgau, and Dave Marsh let it be known that they favored blues-based rock. They viewed rock as deriving directly from the blues.

Marsh insisted that only rock based in the blues was authentic. Lester Bangs preferred the Velvet Underground, the Stooges, and the New York Dolls to complex keyboard figures by Keith Emerson, or the vocals of Jon Anderson and the musicianship of Chris Squire, Steve Howe, Bill Bruford, and Rick Wakeman of Yes. For some listeners, there was a vast gulf between Iggy Pop and the MC5, on the one hand, and the guitar pyrotechnics of Robert Fripp of King Crimson or Renaissance's Annie Haslam's three octave vocal range, on the other. Edward Macan argues for a place for progressive rock's fusion of classical music and rock music and its appeal to mythological imagery.

EMERSON, LAKE, AND PALMER

Emerson, Lake, and Palmer created innovative music that was at the center of progressive rock's merging of science fiction themes and images of the fantastic. Their music was characterized by complex guitar and keyboard runs, shifting time signatures, and sounds from Moog or synthesizers. Keith Emerson (keyboards), Greg Lake (guitar and vocals), and Carl Palmer (drums) made use of banks of amplifiers and stages filled with synthesizers and vast percussion sets. Radio airplay featured Lake's vocal on "Lucky Man," ELP's first single. For their song "Jerusalem," ELP drew lines about England's green and pleasant land from the poetry of William Blake. Yet, it was in extended keyboard driven instrumentals that ELP most idiosyncratically made their mark.

Edward Macan argues that progressive rock's use of science fiction and fantasy was an extension of the hippie ethos of the late sixties. He points to Keith Emerson's interest in the music of Bela Bartok and the music of Alberto Ginastera and asserts that ELP, making the synthesizer central to their sound, "were more responsible than any other band for shaping the progressive style." They made "a truly idiosyncratic use of classical forms and techniques in a rock context."[14]

ELP took up a science fiction theme in their album *Tarkus* (Island [UK] Cotillion [US] 1971), which included a twenty minute piece about fighting a war in the future. The album cover portrayed an armadillo and a First World War tank. The armadillo-like Tarkus, a cybernetic force, battles with Manticore, a mythical creature that is said to represent the counterculture and an idea of naturalness. This represents "a conflict between materialistic and mystic/Gnostic world-views," observes Edward Macan.[15] Their mythic story addresses tensions in the modern world.

ELP's *Brain Salad Surgery* (1973) included "Karn Evil 9," a lengthy musical suite concerning the earth's process from an ice age to the time of a future war that involved computers and humans. While this widely circulated record made a mark commercially, there was some critical resistance to this album. The classical music gestures, stacks of equipment, and fantasy concepts were sometimes considered pretentious. The forward-looking science fiction concept and suggestions of artificial intelligence and human-machine conflict engaged some imaginations. However, the extended keyboard solos and songs couched in science fiction motifs did not appeal to everyone. ELP's most notable recording, *Pictures at an Exhibition*, does not involve science fiction or fantasy themes. It underscores ELP's merger of classical and rock music. The classical music connection also appeared in Emerson's reworkings of Aaron Copland's music in "Fanfare for the Common Man" (1942) on their *Works* album and "Hoedown" for *Trilogy* (1972).

While Greg Lake contributed vocals and classical guitar playing and Carl Palmer was a fine drummer, ELP was primarily driven by Keith Emerson's keyboard playing. Soft Machine's bassist, Hugh Hopper, saw the "rise of the keyboardist at the center" of progressive rock. The keyboard player often substituted for piano, strings, and orchestra the Moog, the Mellotron, and the synthesizer. Robert Moog had developed the large Moog, which was adapted for the stage into a mini-Moog. The synthesizer followed, with strings, horns, and guitar simulation. The synthesizer is an electronic instrument that can be engaged in sound synthesis. RCA Victor created tone generators in the late 1950s. The synthesizer was further developed with the Moog and with the use of sequencers. Robert Moog and Donald Buchla created synthesizer manufacturing companies in 1966. They were soon followed by the Tonus firm and by EMS London. Synthesizers became portable and in the 1970s the synthesizer developed device control with a microcomputer. This was followed in the 1980s by digital techniques.

YES

The visual elements surrounding the band Yes's musical product reinforce connections with science fiction, myth, and fantasy. Roger Dean's artwork for Yes album covers set forth a style for progressive rock imagery. Rick Wakeman of Yes, recalling Roger Dean, has said that "he'd become like a sixth member of the band."[16] Dean's visual iconography helped to create messages that linked fantasy landscapes with Yes's music, lyrics, and performances. Dean's album cover artwork on the *Yes Album* and *Fragile* (1971) and *Close to the Edge* (1972) gave listeners imaginative worlds to place the songs within. Even so, the band's lyrics could be obscure. All good people might turn their heads each day, but what did that mean? How familiar was an American audience with traffic circles called roundabouts? Perhaps that didn't much matter. The musicianship of Yes and the strength and tone of Jon Anderson's vocals could turn singing the words on the back of a cereal box into a hit.

In Yes folk elements and classical guitar met with "symphonic" progressive rock, complex vocals, keyboard arrangements, and electric guitar leads. Jon Anderson's soaring vocals were joined by other band members who also sang. Steve Howe on guitar and Chris Squire, the bass guitarist, composed much of the music. Drummer Bill Bruford contributed the skills he also brought to King Crimson, Genesis, UK, National Health, and his own fusion band. On *Fragile* and *Close to the Edge*, Rick Wakeman's keyboard dexterity complemented the tenor voice of Jon Anderson, the complex guitar-based work of Steve Howe and bassist Chris Squire, and Bruford's drums. Wakeman was able to undertake his own musical innovations with *Journey to the Centre of the Earth* as a solo project and his record rose to the top of the album charts.

Yes's Jon Anderson, Chris Squire, and Steve Howe created "Starship Trooper" (1970), a dynamic composition that was given vague lyrics by Anderson that reflects his interest in mysticism and space. The title comes from a Robert Heinlein novel, but the song lyrics do not correspond in any way with the book. The trooper is an expansive soul who has traveled across the universe. In one sense, the utopian society in Heinlein's story appears to be without racial discrimination or gender discrimination. In another, Johnny Rico learns that military code of duty carries a violence by which he will enforce orders. The restriction of voting rights to those who have been in government service suggests a repression of democracy. Heinlein's *Starship Troopers* dramatized war and some readers saw in it a subtext that was political. Yes steered away from that controversy.

The song "Starship Trooper" has three parts: Life, Seeker, and Disillusion. The opening motif is repeated often in the song's first section. The song is rich with melodic ideas and with Steve Howe's polished guitar playing over the vocal harmonies. There is a bass melody by Squire at 1:41, a bridge at 1:51. Disillusion begins at 3:16. At 5:36 there is a descending three note pattern (D to Bb, resolving on G) and the music winds around these three notes. The final section is carried by Anderson's vocals.

The Yes Album (1971) was built around science fiction concepts and signaled the Yes sound. Songs like "Your Move," "Starship Trooper," "Perpetual Change," and "Yours Is No Disgrace" developed that sound. *Fragile* (1972) followed with science fiction and fantasy elements. Rick Wakeman's synthesizers, Mellotron, organ—all costly—also contributed greatly to the sense of spaciousness. "Roundabout," as an edited piece, became a single that brought Yes widely to public notice. *Close to the Edge* (1972) offered three tracks, with the lengthy "You and I," "Siberian Kaatu" and the side long title track. This became a top five album supported by a long international tour. Hermann Hesse's *Siddhartha* appears in the lyrics of *Close to the Edge*. This is the down by the river of Hesse's novel, where enlightenment is found. Jon Anderson sees the song as engaged in a dialectic of the material-physical and the spiritual. John Covach notes the verse-bridge section contrast in A Dorian, the bridge part in major keys, and metric tension.[17]

With their releases of *Fragile* and *Close to the Edge*, Yes became quite a popular progressive rock band. When Yes released *Tales from Topographic Oceans* (1974) critics called the album overindulgent. The album was musically alive, with Jon Anderson's lyrics which hearkened to Eastern mysticism. Anderson, during this time, made a deeper investigation of myth and Eastern religion. The lyrical approach to the four songs was influenced, in part, by Anderson's reading of Swami Paramahansa Yogananda. Anderson looked through *Autobiography of a Yogi* while on tour in Tokyo. (Yogananda's name is derived from *maha,* or great and *ananda*, or bliss.) Anderson on his search, knowing little about Hinduism, developed a cosmology and unique contribution. The album attempts to represent four interlocking *shastras* and to suggest a path to inner peace.

A few years later, Yes developed *Relayer* (1974). The band was now out of critical favor but they remained popular. This recording alternates dense instrumental sections with vocal/chorale sections. Some critics wanted songs. The band was composing suites. The members of Yes were also engaging in side projects. *Olias of Sunhillow* (1976) was Jon Anderson's mythical concept album. His song "Sound Out the Galleon" expressed a fantasy in which an alien race is forced to abandon their planet and find another. The spaceship is the *Moorglade Mover*, operated by Olias. The album reflects Anderson's speculations in science fiction and his enthusiastic acquaintance with Eastern mysticism. Jon Anderson incorporated neo-pagan elements into his lyrics and a sense of "presence" in nature: pantheism and polytheism.

Rick Wakeman created his solo albums *Six Wives of Henry VIII* (1973) and *Journey to the Center of the Earth* (1974), which takes its title from Jules Verne. He then produced *The Myths and Legends of King Arthur and his Knights of the Round Table* (1975), suggesting a mythical mindset, a *chanson de geste*. His recordings *Lizstomania* (1975), *No Earthly Connection* (1976), *White Rock* (1977), *Rick Wakeman's Criminal Record* (1977), and *Rhapsodies* (1979) followed. For Yes's recording *Going for the One* (1977), recorded in Switzerland, Patrick Moraz left the band and Wakeman returned after a two-year hiatus. The album, with its more commercial sound, was well-received. The content of this album was mystical and abstract on five songs. The songs were melodic, filled with Steve Howe's guitar work and with the band's vocal harmonies. Jon Anderson wrote the title song, which others contributed to and on which Howe played steel guitar. He created the song "Wonderous Stories," which conveys a romantic sensibility. Rick Wakeman played the organ at St. Martin's Church in Vevey, Switzerland. *Drama* (1980) shifted the sound to harder rock. Howe played more electric guitar. John Anderson and Rick Wakeman were missing. Geoffrey Downes and Howe then joined the band Asia and Yes unraveled. When Yes returned they went through changes in their sound across the next decade. They made use of Digital Performer technology in recording sessions. Steve Howe, who was central to the band's earlier sound, did not like the new Yes sound.

JETHRO TULL

Jethro Tull emerged between 1968 and 1970, then ascended on the charts in the 1970s. The band had a gig at the Marquee Club on February 2, 1968. They began to play there regularly. Ian Anderson wore his long overcoat, and performed animatedly: bug-eyed, leaping about with his flute. The band at this time included Mick Abrahams (guitar), Ian Anderson (vocals, flute, harmonica), Glenn Cornick (bass), Clive Bunker (drums). Guitarist Martin Barre entered the band in February 1969. (John Evan joined to play piano in 1970.) They combined folk, rock, and the blues into their own form of progressive rock.

In Hyde Park in June 1968 Jethro Tull played a free concert with Pink Floyd. The Sunbury Festival went across three days in August. It included Deep Purple, Fairport Convention, John Mayall, the Spencer Davis Group, Traffic, and the Incredible String Band. Jethro Tull did a broadcast on September 22. In 1968 at Abbey Road, they were under contract with MGM. They recorded a Mick Abrahams song called "Sunshine Day" and coupled it with "Aeroplane." The year 1969 brought the album *This Was*, with a Brian Ward photo of the band in theatrical makeup. "Move on Alone" and "Jeffrey" were released as singles. "Living in the Past," the band's first hit, was released in May 1969.

In the United States, Jethro Tull played at the Fillmore East and opened for Blood Sweat and Tears, Fleetwood Mac, and Vanilla Fudge. Their *Stand Up* album (released in the United Kingdom in August, and the United States in September) went to number one in Britain. There was an apparent influence of Bob Dylan on some of Anderson's lyrics. Jethro Tull scored hit singles with "Aqualung" (191) and "Bungle in the Jungle" (1974). The band's musicianship blossomed at live performances across the years and the singles became a staple of "classic rock" radio airplay.

GENESIS

When Peter Gabriel and Tony Banks met with Anthony Edwin Phillips and Mike Rutherford at the Charterhouse preparatory school two bands, The Garden Wall and The Anon, merged. They became Genesis, a band that would explore progressive rock territory. Jonathan King at Decca Records produced the band's first album, which sold few copies and received little airplay. Strings were added to songs by Arthur Greenslade. The band released the cosmic titled "The Silent Sun" and "That's Me" on the B-side. Peter Gabriel sang the vocal on "The Silent Sun" in an early Bee Gees influenced style. The young band replaced drummer Chris Stewart with John Silver and then replaced Silver with John Mayhew by the time they recorded their second album. Tony Stratton Smith worked with Genesis on Charisma Records. They played on the BBC, opened for Deep Purple and for Caravan, and on March 11, 1970, opened for David Bowie.

Trespass (1970), their second album, featured "Knife," a seven-minute piece that they played in concert. "Knife" signaled that Genesis was a band that was ready to indulge in extended compositions. "Looking for Someone" is rather orchestral with its tempo changes, organ and guitar, and musical climax. "White Mountain," opens on guitar and adds flute and Tony Banks' Hammond organ as Peter Gabriel sings a myth that includes woods and wolves and foxes. "Visions of Angels" was another extended composition with a Peter Gabriel vocal and Tony Banks' Hammond organ. Stagnation brings an acoustic guitar intro. "Dusk" is a shorter piece on acoustic guitar with flute. Then comes "Knife" and Peter Gabriel calls out "now" and the band breaks into an ambitious arrangement which conveys a sense of fighting. The song has a quieter passage that contrasts with all of that energy.

With *Nursery Cryme* (1971) came a new sound with the addition of Phil Collins on drums and Steve Hackett on guitar. John Anthony and recording engineer Dave Hentschel produced the album. *Nursery Cryme* begins with "The Musical Box," opening on chords softly played high on the keyboard. This introduces a Peter Gabriel vocal, which is mixed forward and very present. Phil Collins makes a difference with his drumming staccato and crescendo. "For Absent Friends" is Collins's first vocal with Genesis. "The Return of the Giant Hogweed" offers an odd tale with a comic edge about a Victorian explorer that has brought back troubling weeds. This peculiar ecological tale—if it is that—includes passages on flute and guitar, a march beat, then piano and Collins's drums. "Seven Stones" brings an old man figure and Tony Banks playing the Mellotron. Then "Harold the Barrel" introduces more peculiar characters and British humor with Mr. Plod the mayor and Mrs. Barrel the mother. "Harlequin" changes things with acoustic guitar and vocals. Then it's time to get mythical again with "Fountain of Salmacis," in which Hermophrodis meets with a wood nymph. We hear guitar leads by Hackett.

It was with *Foxtrot* (1972) that Genesis began to hit an innovative peak with lengthy pieces like "Supper's Ready" and "Watcher of the Skies." When *Foxtrot* opens the listener enters a space that is immediately filled by keyboards/organ chords in an overture. In "Watcher of the Skies" a Mellotron opens with minor chords. Peter Gabriel takes on the role of the watcher. The song draws upon Holst's "Mars" in *The Planets*. Drums and guitar respond to Banks' keyboard chords and Collins rolls the tom-toms. Next, the listener is given "Time Table" with Peter Gabriel's vocals and a bass lead by Mike Rutherford over the piano in the center of the song. On this album Steve Hackett provides his guitar on "Horizons." Across Side Two is "Supper's Ready," a fine dish indeed in seven musical sections.

The classic Genesis album *Selling England By the Pound* (1973) begins with Peter Gabriel's vocal. The ambitious double album, *Lamb Lies Down on Broadway* (1974), begins with a rapidly played figure on piano, joined by drums and bass and vocals, beginning with the words of the title as the tempo increases. Genesis was being described as innovative, a band that engaged with the English folk and neo-classical soundscapes. However, Peter Gabriel left the band in 1975, after this concept album. The next three albums were more introspective than Peter Gabriel's theatrical style. Steve Hackett left in 1978. Phil Collins, with his vocals, sure drumming, and Motown memories, moved the band toward further commercial successes. By 1980 Genesis was shifting out of progressive rock expectations into rock with Phil Collins's vocals, brass, drum machines, and less keyboard solos. *Abacab* (1981) opened with the pulse of the title song, a commercial hit. We hear drums and bass with guitar riding over the top joined by keyboards. The guitar, dirty and buzzing with an effects pedal, plays a distinctive four-note hook and is answered by the keyboards. Genesis had entered a techno phase, perhaps in keeping with industry changes. Across the years, they had produced the singles from "I Know What I Like" (1974) to "Mama," "Invisible Touch," and "I Can't Dance," (1992). They finally called it quits after reuniting for *Calling All Stations* (1997). Each of the key members of Genesis recorded solo albums. Peter Gabriel and Phil Collins, of course, were highly successful, creative recording artists throughout the 1980s and 1990s. Peter Gabriel's first solo single was "Solesbury Hill" which reached number thirteen on the UK charts. Songs like "Biko" concerned world issues. "Games Without Frontiers" was number fourteen in the United Kingdom. "Red Rain," "Sledgehammer," "In Your Eyes" (1986), and "Digging in the Dirt" (1992) were top hits in the United States on the *Billboard* charts. Phil Collins has produced numerous hit songs in his impressive solo career. He recorded "In the Air Tonight" in 1981. A wave of Phil Collins popularity crested in 1985 with a string of hits including "Take Me Home," "Sussudio," "One More Night" and "I Don't Care Anymore" and many other hit songs followed in subsequent years.

QUEEN

The film *Bohemian Rhapsody* has brought Queen back front and center to public attention. With the Golden Globe winning film showcasing Freddie Mercury's talent alongside those of Brian May, Roger Taylor, and John

Deacon, the songs of Queen climbed back up the *Billboard* charts. Queen links with classical repertoire with their chorale vocals on "Bohemian Rhapsody." The conspicuously operatic vocals of Queen combined with science fiction themes on their album, *A Night at the Opera* (1975). It was a sure recipe for pop music magic. Freddie Mercury's vocals rested upon the layered guitar work of Brian May and were surrounded by the band's rich background harmonies. Queen songs have less complexity about them than orchestrated classical music. Yet, there seems to be a classical texture or quality to some of their work. Songs like "Slightly Mad" and the introduction "It's a Hard Life" suggest some classical influence. Freddie Mercury's expressive vocals and the chorale vocals of Queen are reminiscent of Monteverdi. "Bohemian Rhapsody" circles and rises vocally in almost Mozart-like form.

Queen (1973), the band's first album, reflects the progressive rock of the period. *Queen II* (1974), containing fantasy themes and virtuoso musicianship, reached number five on the British album charts. It featured the mythically oriented single "The Seven Seas of Rhye" and the six-minute long "The March of the Black Queen." *Sheer Heart Attack* (1974) showed experimentation with hard rock, heavy metal, ballads, and the English music hall tradition. The single "Killer Queen" suggested the layered music and vocal sound that would appear on their next recording, *A Night at the Opera*. That album launched Queen as one of the most successful pop rock bands of its day. The record contained the hit "Bohemian Rhapsody" (1977). With their operatic vocals, Queen's *A Night at the Opera* offers a narrative of characters that set off and reached a new world. Upon their return one year has gone by for them but a hundred years have passed. Queen's *News of the World* contained the anthems "We Will Rock You" and "We Are the Champions."

Freddie Mercury, a former art student, designed the Queen logo. The logo includes the zodiac signs for the four band members: two lions for Leo (Deacon and Taylor), a crab for Cancer (May) and two fairies for Virgo (Mercury). The lions wrap around the Q. The fairies lie beneath one of the lions and the crab sits above Q. A Phoenix rises above this. The design appears to represent the royal coat of arms of the United Kingdom, as much as the band it designates.

Between 1968 and 1970, Brian May and Roger Taylor played in a band called Smile. They joined with Freddie Mercury to form Queen and added John Deacon on bass guitar. May's guitar sound is layered and has a distinctive tone. He sang the bass parts on "Bohemian Rhapsody." As a trained physicist, his knowledge of sound waves, timing, and distance contributed to studio work with Queen, such as on the clapping sequence on "We Will Rock You." For this song he relied upon his sense of the correlation between music and mathematics. The stomps were based upon prime numbers and repetitions. The use of delay created the effect of sounding as if many people were involved in the clap and stomp sequence. May reflected upon the possibility of uniting the audience by developing the rhythmic ideas. The band worked the song rhythms out in an old London church. This audience participation broke down the distance between band on stage and the audience. The pulse of "We Will Rock You" is used to build crowd enthusiasm in sports contests. It is heard today chanted by crowds in stadiums throughout the world.[18]

TODD RUNDGREN AND THE SOLO MAGIC OF *SOMETHING/ANYTHING?*

The music of Todd Rundgren has included forays into progressive rock with his band Utopia, Philadelphia sound soul with The Naz, and everything from pop charting singles like "Hello, It's Me," to hard rock, glam, funk, dance, parody, and R&B. Immediately before Rundgren's turn toward progressive rock on *A Wizard/True Star*, the solo magic of Todd Rundgren appeared in full force on his landmark *Something/Anything?*: a double album released in February 1972. It was a recording that he produced and arranged, for which, across three album sides, he wrote all of the songs, played all of the instruments, and sang all of the lead vocals and background vocals. Rundgren was joined by other musicians on the fourth album side. The album appeared at a time when he was producing the albums of other artists and it is a key example of his work as a producer and arranger, as well as a collection of many of the best of his songs from the early years of his solo career. Here we will explore *Something/Anything?* with attention to the solo accomplishments of Todd Rundgren as a songwriter, musician, arranger, and producer. The progressive rock of the band Utopia is only one of the many facets of this musician's considerable creativity. To the extent that rock is a hybrid and romanticism expresses intermedial art, Rundgren is one of rock's truly imaginative, eclectic romantic creators.

Recognized as a creative producer, in the autumn of 1971 Todd Rundgren recorded the sessions with Badfinger that brought "Day After Day" and "Baby Blue" before he began recording *Something/Anything?* In June 1973 he produced the Grand Funk album single "We're an American Band." Todd Rundgren was also behind the August 1973 New York Dolls' album, a seminal recording for the rock underground. Along with this, Rundgren created records with The Band and Sparks. *A Wizard, A True Star*, at 55:56, pushed against the technical limits of how much music was possible to fit on a single LP at that time.

Todd Rundgren could change like a kaleidoscope, or like a chameleon, from album to album. *Something/Anything?* represented a rich palette of musical variety before Rundgren's radical shift on *Wizard-True Star* to extended forays into progressive rock. *Something/Anything?* had scored three top 100 singles: "Hello, It's Me" (number five), "I Saw the Light" (number sixteen), and "Couldn't I Just Tell You" (number ninety-three), which just broke through. Yet, the album was hardly all pop. It was an eclectic, playful menagerie—like that salad into which you might toss . . . well . . . something, anything.

Side One of *Something/Anything?* opens with the single, "I Saw the Light." The song begins with a run of three descending notes in the bass and bright keyboards and a wistful romantic story follows: "It was late, last night." The lyrics are moon-June-spoon but the sentiment in them communicates well and the production is decidedly catchy. There is a simple drum pattern and a classy doubled octave lead on the guitars. "I Saw the Light" has an airy, Carole King pop song quality. Rundgren, however, was more adventurous than those talented songwriters who craft top forty pop singles. "Couldn't I Just Tell You," shifted the tone and attitude toward power pop, injected with a strong guitar lead.

"It Wouldn't Have Made Any Difference" gathers richly layered harmonies, all sung by Todd Rundgren. We can hear wind chimes and percussion from a conga drum, high vocal harmony and piano-keyboard chords. The vocal is in front and the notes are extended as he sings "Do you remember." Then, suddenly, the earth shifts on the third track, "Wolfman Jack," and we are hearing "Hey, baby," a kind of talk-singing that predates rap. One hears a Motown-like sound and background vocals that sound like the Supremes, or Martha and the Vandellas. Rundgren had created a hermaphroditic wonder. Were those female background singers from Detroit singing a Holland-Dozier-Holland song? No. Behind his lead vocal, Todd Rundgren had morphed into some extraordinary vocal group of hot black chanteuses all by himself. The fourth cut, "Cold Morning Light," emerged with a flute sound and guitar parts to which he joins his voice. The tempo changes to 3/4 time and slows and piano, guitar, and that woodwind sound merge as he sings "I was yours. . . . You were mine." The organ introduces the next song "It Takes Two to Tango" and the tempo accelerates with a variety of percussion elements and rhythmic changes. The background vocals are layered and again I was feeling "this cannot be . . . one guy is doing all of this?" "It Takes Two to Tango" begins on the keyboards and the tempo gradually increases. Background vocals sing the title. Joining the lead voice and in chorus they sha-la-la, with almost a touch of Beach Boys, *Pet Sounds*. A listener hears kabasa and other percussion effects, as vocal harmonies sing the lines. The chorus resolves on an open final chord. "Sweeter Memories" concludes the side with a pretty guitar sound, with an effects pedal playing a slow blues, joined by keyboard-organ and big vocals joining together: He points out that there's a big cloud in the sky but you can set your mind at ease. There are obvious cymbal hits, harmony vocals, a blues texture that is played soulfully.

The diversity of *Something/Anything?* is already evident by the time a listener reaches the end of Side One. Todd Rundgren launches into a variety of styles that mark him as an unpredictable creative force. *Rolling Stone* called this album "a kaleidoscope of rock genres."[19] Rundgren has said that he wrote the music and often set out the music tracks first.[20] *Something/Anything?* was an extension of the magic he had been creating all along. Rundgren had previously laid down music tracks, vocal harmonies, and percussion for "We Gotta Get You a Woman" and songs for the *Runt* album. Besides this, among the most astounding elements of *Something/Anything* is that layering of vocals: all of which are Todd Rundgren's singing. Listen and you will hear an amazing background singer, placing those vocals well, without cluttering them. There is an organic quality to this record. This is not a songwriter aiming for hits but, rather, one who is letting out the images, sounds, and the feeling within him.

Something/Anything? runs the gamut from serious to wistful to playful and from pop to rock to progressive. *Billboard* magazine, in March 1972, said in its review that Rundgren's songs "have the aura of being irreverent little ditties, while in reality they are penetratingly strident observations."[21] That irreverent humor burst forth in his sounds of the studio game on "Intro" at the top of side two. Turn the LP over and one can hear Todd Rundgren presenting tape hiss, hum, bad editing, the mangling of tape, and punch-in clicks. "Before we go any further," he says, and a listener is instructed to locate sounds on the record. Then one is treated to music patched together in a variety of styles: guitars, piano keys run wild, surfer riffs, and a synthesizer feast. These were the days of analog tape, in which Todd Rundgren began to make his significant contributions as a producer and engaged in studio experimentation. It became obvious that he knew how to get sounds. He did not just write songs and play and sing well on them: he knew how to make records.

Rundgren recorded three-quarters of *Something/Anything* completely by himself. He played all of the instruments and sang all of the vocals. Only later, for side four, were musicians gathered for the final songs for the double-album. The last quarter of the album is filled with songs recorded live. Into this mix he weaved some archival recordings he had saved from his band in 1966.

Rundgren began recording in Los Angeles, in his home. He multitracked his work passage by passage, with his focus aided by taking Ritalin, which is often prescribed for Attention Deficit Disorder, and he mellowed out with marijuana, which may have helped along his lyric writing, or at least helped him to get out of his own way. With multitracking it is possible for a musician to outline an entire album, track by track, and carefully assemble the music, joining the instruments into a rough mix that one can sing over. Rundgren set up most of *Something/Anything?* while he was in the L.A. area.

When he was in Los Angeles, Rundgren had been creating more songs than he could fit on a single album. In his home, his synthesizers, eight track, mixing board had been getting a daily workout each afternoon and evening. It usually makes the most sense to record drums first when one is building a recording in the studio. Capable of playing drums, although not a stellar drummer, he had to build up the songs on the rhythm parts. In the studio, engineer James Lowe looked on as Rundgren maintained the tempo, hummed the song, working without a click track. Taking some Ritalin focused Rundgren as the three solo sides were recorded at I.D. Sounds.

Todd Rundgren gravitated toward C major 7th, in the middle of the keyboard, as he began writing the songs for *Something/Anything?*. This is a chord that is a little more opened out, a little more dreamy than the C major. The C chord is a triad with three main tones: the root or tonic C, the E, which is two steps higher, and the octave of the C, which sings out eight tones higher. The C scale is eight notes that are played along the center of a keyboard, or in other positions: no flats, no sharps, all white keys. To this is added a major seventh, which tends to soften the chord. Rundgren's songs emerged as he played keyboard or guitar, moving his hands around in chord patterns.

The drums were one of the songwriter-producer's biggest challenges. To get the right rhythmic structure and to provide a pulse and bottom for the songs he had to start with the drums. He worked without a click track, keeping a sense of the rhythm steady in his mind. He hummed aloud as he played, and he tried to play the song straight through. Most of the drum playing is rudimentary but it is solid and sufficient. His goal was to make the final recording sound like a band was playing. So, he layered the tracks. Rundgren was wise to leave space on his tracks, to not clutter anything as he overdubbed instruments. His arrangements were spontaneous. He did not plan much in advance. Instead, he created the songs and their sound as he went along. Once he had gotten a few overdubbed tracks down, the process moved past the incubation phase and the sound of each song started to become clear.

He worked alone, in his house in Nichols Canyon, with an eight track recorder. Maybe the name of the street—Astral Drive—served as an inspiration for the more ethereal moments. Maybe not. In any case, he recorded his "Intro" and "Breathless" there by layering keyboards and guitars. The techniques of recording technology—those available in 1971—were all-important in this process and he was not shy about adding effects. He had to work from channel to channel on the recording equipment, setting up his VCS3 synthesizer, running the wires for the guitars and the amplifiers. Like a slightly mad scientist in his laboratory, he conjured his alchemy. *Rolling Stone* would later applaud his command of the studio.

The solo mastery of Todd Rudgren's effort on *Something/Anything?* is not diminished by his turning to recording engineer James Lowe and his assistant John Lee to capture his sound in the I.D. Sound Studio in Los Angeles. This was an independent studio, one that functioned apart from any record company. This creation was one of prodigious musical versatility. "The many good songs span styles and subjects in a virtuostic display," rock critic Robert Christgau has written, "and the many ordinary ones are saved by Todd's confidence and verve."[22] Of course, one might ask: which ones are ordinary? Everyone hears things a little differently and your sense of the songs may or may not mesh with Christgau's sense of them.

"Breathless" follows the musical play of "Intro" with nothing less than verve. Then comes one of finest artistic achievements on the record: "The Night the Carousel Burned Down." This piece begins in keyboards. The music shifts to 3/4 time, into mechanical sounds and percussion sound, as if a carousel is in motion. One might be vaguely reminded of the circus motif in John Lennon's "For the Benefit of Mr. Kite," or of "A Day in the Life" on The Beatles' *Sergeant Pepper* album. This song is bright, a beautifully captured merry-go-round that circles with a nostalgic air. We are taken up into this ride on a mechanical, steam-driven calliope, and drawn into the effects and patterns on the keys that slow gradually to conclude our ride as the background vocals repeat "We all left town the next day."

After "Saving Grace" comes "Marlene": a bright, simple, youthful love song. It is melodic, memorable, and was written quickly. The speaker says that she is the prettiest girl he has ever seen and he just doesn't care who knows it. The chorus is filled with soft harmonies that repeat her name. The "ene" of her name rises in pitch, as if rejoicing in the heaven that is Marlene. But oh, the comic jaunt that follows it! "Song of the Viking" is a comic romp that belongs to the music hall—or maybe to a beer hall. This first person telling of a saga of a Viking crew pulses along into a rapid operatic vocal chorus, a Viking chorus in which Rundgren harmonizes with himself. The tempo is Conan the Barbarian on speed and Leif Erickson unleashed: a mad warrior's primal dance after slurping pure vodka and pep pills. The chorus sings "lo, lo, lo," and Thor, Odin, and the Valkyries must not be far off as piano chords hold this raucous riot down.

"I Went to the Mirror" follows. "Black Maria" is power pop-rock. The high pitches of guitar pierce over the rhythm section. The pulse of the song is punctuated by smacks of the bell on the drum cymbal. Todd Rundgren gives us a guitar lead that would do Robin Trower or Carlos Santana proud. This song is a feast of Todd Rundgren the exceptional guitar player. The vocal is strong, assertive, plaintive: "Oh, I'm going down slow," it declares in blues rock clichés: Attention goes to the guitar lead, which is out front. The vocal growls, "You're a liar, this I know." The production seems to anticipate

Grand Funk and other rock projects. The backing vocals "ooo" sound a bit like The Eagles. Every bit of it is Todd Rundgren.

"One More Day," "Couldn't I Just Tell You," and "Torch Song" complete the work Rundgren did by himself. "Couldn't I Just Tell You" is a power pop-rock song that crackles with guitar energy and it is one of my favorites. It was released as a single in July 1972. I wonder what it might have sounded like if it had been also covered by Badfinger. The song, played by Rundgren, rips along brightly in chord-driven guitar tones. The vocals, layered along with the guitars, create a tune that just had to be a power-pop standard for many musicians.

Among the many fine features of this album are the background vocal textures that Rundgren develops. "One More Day" (No Word) takes us to a gentle, Spanish sounding rhythm: maybe a breezy day on an island somewhere. Vocal harmonies begin on the title and it becomes clear that the singer of the lyric is waiting, for Christmas, for someone. The lead vocal is provided with pleasant support from the array of backgrounds that Rundgren creates. We hear about the hope of some people getting a contract soon so they can stay. Even so, there has been "no word." Times is going by and "friends are gone" but there is only more waiting.

On "Torch Song," the track begins quietly and then is pulled up, with the piano leading the ballad along and an organ overtone above it. The word "Some-where" opens up with one chord hit for each note and a pretty-sounding lament follows.

A WHOLE LOTTA SHAKIN' GOING ON: SIDE FOUR

Early in 1972, the recording process for *Something/Anything?* was disrupted by an earthquake that shook Rundgren's rented Nichols Canyon house. Distressed by this, he decided that it was time to pack up and leave for New York. He had completed three sides of a recording on his own and it was time for something different. He headed for New York, where he joined Moogy Klingman. Once in New York, he shifted into recording his final songs with session players. The New York sessions were recorded live, with Rundgren playing a Neumann U67 keyboard/synthesizer. The vocals were recorded at The Record Plant in New York and at Bearsville, in Woodstock.

When we listen to side four, we hear songs played by Todd Rundgren with a variety of musicians. Rick Derringer played guitar on one song. Randy Brecker and Michael Brecker joined Barry Rogers to create a horn section and Jim Horn and John Kelson also joined them. For the session at the Record Plant in New York City, Moogy Klingman brought in John Siomos on drums and Robbie Kogale (guitar) and John Siegler (bass), who were soon followed by Derringer (guitar) and Stu Woods (bass). The sound was filled out by singers Richard Corey, Cecelia Norfleet, Vicki Sue Robinson, Hope Ruff, and Dennis Colley, who added their background vocals to "Dust in the Wind" and "Hello, It's Me," all very spontaneously. "Hello, It's Me" was recorded during a sixteen-hour session along with Klingman's song "Dust in the Wind" and "You Left Me Sore." During these sessions, Rundgren would move back and forth between singing and playing and engineering in the booth along with Dan Turbeville.

Studio chatter brings us into the spontaneity of the sessions on Side Four. There are count-offs and there is laughter. This provides the listener with a "you are there" listening experience. Rundgren sings the song and then playfully extends a note on the word "you" a bit too long and this is met by laughter in the studio. The female background vocalists work superbly.

"Little Red Lights" is all about the energy of rocking out. The song is a scorcher. Guitar kicks into gear, with a slide and the sound of an engine that then moves into a riff that then falls behind Rundgren's vocal. We're off into a power trip romp. Drums punctuate and break up the pattern and the guitar lines soar.

Studio talk precedes "Piss Aaron." Suddenly, we are at a high school with the junior class of 1932, where Piss Aaron is notorious for pissing in the hall. The music swings and a second major character enters: Dumb Larry. He is accompanied by other fools at the school. Piss Aaron precedes the hit "Hello It's Me."

The radio hit "Hello, It's Me" is live and spontaneous. "Hello, It's Me" was a refurbished version of a song Todd Rundgren had played with Nazz. The horn lines and vocals were freely improvised. We can hear the freedom of the recording in the horns circling and vamping and singers improvising "think of me" at the end. The musicians played through the Nazz song and just let it happen. What happened was a hit: the song which to this day is most often identified with Todd Rundgren by casual listeners.

"Dust in the Wind" is a Moogy Klingman song and quite a good one. "Here we go," chimes a voice that sounds like that of a cartoon character, and they are off into a great song. There are some little horn touches at the beginning and we hear piano and the vocal speaking of being "sorry, truly sorry." The band is tight as the horn section enters. The backing vocals sound live and not edited and we listen to another a charming pop song.

"Piss Aaron" and "Some Folks is Even Whiter Than Me" were recorded at Woodstock, in Bearsville Studio. The cast of musicians for these songs include Billy Mundi on drums, Amos Garrett on guitar, Ben Keith on pedal steel, Jim Colgrove on bass, and Todd Rundgren doing most everything else. On "Some Folks is Whiter Than Me" the Paul Butterfield Band joined Rundgren and Moogy Klingman on piano. "You Left Me Sore" follows, with a shuffling recognition of a romantic experience gone bad, or a sexual experience resulting in STDs, if one prefers to read this as a double-entendre. Then we hear studio talk about "sugar in that water" and the encouragement to "throw money" and "Slut" begins. The horn section and rhythm section are each apparently recorded live and they are masterful. Background vocals move into a call and answer. The Rolling Stones Honky Tonk Woman she is not. She might be a slut but, from his point of view, the speaker says, she looks okay.

That last song on the album, "Slut," made use of a L.A. session with Tony Sales and Hunt Sales, the sons of comedian Soupy Sales (the Runt band of 1970). Rick Vito played guitar. We hear Jim Colgrove on bass and Charlie Schoning on keyboards. Jim Horn and John Kelson added horn parts. Edward Ames Volmos contributed backing vocals. So, one has to acknowledge that on the fourth side of this double-album, Todd Rundgren does have some musical help. The non-solo songs are: "Hello, It's Me," "Money," "Dust in the Wind," "Piss Aaron," "Some Folks Is Even Whiter Than Me," "You Left Me Sore," and "Slut." However, three sides of this double-album can be considered completely a solo effort.

Something/Anything? reached number twenty-nine on the *Billboard* charts and number thirty-four in Canada. The single, "Hello, It's Me," reached number five and "I Saw the Light" went to number twelve. But it is the longevity of this album that marks its importance within Rundgren's varied catalog. He then said goodbye to the pop charts and is today only recalled by the common listener for a later single in which he says he does not want to work and wants to bang on a drum all day.

Todd Rundgren took a new turn in the musical cosmos with *A Wizard/ True Star* (1973). The album is a medley that weaves together a quilt of sounds. For this, he moved to sixteen track recording. The five or six minutes of music that went beyond typical recording limits may have suggested Rundgren's desire to transcend limitations. Patti Smith's review of the album appeared in *Creem*. Poetic, abstract, impressionistic, in her review she said that Todd Rundgren had anticipated a generation of "frenzied children who will dream in animation."[23] "Side one is pure brain rocket," she wrote. "Rock and roll for the skull. Todd Rundgren's season in hell." As if her reference to the French poet Arthur Rimbaud's work was not enough, she added the observation that: "Internal voyage is not burnt out."[24] Like Baudelaire, Todd Rundgren had given us, with "I Know, I Know," a journey "into the realm of pure intellect" and a "further mystery than Greek." Patti Smith waxed eloquent over the album. "Am I getting abstract? It doesn't matter. Music is pure mathematics," she told her readers in *Creem*. "He has always been eclectic. Something magical is happening." The album was "like a coat of many colors."[25]

The amazing dream-coat of this artist's designs has remained very much with us. Fresh innovation, from *Utopia* (1974), *Initiation* (1975), and *Utopia Another Live* (1976) brought us to cosmic reflection, Eastern spirituality, psychedelic spaces, something like jazz fusion, and progressive rock. In the several decades since then, Todd Rundgren has been self-creative, innovative, and constantly renewing.

As a producer, Todd Rundgren's accomplishments seem almost legendary. In the 1970s, he produced *Straight Up* by Badfinger, *We're an American Band* by Grand Funk, the New York Dolls self-titled *New York Dolls*, and *Bat Out of Hell* by Meat Loaf with Jim Steinman's fine array of songs. He has produced many more records since that time, including intriguing interactive work. His creative work continues to show his technical skills, such as his development of an extraordinary website. He offered a music revival camp across two summers in New York state to serious fans, with Mark Volman of the Turtles, Greg Hawkes of The Cars, and Lenny Kaye among the guests.

In 2010, Todd Rundgren brought the *A Wizard/True Star* album back into his shows. He teamed up with Greg Hawkes and Ralph Schuckett on keyboards, Prairie Prince on drums, Kasim Sultan of Utopia, Jessie Gress on guitar, and Bobby Strickland, who played wind instruments and keyboards. As a guitarist, he recalls influences like Jeff Beck, Eric Clapton, and Paul Butterfield. He plays keyboards with the best of them. He involves excellent musicians in his musical explorations and remains a studio wizard. Most of all, even amid his collaborations, Todd Rundgren remains a model for solo work: the art of the Renaissance man or woman who practices the sublime art of singing all the vocals, playing all the instruments, and producing all the tracks on an album. He is a musical cosmos: a microcosm of the creator, a force to be reckoned with.

NOTES

1. See Edward Macan, *Endless Enigma: A Musical Biography of Emerson, Lake and Palmer*. Chicago: Open Court, 2006.

2. British progressive rock included: Genesis, Procol Harum, Renaissance, Moody Blues, Gentle Giant, King Crimson, Jethro Tull, Yes, Renaissance, and The Nice which evolved into ELP. In Britain in the 1980s progressive rock returned with Marillion. In the late 1970s into the 1980s noted progressive rock bands created singles rather than extended play. Gentle Giant made use of counterpoint, as John Covach observes. Steve Howe and Robert Fripp were classically trained guitarists. Keith Emerson in The Nice revisited classical music, as did Rick Wakeman, who joined Yes for the Fragile album. On Five Bridges (1969) "Five Bridge Suite" is side one. Side two turns to Sibelius, Tchaikovsky, and Bach. Progressive rock uses Baroque counterpoint. (Covach p. 8) John Covach and Graeme Boone. See *Understanding Rock: Essays in Music Analysis*. New York and Oxford: Oxford University Press, 1997. Classical guitar enters the introduction to "Roundabout." A solo piano lead comes to us in "South Side of the Sky." There is a harpsichord solo on "Siberian Khatro." Steve Howe left Yes to create Asia with Geoff Downes, Carl Palmer, and John Wetten. Their major hit was "Heat of the Moment."

3. Edward Macan, *Rocking the Classics*. Oxford and New York: 1997, p. 4.

4. Progressive rock is examined in Paul Stump, *The Music's All That Matters: A History of Progressive Rock* (London: Quartet, 1997); Carol Selby Price and Robert M. Price, *Mystic Rhythms: The Philosophical Vision of Rush* (Rockville, MD: Borgo, 1998); Bill Martin, *Listen-*

ing to the Future: The Time of Progressive Rock, 1968–1978 (Chicago: Open Court, 1998); Kevin Holm-Hudson's edited collection *Progressive Rock Reconsidered* (London: Routledge, 2002); and Robert McParland, *Science Fiction in Classic Rock: Musical Explorations of Space, Technology, and the Imagination, 1967–1982* (Jefferson, NC: McFarland, 2017).

5. Kevin M. Moist, "Global Psychedelia in Counterculture," *Rock Music Studies* Vol. 5, No. 3 (October 2018): 197–204, p. 197. This is particularly true with attention to psychedelia as an international phenomenon.

6. Michael J. Kramer, *The Republic of Rock: Music and Citizenship in the Sixties Counterculture*. New York and Oxford: Oxford University Press, 2013, p. 23.

7. David Malvinni, *The Grateful Dead: The Art of Rock Improvisation*. Lanham: Scarecrow Press, 2013, p. 36. "Dark Star" may be representative of the band's cosmic reference.

8. Jerry Garcia, Charles Reich, Jann Wenner, "Garcia: Signpost," *Rolling Stone* (pp. 100, 58). The song "reflects the metaphysical world in which the Dead live." p. 35. David Malvinni, *The Grateful Dead: The Art of Rock Improvisation* (Lanham: Scarecrow Press, 2013) relates "Dark Star" to acid tests and a cosmic frame (p. 73). He notes that the Dead performed the song mostly between 1968 and 1974, the height of the sixties era. He notes that Deadlist says they played the song 213 times. Malvinni observes that Phil Lesh drew upon Charles Ives' 4th Symphony ideas for tone clusters, unmetered barring, and free polyphony, p. 83.

9. Sheila Whiteley points to "psychedelic coding" with fuzz boxes, phase shifters, and delay. *Progressive Rock and Psychedelic Coding in the Music of Jimi Hendrix*. Cambridge: Cambridge University Press, 1990.

10. "Critical response to 1970s progressive rock was often brutal," writes John J. Sheinbaum, "Critics decried the genre's virtuosity, complexity and indebtedness to classical or art music as a betrayal of rock's origins." John J. Sheinbaum, *Good Music: What It Is and Who Gets to Decide*. Chicago: University of Chicago Press, 2019. Paul R. Kohl, in a review of Endless Enigma, Edward Macan's book on progressive rock, asserted, "The progressive rock movement of the 1970s is one of the most reviled musical genres of all time." *Popular Music and Society* Vol. 32, Is. 3 (2009): 437–39. See Edward Macan, *Endless Enigma*, p. 196.

11. Kalefah Sanneh, "The Persistence of Progressive Rock," *New Yorker* (June 19, 2017).

12. Ibid. The article refers to *Washington Post* writer David Weigel's recent book *The Show That Never Ends* (New York: Norton, 2017) and to Will Romano's book *Close to the Edge: How Yes's Masterpiece Define Prog Rock* (Backbeat, 2017). Sanneh makes reference to King Crimson's *In the Court of the Crimson King*, Genesis' "Watcher of the Skies," Yes recordings, Radiohead's *OK Computer*, Kansas and Styx in the 1970s. Kalefah Sanneh, *New Yorker* (June 19, 2017).

13. Hackett told interviewer Dave Thompson that while he was not classically trained, he has enjoyed his times with people who are and being around orchestral music. Thompson 2005, p. 64. Edward Macan addresses the "classicalization" of progressive rock, which has slipped in popularity from the "cultural relevance" it had in the late 1960s. Macan 1997, p. 151. English progressive rock bears a relationship with Anglican Church music and it is a "secularization" of this, asserts Jim Curtis. Peter Gabriel of Genesis and Chris Squire of Yes sang in choirs and Squire spoke of a spiritual feeling in music. John Wetton assisted his brother who was an organist-choirmaster.

14. Macan, *Endless Enigma*, p. 24. Edward Macan analyzed the group through a musicological lens in *Endless Enigma: A Musical Biography of Emerson Lake and Palmer* (Open Court, 2006).

15. Macan, *Endless Enigma*, p. 33.

16. Bill Martin, *Music of Yes: Structure and Vision in Progressive Rock*. Chicago: Open Court, 1997, p. 133–34.

17. John Covach, "Close to the Edge and the Boundaries of Style," *Understanding Rock: Essays in Music Analysis*. Ed. John Covach and Graeme Boone. New York and Oxford: Oxford University Press, 1997, pp. 17–20.

18. Some of these notes on Queen also appear in my book *Science Fiction in Classic Rock: Musical Explorations of Space, Technology and Imagination*. Jefferson, NC: McFarland & Company, 2017. Brian May's academic work was on hold for the two decades that he was involved with Queen. May's dissertation, completed in 2007, inquired into interplanetary dust.

This has been described as "a survey of radial velocities in the zodiacal dust cloud." (See Brian May, *Bang! The Complete History of the Universe*. London: Carlton, 2006.) May theorizes that the earth moves through this dust and May wanted to figure out the motion of the dust. He asked if this dust has anything to do with the origin of the solar system. May's website brings together music and astrophysics. Commenting on the guitarist, *The Guardian* noted May's discussion of "hyperbolic orbits or interstellar particles." See Brian May's interview with Fresh Air host Terry Gross. www.npr.org Also see reporting in *The Guardian*: www.theguardian.com

19. Todd Rundgren, *Something/Anything*. Review. *Rolling Stone* (March 1972).

20. Paul Myers, *A Wizard, A True Star: Todd Rundgren in the Studio*. London: Jawbone Press, 2010, p. 174.

21. *Billboard*. Todd Rundgren, *Something/Anything?* Review. *Rolling Stone* (March 1972): 1–2; 18.

22. Robert Christgau, CG Artist p.17. CG Artist 1593. http//:robertchristgau.com

23. Patti Smith, "Todd's Electric Exploration: Rock and Roll for the Skull," *Creem* (April 1973): 56–57.

24. Ibid.

25. Ibid.

Chapter Four

The End of the World as We Know It

Rock Music Dystopia

A narrative of idealism, expectation, and ascent followed by one of disillusionment and decline characterizes some accounts of the sixties generation. The promise of transformation, the hope for an alternative culture, is challenged by a persistent war, political assassinations, tragedy at Kent State, and the loss of confidence that arose with Watergate. Of course, the picture is a bit more complicated than this declension thesis assumes. For along with the countercultural sixties there was the conservative sixties and there were a variety of global changes. The years 1974–1975 do not mark an ending but a transition. The counterculture did not simply fade away into oblivion. Some aspects of counterculture persisted and survived the 1970s and have returned in subsequent generations.

Yet, fifty years after Woodstock, we may ask: what has become of the utopian vision of the Woodstock generation? Utopia, in formulations by Frederic Jameson and Ihab Hassan, includes the refusal of co-optation and the search to transcend alienation and the quotidian in a movement toward utopia. How have "the sixties" been co-opted, absorbed in the system's machinery, in consumerism, or in business as usual? Theodore Roszak once suggested that the counterculture emerged from opposition to technocracy and from disenchantment with a Cold War culture in which consensus was built upon conformity. Historians point out that the post-war period was a time of economic growth and prosperity, stability, and suburban expansion. This security enabled the baby-boom generation to grow up free from the concerns that hovered over the previous generations. Experiencing alienation in a Cold War context, they attempted to create an alternative culture and consciousness. Seeking authenticity, they turned toward communal living,

Eastern religions, challenging societal values, or creating alternative lifestyles. One of their key vehicles for this was rock music.

What were these rock and roll dreams? In rock music we hear the claim of Chuck Berry that rock and roll will lead to the promised land. The sentiment is later echoed by Bruce Springsteen. There is a desire to seek illumination, to use Walter Benjamin's term, rather than only surrealism. Jimi Hendrix in "Purple Haze" gestures to "kiss the sky." There is a longing for freedom and for something higher and more expansive, not only hopeful dream but transformation. In Paul Kantner and David Crosby's "Wooden Ships," sung by Crosby, Stills and Nash, the alienated will remove themselves from society. They are "leaving" and taking off to ascend to a better life. When the page is turned to the 1980s, where might transformation be in Sting singing that he wants his MTV? When Mark Knopfler's jotted down a consumer's comments in an appliance store he might have characterized some of the tone of the commercial rock market in the 1980s. Rock was a packaged commercial product whose sales were calculated by accountants.

Indeed, as filled with aspiration as rock music is, it frequently has faced the dark side of dystopia. Dystopia is a word derived from the Greek meaning bad place. It reverses the word utopia, which refers to an idyllic world that is nowhere to be found. The dystopia is a place that is alienating, dehumanizing, totalitarian, or tyrannical. Often the dystopian fiction has an apocalyptic scenario attached to it. The dystopian song or album may draw attention to real world problems in society, politics, technology, science, or religion. Dystopian places in rock songs act as commentaries on society and social behavior. The Eagles' "Life in the Fast Lane" critiques hedonistic behavior, with its story of jet-setters in the fast lane of life. Equally trenchant is the symbolic "Hotel California," which begins on a desert highway where scents catch on the breeze. One is drawn by a light up ahead to a place of enticements, an underworld from which one can never leave. The winding octave guitar lines trade off with each other, complementing this Dantesque journey. Some critics have suggested that through the figure of this bewitched hotel The Eagles were taking aim at the music industry itself. Ironically, this well-crafted song, filled with disillusion, became one of their greatest hits.

The Rolling Stones' "Gimme Shelter" is a song in which the blues become apocalyptic. The Doors, The Velvet Underground, and Creedence Clearwater Revival, likewide, at times expressed dark visions. "Riders on the Storm" and "The End" dwell upon being thrown into a world of uncertainty. John Fogerty's song "Who'll Stop the Rain" was heard by many listeners as a war protest song. Its topic may be more broadly viewed as a lament about humanity's inability to resolve longstanding problems.[1] Fogerty's jeremiad, or apocalyptic vision, appears in songs like "Bad Moon Rising" and "Who'll Stop the Rain." There are echoes of such dark vision in Ginsberg's "Howl," or in aspects of Poe, Hawthorne, and Melville, Springsteen's "Darkness on the Edge of Town," or Bob Dylan songs like "A Hard Rain's a Gonna Fall," "Subterranean Homesick Blues," "Tombstone Blues," or "All Along the Watchtower."

Rock has turned toward science fiction to question society, tapping into issues of alienation and images of monstrosity. Through songs it has presented a challenge to social norms. Bands like Rush, Nine Inch Nails, Black Sabbath, Judas Priest, and Iron Maiden have utilized apocalyptic and dystopian narratives. Rush, in *2112*, rejects all forms of totalitarian control that would impose upon the individual and limit individual expression. In Rush's *Clockwork Angels*, amid an opposition of city and country, Owen confronts the Watchmaker, an oppressive central power who reflects rational control. Rush's Neil Peart, in collaboration with science fiction novelist Kevin J. Anderson, recalls science fiction dystopias.

In his science fiction, H.G. Wells presented apocalyptic scenarios in *War of the Worlds* and in *When the Sleeper Wakes*.[2] Dystopian situations appear in George Orwell's *1984*, Aldous Huxley's *Brave New World*, Yvgeny Zamyatin's *We*, Arthur Koestler's *Darkness at Noon*, Ray Bradbury's *Fahrenheit 451*, Kurt Vonnegut's *Player Piano*, and more recently in *The Hunger Games*. In rock they are evident in Rush's *2112*, Iron Maiden's *Brave New World*, Megadeth's *Dystopia*, songs like "London Calling" by The Clash, "Eve of Destruction" by P.J. Sloan (sung by Barry McGuire), Metallica's "My Apocalypse," and sociopolitical critiques like "Darkness (Of Greed)" and "Testify" by Rage Against the Machine. David Bowie attempted to adapt *1984* and included his dystopian songs on *Diamond Dogs*. Joy Division's Ian Curtis read dystopian fiction like *A Clockwork Orange* and *Brave New World* on his way to creating "Transmission." Bruce Dickinson reread *Brave New World*. From Bob Dylan's "Talkin' World War III Blues" to Prince's "1999," Jethro Tull's "Protect and Survive," and Radiohead's "Idioteque" and "2+2+5," rock bands have imagined dystopian worlds.

Black Sabbath is the chief British contribution to existentialism, says William Irwin. He defines existentialism as a perspective on "a world emptied of meaning—causing despair" or as a need for freedom and self-actualization. Black Sabbath are "unwitting existentialists."[3] Their existentialism is "more emotional than intellectual," says Irwin. Black Sabbath deals with "fate," death, disenchantment. "Wheel of Confusion" will still be turning when you are gone. The alienated Ozzy Osborne absorbs Geezer Butler's lyrics. The narrator of "Lord of This World" has an ill-soul and is stuck and searching. In "Children of the Grave" the speaker tells us of those who are seeking a better world to live in. If unable to realize this, they will all be children of the grave. Irwin cites Nietzsche's position that "creativity . . . is the proper response to pain and difficulty in life."[4] This includes self-overcoming and self-making, or self-creation.

DAVID BOWIE'S *DIAMOND DOGS* AND GEORGE ORWELLS'S *1984*

David Bowie's *Diamond Dogs* arose from his reading of George Orwell's *1984* and his imagining a musical based upon the novel. Bowie's science fiction interests informed the project, along with his rejection of conformity and totalitarianism. We can chart Bowie's movement toward *Diamond Dogs* from October 1973 to February 1974. In late 1973, David Bowie met William S. Burroughs, at a time when the spirited hopes of "the sixties" were fading. It was during a time when, on a personal level, Bowie appeared to be reflecting pessimistically on his sense of civilization falling apart. *Diamond Dogs* was a Bowie universe, a vision of a future world facing the collapse of decadence. Unlike Orwell's *1984*, it avoided obvious political comment. Bowie's palette of musical colors lived in fragments, envisioning a dystopia. The album explored Pop Art from the 1950s and the contact between science fiction, consumerism, and Western society's potential for catastrophic events. Bowie dreamed something filmic in which cyborg punks moved through apocalyptic visions. Bowie wrote "We Are the Dead," "Big Brother," and the "1984/Dodo" theme with Ken Scott producing and his band, the "Spiders from Mars," accompanying him. On "1984" and "Dodo," which were linked, one hears cinematic scoring and the incorporation of fragments of reference to the novel. "Dodo" is at first focused on Winston and Julia, the would-be lovers of *1984*. It then turns to the character of Mr. Parsons, their neighbor who was betrayed by his own child. On the final track of the album, the chant of humanity is comparable to the "Two Minutes Hate" in George Orwell's novel, when the citizens of Oceania vent their anger at the enemies of Big Brother. (Sonia Orwell, who had disliked the 1955 film adaptation of the novel, rejected any adaptations into other media and refused to allow rights for a musical.)

George Orwell did not seek the utopian path of William Morris's *News from Nowhere*. In considering the future in his dystopian novel, Orwell looked at the past. *The Last Man in Europe*—his original title—finds its precursors in Mary Shelley's *The Last Man* (1826), a novel written a decade after *Frankenstein*, which describes human extinction by plague. While Mary Shelley's books do not directly resemble Orwell's, they do present interesting parallels. Both may be read as cautionary appeals to humanity. Meanwhile, contemporary works like Olaf Stapledon's *Last and First Men* (1930) and *Darkness and Light* (1942) are futuristic stories much like *1984* which appeared in Britain. C.S. Lewis's *That Hideous Strength* (1945), a book which Orwell reviewed, may also be considered by those curious about intertextual sources for Orwell's novel:

> A company of mad scientists—or perhaps they are not mad, but merely have destroyed in themselves all human feeling, all notion of good and evil—are plotting to conquer Britain, then the whole planet, and then other planets, until they have brought the universe under their control . . .[5]

Orwell was a writer of conscience, an ethical model of the relation of the writer to public issues. His clear and relentless opposition to totalitarianism in all its guises continues to serve as a guide for us in our changing situation in the twenty-first century. Orwell is also a striking test-case in the political sociology of British left-wing intellectuals, as John Rodden has observed.[6] He was markedly different in temperament, style, and experience from his literary contemporaries. Orwell stood both inside the political left and outside it as one of its keenest critics. Orwell may be regarded as progressive yet, in some respects, Orwell is "conservative": defending and honoring the past. Orwell wishes to preserve the English language. Orwell cherishes a past time, for the past gives meaning and connects one to a history.

FROM MAJOR TOM TO ZIGGY STARDUST

Can art and rock music transcend the features of an Orwellian world? David Bowie's "Space Oddity" in 1969 suggested Bowie's interest in other worlds and science fiction. Re-released in 1972, the single about Major Tom became a popular hit and a signature song for Bowie. RCA Records released *Hunky Dory* in November 1971, with the single "Changes." RCA executives were not enthusiastic about the album. In February and March 1972 Bowie's management sought to develop publicity for Bowie's concert dates in the United States. Bowie transformed his persona, creating Ziggy Stardust: a mythical creature through which his art could speak. His band, including guitarist Mick Ronson, became the Spiders from Mars. Theatrical, costumed, playing with artifice, the band wore gold suits and gave a nod to glam. Bowie developed his androgynous character of Ziggy: an otherworldly hermaphrodite, a gender-bending guitar playing creature somewhere in between male and female. Musically, he expressed his respect for Lou Reed, as the band played "White Light, White Heat" and "Waiting for the Man" alongside Bowie singles like "Suffragette City." He took cues from Marc Bolan, Iggy Pop, the New York Dolls, and Alice Cooper's shows. *Melody Maker* called David Bowie and his band "superb parodists."[7] Bowie used the rock star as outsider and extra-terrestrial theme in *The Rise and Fall of Ziggy Stardust and the Spiders from Mars*. Bowie told a *Rolling Stone* magazine photojournalist that his character of Ziggy was a cartoon. Yet, there was uniqueness and drama to this otherworldly character, this comic book creation. There was also in Ziggy Stardust an expression of Bowie's creativity and the malleability of his art. David Bowie fascinated audiences and critics because he continually revised and recast himself and was always an artist engaged in self-discovery.

The science fiction figure of Ziggy Stardust welcomes us to think about aliens and alienation and about the reinventions of the human that run through science fiction stories. This articulation of alienation is a form of contemporary dystopian vision. Bowie drew upon writer William S. Burroughs to create a character who is persuaded by aliens. Bowie's persona highlights media constructions of celebrity and the disintegration and eclipse of the pop star. In March 1972, "Starman" was the first single from *The Rise and Fall of Ziggy Stardust and the Spiders from Mars*. "Five Years" begins the recording ominously with a note of world crisis, the news that the world has only five years of existence left. In "Starman" the narrator is a child who sees a UFO. He tells his friends and he makes contact with the Starman. At the center of the record are the songs "Ziggy Stardust" and "Suffragette City." Underlying this recording is a critique of art and the recording industry, of creation, construction, and manufacture. Bowie appears to reflect upon his own constructed image and upon the ways in which the industry and society creates pop stars. Bowie's acoustic guitar playing is heard throughout the album: a twist on the notion of folk music authenticity. Bowie clearly can rock. "Rock n' Roll Suicide" brings the album to a strong conclusion.

Some critics have asserted that Bowie's alien figures reflect his own sense of alienation. Bowie said in a 1977 interview: "They were metaphysically in place to suggest that I felt alienated."[8] Bowie's Ziggy Stardust and his "Spiders from Mars" raise questions about alterity, or "the other" and alienation. In what ways do we project aspects of ourselves onto the alien? How does the alien represent the unknown, or what we don't understand, or a figure to place our prejudices upon? Is the alien friendly, or a monster and a symbol of fear? Is the alien "other," or is it a reflection of us?

At times, early in his career, Bowie appeared as an image of urban alienation. Ian Chapmen points out that Bowie addresses alienation of British youth and offers dreams. He focuses on alienation in the urban environment. The cover of *The Rise and Fall of Ziggy Stardust*, Chapman observes, is filled with industrial brick walls and a cloudy rainsoaked sky. Bowie is the other, an outsider. He is liminal, transitory, a reflection of estrangement. Bowie strikes a figure of alienation in a contemporary urban milieu.

Bowie experimented with constructions of identity and character throughout his career. He carried this mythical mode from the height of his acclaim with records like *Alladin Sane* and *Young Americans* in the 1970s into other phases of his work. This mythical mode was present in the revival of his work in the 1990s and the farewell that he created for his final album when he knew that his death was imminent in 2016. Across this span of more than forty years, Bowie's characters represent the rebirth of a Dionysian figure, a Phoenix that renews himself. "His other great inspiration is mythology," stated Gordon Coxkill, an early interviewer. The interviewer said that Bowie had a need to believe in legends like Atlantis and that "he has crafted a myth of the future," of a superior race. He placed Bowie within rock's history of "shock and outrage."[9]

David Bowie was an inventive songwriter who drew upon the unconscious and upon the music of The Velvet Underground, Iggy Pop, The Rolling Stones, and many other artists whose work he absorbed. He explored visual art, mime, theatre, and dance, film, and pulp science fiction, comics, and literature. "Literary tradition . . . is the collective unconscious writ large," observes James T. Jones. The art that incorporates myth is one that he describes as "a poetics of integration of archetypal imagery within individual expression."[10] This reflects the art of David Bowie. Bowie's individual expression across the many phases of his career was like the collective unconscious writ large. He was himself at times like a mythical creation. At the intersection of gender, art and artifice, his creativity extended across music, culture, fashion, film, and theatre. Bowie was not actually from outer-space but his creative gifts were evidently as significant as any that his space characters could bring to make the earth a brighter and more interesting place.

THE VELVET UNDERGROUND AND DOWNTOWN DYSTOPIA

The Velvet Underground expressed rough, concrete realities rather than airy liberation. The Velvet Underground's embrace of rock minimalism, concrete surfaces, deviance, and depression contrasts with pop. Disenchantment and the dark side of punk, metal, and Goth contrasted with the perceived emptiness of some commercial pop and with the idealism of the sixties and progressive rock's utopian dreams. The title of a 1963 paperback by Michael Leigh became the name of a band that coalesced around the unique talents of Lou Reed and John Cale and the rhythm section of Sterling Morrison and Maureen Tucker. In March 1967, they added the German model Nico (Christa Paffgen) (*The Velvet Underground and Nico* [1967]). Their songs were dark and assertive: "Waiting for the Man," "Heroin," "Femme Fatale," "White Light, White Heat." Transgressive, rhythmic, and minimalist, conveying an underground harshness, their sound set the tone for many subsequent bands. This was music that was raw, edgy, dissonant, quite unlike the polished neo-classical forays of progressive rock. It flew in the face of counterculture utopian dreams. The Velvet Underground were surely anti-utopian and showed it songs like "Heroin" and "Walk on the Wild Side." Ellen Willis wrote that "the Velvets music was too overtly intellectual, stylized, and distanced to be commercial."[11]

David Fricke writes: "Just about every band that has subscribed to the avant-garde ideals of 1970s and 1980s rock owes a great debt of influence and sacrifice to the Velvet's. Covering Velvets songs has, for many of those acts become a major industry and art form in itself." Ellen Willis put it this way: "The Velvets broke up in 1970 but the aesthetic punk connection was carried on mainly in New York and England by Velvets-influenced performers like Mott the Hoople, David Bowie (in his 'All the Young Dudes' rather than Ziggy Stardust mode), Roxy Music and its offshoots, the New York Dolls and lesser protopunk bands."[12] This connection resurfaced by 1975–1976 as new wave. Willis observed that The Velvet Underground crossed categories, from Dylan to Townshend, from Andy Warhol to John Cage, noise for noise sake, folk-like melodies, and "demented feedback."[13] They played "White Light/White Heat," "I'm Waiting for the Man," "Beginning to See the Light." The music was "anarchic energy [that] contained repetitive structure" and the lyrics portrayed their urban hard-edged dimension.[14]

The Velvet Underground's authenticity was contrasted with commercial pop. Lou Reed, following the Beats stripped down rock to a minimalism and created the ground for punk. This was "real" rock, not manufactured pop, some commentators insisted. Authenticity was used as a term to distinguish this distinctive expression from pop commercialism. Music for meaning was something other than music tailored to the market.[15] The band created raw, primal rock music.

THE RAMONES EMERGE FROM HILLY KRISTAL'S TEMPLE OF PUNK

The Bowery homeless and the 1975 fiscal crisis hovered around CBGBs. On the Lower Eastside, Manhattan melted away into pale lamplight on dingy blocks, life suspended amid boxes and stained sheets, and ragged ash-men flattened out like their cardboard makeshift beds by the curbs. New wave declared its opposition to mainstream pop-rock which appeared to have lost its authenticity. The Blank Generation, as Richard Hell explained, didn't mean they didn't care. They were looking for a way to fill in the emptiness, create new identities, and make new worlds for themselves.[16]

Bold energy, loose force, three chords, and a bass pulsed through a long room, graffiti stricken, drenched with fallen angels, chairs, and beer signs. Outside one night, piss showered down from the Palace flophouse above CBGB's, urine spray followed by laughter and the voice of the homeless man who had baptized the night air. Inside, punk rock declared vengeance; guitars and drums affirmed life against alienation, cold concrete cinder-shadows, and the ghostly wraiths of the Bowery.

Punk rock was not necessarily dystopian, but it was forceful and determined to return to roots. Nothing was more basic than The Ramones in-your-face sonic assault of two and three chord statements. The Ramones' first album appeared April 23, 1976. They were from the Forest Hills area of Queens. Monte Melnick managed The Ramones. Joey Ramone was Jeffrey Hyman. Hilly Kristal owned CBGBs. Jonathan Richman and the Modern Lovers. Chris Stein of Blondie, Lenny Kaye of the Patti Smith Group: all were Jewish. Tommy Erdelyi was Tommy Ramone; his family was Hungarian. Tommy Erdelyi was born in Budapest, Hungary in 1949. He had gamily lost in the Holocaust. He helped in creating the band. John Cummings was Johnny Ramone. His father was a construction worker of Irish background and his mother was from Lithuanian-Ukranian background. With his longish mop-hair he was a bit taller than Tommy. He was conversational. Some have mentioned that he had a wellspring of anger within him. Yet, he had a sense of humor and knew the darkness of an outsider.[17] Douglas Colvin was Dee Dee Ramone. He felt the press of his German background, alienation, conflict, rebelling, an ambivalence about Nazi imagery. Their look was ironic punk: leather jacket and blue jeans. They bonded over glam rock and moved together toward punk, wrote Larry Getham in "Meet the Groupie Who Came Between the Ramones" *New York Post* (April 10, 2016). The Ramones were 2002 inductees into the Rock and Roll Hall of Fame.[18]

BRITISH PUNK

Punk began creating a scene in Britain around 1976 with Johnny Rotten and the Sex Pistols, Billy Idol, Joe Strummer, Hugh Cornwell, and others. Patti Smith gave her first performance in Britain in May 1976, bringing along Lenny Kaye, Ivan Kral, J.D. Daugherty, Richard Sohl. They played songs like "Gloria," Redondo Beach," "Land," "Pissing in the River," and the encore of "My Generation."[19] In the British rock press, Charles Shaar Murray wrote with high praise for Patti Smith and mentioned New York bands like Tuff Darts, Talking Heads, Ramones, Dictators, Blondie, and Television. The work of Lenny Kaye and Patti Smith together goes back to about 1974.

In November 1975 The Sex Pistols were opening for Eddie and the Hot Rods at the Marquee. Joe Strummer was with the 101ers. (There was then Heartdrop which led to The Clash.) Glam rock persisted in Britain with Bowie, Gary Glitter, Roxy Music, Sparks. Bowie led this toward Iggy Pop, the Stooges, Lou Reed and The Velvet Underground, John Cale, and Nico. As punk emerged, bands were covered in *Melody Maker* and *New Musical Express* and *Record Mirror*. The Sex Pistols were loud and Sid Vicious and Johnny Rotten became notorious. The Ramones brought aggressive playing, attitude, and speed to London's Roundhouse on July 4 with songs like "Blitzkrieg Bop." Critics noted that The Ramones played sixteen songs in thirty-five minutes and Nick Kent interviewed them in *New Musical Express*. The Ramones pulsing manic energy and drive recalled the loudness of MC5.[20]

The Clash formed in London in 1976 with Joe Strummer (vocal/rhythm guitar), Mick Jones (vocal/lead guitar), Paul Simonon (bass), and Nicky "Topper" Headon (drums and guitar/bass/keyboards). Their British punk energy and rebellious attitude emerged with their first album in 1977. Their third album *London Calling* (UK, December 1979) was a breakthrough record. In 1982, *Combat Rock* featured the single "Rock the Casbah." The Clash's first single "White Riot" (March 1977) set the tone of political anarchy, calling for disaffected whites to riot. The first album, *The Clash*, followed in April 1977. "Remote Control," the second single, was chosen by CBS, their record company. Blue Oyster Cult producer Sandy Pearlman was selected to produce the second album, *Give 'Em Enough Rope* (1978). *London Calling* followed, produced by Guy Stevens and incorporating sounds from punk rock, rockabilly, Jamaican ska, and reggae. It was released in the United States in January 1980. *Combat Rock* (May 1982) brought them back onto the singles charts with "Should I Stay, or Should I Go?" (released June 1982) and "Rock the Casbah." The Clash has influenced alternative rock and American punk bands with a political edge like Black Flag and Green Day.[21]

GARAGE ROCK

It has been suggested that Lenny Kaye's *Nuggets*, a collection of no-frills rock of the 1960s, anticipated punk and postpunk garage rock. Eric Abbey recognizes "nostalgic representations" of "garage rock," recalling British Invasion and Mod cultures of the 1960s and early 1970s. They see in bands an effort "to reclaim the naivete of the original rock groups" and "a drive toward cultural rebellion."[22] Abbey recognizes a constructed individualism and makes a claim for the value of nostalgia in this process.

"By asserting specific traits of the 1950s, 1960s, and events the 1970s contemporary garage rock reaffirms the rebellion of the past and restates it for today."[23] "The concept of aggression in society is often viewed with disdain," Abbey writers in the introduction to *Hardcore Punk and Other Junk*. The collection will demonstrate that aggression is a positive and necessary element of music and in life. Without it, people may repress emotion and "become withdrawn and possibly violent and depressed." Thus, playing music with force is a way of venting and expressing creativity. Such aggressiveness in performance, in chord structures and lyrics, is different from violence. Freud would have called this sublimation.[24] These writers point out that there are people who become angry at government, established rules, or society in general. They refer to the social psychologist Konrad Lorenz, who held a view of the positive benefits of appropriate release of aggression. Eric Abbey offers the view that aggressive release in rock music may help to overcome violence and move individuals and society toward peace.[25]

David Easley points to riff schemes form and gestures in the punk rock of Black Flag and the Dead Kennedys. These are organized patterns of repetition and transition, contrast and alteration.[26] The Ramones played power chords in fast tempos with raw intensity and aggressive energy. Steve Waksman makes the observation that in punk there is less differentiation between the instruments of the players. They blend and work together.[27]

NEW WAVE GOES POP

In America, new wave influences gained radio airplay through Blondie, The Ramones, The Talking Heads, the Patti Smith Group, and the pop strands of The Cars. Patti Smith bowed out of the music business, moving to Detroit in 1980, as new wave and punk elements were mixing into the mainstream. Duran Duran and Culture Club were decidedly commercial. There was now the MTV video—and one might wonder: what about the music?

The Cars, from the Boston area, hit the charts with "Just What I Needed" in 1978. In the song four chords cycle around beginning with movement of the tonic, or root chord, to the dominant. We hear the tune in E major shift to C sharp minor (tonic-dominant). Then we come to a chorus that seems to be in E major, although as one critic points out "its phrases cadence on the C# chord." In the third verse, after this harmonic ambivalence, the drummer moves into a backbeat of one and three.[28] Theo Cateforis compares this with the single "Hot Blooded" by Foreigner, with its riff-rock rooted in the blues, leaning toward hard rock. The Phil Gramm vocal and the lyrics are described as all libido. He examines Orr's vocal for the Cars' song and its tonal ambiguities. Powers points to The Cars' vocal arrangements, a style of "staccato notes with air between them." He asserts that Steely Dan, The Eagles, or Fleetwood Mac do not have this "breathing room." He suggests that smaller studios led to a tighter drum sound and less ambient room sound.[29]

Around 1984, there is some difference between The Smiths and REM. At that point there had been a return to roots and guitar driven rock. A kind of post-punk began to emerge. There was a shift in the 1980s from the 1970s album model back to the goal of releasing singles and aiming for airplay and the charts. This led to more flitting moth-like turnover of popular music acts.[30] In the 1970s record companies and management emphasized creativity and career longevity and in contrast in the 1980s there were increasingly more ephemeral one hit wonders.

Yet, there were other musical possibilities emerging. Heavy metal rose from its predecessors—Black Sabbath, Led Zeppelin, Deep Purple, and others—into commercial visibility with Judas Priest, Iron Maiden, Def Leppard, Metallica, Slayer, and a host of lite-metal commercial bands like Bon Jovi.[31] Rap/hip-hop gathered strength with Run D.M.C., L.L. Cool J, Doug E. Fresh, and the rise of Def Jam Records. MTV appeared to take over pop music. Then all hell broke loose: the world went digital.

IRON MAIDEN AND ALDOUS HUXLEY'S *BRAVE NEW WORLD*

Iron Maiden's twelfth studio album appeared at the millennium, in the year 2000. Apocalyptic imagination associated the date with cataclysm. Vocalist Bruce Dickinson returned for the album. Dickinson reread Aldous Huxley's *Brave New World* and was involved with the album concept. The songs do not make direct reference to Huxley's novel but the narrative voice in the title song sounds like it comes from the point of view of a key Huxley character John the Savage, toward the end of that novel. Iron Maiden's *Brave New World*, produced by Kevin Shirley (rather than longtime producer Martin Birch) features the leads of three guitarists: Dave Murray, Janik Gers, and Adrian Smith who had returned to the band. Artists Derek Riggs and Steve Stone created the cover art of a futuristic technopolis: London in a future time. The album was reissued by Warner on Parlophone, June 23, 2017.

"Wicker Man" is a rocker that starts off the record. We hear "Ghost of the Navigator." "Brave New World," the third track is suggestive of a dystopian reality and immediately refers to a "garden of fear" but the lyric is oblique. Described by some as an anthem, the song looks to the brave new world with guitar energy and an expansiveness of sonic space. Steve Harris's "Blood Brothers," a song written for his father, was dedicated to Ronnie James Dio. The song provides a theme of brotherhood and fellowship and well represents Iron Maiden's reunion of its members. Iron Maiden includes on the album three songs that run more than eight minutes: "Dream of Mirrors" (9:21), the Arabian sounding "Nomad" (9:06), and "The Thin Line Between Love and Hate" (8:26).

The novel *Brave New World* is critical of conformity. Huxley attacked a conforming society based upon the pleasure principle. Huxley would no doubt sharply criticize the frivolity and narcissism of "selfies," repeated Twitter hashtags, or Facebook reports posted about what one has had for breakfast. Iron Maiden obviously does not take their album in this direction. They appear more concerned with futuristic drama. Yet, it is perhaps instructive to take a closer look at Huxley's novel for what it shares with the spirit of rock in its affirmation of authenticity and imagination and resistance to authoritarianism.

Huxley launched a scathing satirical critique of one-dimensional thinking. In the 1960s, Herbert Marcuse presented a critical assessment of "one-dimensional man" that appealed to the countercultural generation. Marcuse emerged from the Frankfurt school of neo-Marxist thought, following Theodor Adorno and Max Horkheimer, who gave considerable attention to Huxley's work. Early on in the twentieth century, Huxley expressed concern that Western society was losing its depth dimension to superficiality and that people were living on the surfaces of life. He did not anticipate iPhones, texting, or people walking zombielike across parking lots with their eyes focused on electronic devices rather than attentive to the people and motion of vehicles around them. As a person inclined toward meditation, rather than the "sick hurry" that his grand-uncle Matthew Arnold lamented in the nineteenth century, he did not anticipate the early twenty-first-century celebration of faster Internet connections and the denigration of the "half-fast." Huxley never encountered students whose parents pay thousands of dollars for them to sit in a college class in which they text messages to their Facebook "friends." Yet he, like Adorno, prophesied that clever capitalist-sponsored technological innovation would enchant consumers. What Karl Marx called "false consciousness" Huxley satirized mercilessly in *Brave New World*. Society's greatest aspirations had been trivialized, reduced to mind-numbing soma, sense stimulating Feelies, and excited engagements with Centrifugal Bumblepuppy.

Deeply fascinated by music, Huxley encouraged the use of the phonograph and creative technologies for music reproduction. Yet, he may well have sided with Adorno's criticisms of the popular music market with respect to mechanical repetition of formulas in pop music. Huxley was a significant source for Adorno and Horkheimer's essay *Culture Industry*. John the Savage laments that the things that once were called "high art" do not matter anymore in the new world society. They have been replaced by products that "don't mean anything."[32]

Obviously, Huxley's *Brave New World* was critical of trivial pop commodities. However, rock that makes meaning, rock that is authentic and vital, may have ultimately appealed to Huxley. The spirit of his character John the Savage becomes one of rebellion against a conformist totalitarian system. Totalitarianism appears in many different forms, as Hannah Arendt pointed out in her study, *The Origins of Totalitarianism*. Huxley challenges the notion of a select minority of technocrats controlling society: something we also see as a theme in Rush's album *2112*. Huxley was quite critical of his brother Julian's friends who took this position, of the biologist Haldane, and of the dreams of H.G. Wells. In *Brave New World*, his test-tube society is dedicated to conformity, complacency, and a pacification of human wants. Political repression begins in a production line in which scientists plan human life through the Bokanovsky process that forms standardized humans.

Each enters life destined for a specific social class and a life defined by work, sex, and sport. This continues in social conditioning through sleep training, a process for which Huxley coins the word hypnopadeia, from the Greek word for education, *paideia*, and an abbreviation of the word "hypnosis." In the new Fordian calendar the year is A.F. 632: that is 632 years after Henry Ford invented and produced his Model T. The conveyor belt, assembly-line process of birthing life has replaced human sexuality and motherhood. The Taylor method of industrial production has been implemented and "happiness" has been achieved by prenatal means that is followed by hypnotic suggestion and brainwashing. Huxley begins his novel by showing this antiseptic environment of mechanical control. It is only when the narration and first scenes of the novel have suggested that the people are satisfied with this state of affairs and with their positions in life that Huxley introduces those who are not: the peculiar and troubled nonconformist Bernard Marx and the overabundant genius Hemholtz Watson. They are eventually followed by the fiercely individual outsider John, who has lived on an Indian reservation and quotes Shakespeare. These three characters that discover their identities apart from the controlling state are the center of interest in the story. They seek understanding and seek change and we are each ultimately exiled, for their uniqueness is a threat to the society whose motto is "Conformity, Identity, and Stability."

Rock music could not exist in Huxley's brave new world. The new world is concerned with efficiency, enrapt with its sense of the potential of technology. Its educational system is oriented toward producing competent technical workers who have little grasp of their own identity and none of the range of history, art, or human experience that has gone before them. In the Fordian world, "history is bunk" and, at best, is known vaguely as what occurred "back in the day." History, literature, and art programs can be safely eliminated to secure mindlessness, complacency, and conformity.

The true threat of the brave new world society is outside the minds of characters like Bernard Marx, Hemholtz Watson, Linda, or John the Savage. It lies in the totalitarian assertion of "Community, Identity, Stability" that infantilizes the population. Huxley wrote against the Fascism that was very much in the air of the 1920s in which myth was fashioned in support of the triumphant state. Implying this political concern, *Brave New World* enters a dialogue with George Orwell's *1984* that has been examined by Gavin Miller, Angelo Arciero, and others.[33] Max Weber wrote of the increasing bureaucratization of modern society. Huxley and Orwell warn of the disappearance of the individual in the organization which has an overwhelming emphasis upon conformity. One has little choice or autonomy when an administration is making all decisions, pulling levers from behind a curtain like the Wizard of Oz. Huxley wrote in a letter of May 18, 1931: "I am writing a novel about the future—on the horror of the Wellsian Utopia and a revolt against it."[34]

Insofar as rock music, as a commercial enterprise, submits to *exclusively* being a matter of selling units it loses its revolutionary spirit. In Huxley's novel, the goals of material comfort have supported Ford's pragmatic appeal for productivity and efficiency. Fordian emphasis upon uninterrupted production has led to the control of workers both inside the factory and outside it in daily life. Intellectual activity not focused upon efficiency, material productivity, and one's assigned professional role is wasteful and unnecessary. (Therefore, why create art?) High wages will compensate for monotony. One can then be fulfilled by buying commodities. The iconic Ford reigns over this standardized mechanism for social prosperity.

Fordism aims at producing a reliable workforce. The manufacture of embryos and their future education will fulfill the needs of business, improve efficiency, and regulate their future lives as workers. They will earn a living in the marketplace and benefit from the material comforts and pleasures it has to offer. They can study in school to be cogs in a machine rather than individuals in a society. Of course, they will work in cubicles, barely know themselves, and be controlled by forces that they will not bother to understand. Ah, but, no matter, they will be happy.

In the first three chapters of *Brave New World* we see the reproduction factory in which embryos are decanted. We observe the Bokanovsky Process which produces "Standard men and women, in uniform batches."[35] Interpersonal intimacy has been replaced by a sterile method of reproduction. Biological determinism will ensure that future workers are predestined to belong to one of five castes: Alpha, Beta, Gamma, Delta, Epsilon. The Epsilons will have the menial jobs and will be satisfied with them because they have been deprived of oxygen and are bereft of education. Members of other castes have defined career trajectories that have been manufactured in advance. The Alphas are designed to be society's leaders. "Happiness" is achieved through biological conditioning, job security, leisure time to go to the mall, and mass conformity.

Deltas and Epsilons in the world of this novel are "bred to be just intelligent enough to do the job they are predestined for and to be too stupid to understand or want to understand anything else," observes Peter Firchow.[36] A society that does not encourage the liberal arts, critical thinking, and divergent and metaphorical thinking is one that develops only limited understanding. While gaining specialized knowledge in trades is quite valuable for a student, technical training alone falls short of educating people who have to negotiate the complexities of twenty-first-century society. Dickens saw the need for humanistic education as he wrote *Hard Times* in 1854, satirizing Mr. Gradgrind's dismissal of Sissy Jupe's imagination, that instructor's reducing her to a number as Girl number twenty and insisting upon a world made up only of concrete facts. Huxley's *Brave New World*, like Dickens's

Hard Times, reveals that when the human spirit and its potential scope is reduced by an emphasis on utility the result may be disastrous.

Brave New World appeared in Britain and in America during the Great Depression. Humanist concern in the story was evident enough. However, criticism arose that Huxley was not addressing the pressing economic issues of the day, as Scott Peller has pointed out.[37] He cites a comment from Granville Hicks: "With war in Asia, bankruptcy in Europe and starvation everywhere . . . what do you suppose Aldous Huxley is now worrying about? He is worrying about the unpleasantness of the life in utopia."[38] Of course, such a comment minimizes the abundant evidence of social concern in Huxley's novel. It is true that buying Huxley's novel was an economic stretch for a displaced worker and that there were many serious global issues that he did not treat in this novel. However, his worry about a dystopia was a reading of the cultural and political trends of his times which has had lasting resonance. Dreams of salvation by progress had elevated a new hero, pragmatic Henry Ford, and lifted a new cross of the Model T as a symbol for communal worship. The future would be built on Taylor's assembly line: biology would submit to mechanism.

Bernard Marx derives his name from the socialist thinker Karl Marx and likely from the playwright Bernard Shaw. He is considered odd. He is an Alpha male who is highly self-conscious, He doesn't like playing obstacle golf. He "spends most of his time by himself alone," which seems obscene in a society in which everyone is kept busy and engaged in sociable activities.[39] Hemholtz's name comes from a great scientist and from Watson the behaviorist. Hemholtz is a man of extraordinary sexual prowess, athletic and intellectual ability and masterful excess. He is a lecturer in emotional engineering and seeks to create phrases that will call his students to look within themselves: something that students in this brave new world never do. John the Savage is the consummate outsider, born on a reservation where he is not welcome because his mother is from the new world, he is then inserted into the new world society that regards him as a fascinating freak. To name John "Savage" immediately casts him as the other, in opposition to "civilized" society. He and Bernard befriend each other because each is an outsider, sensitive to how other people see them. John attempts to toss out his soma, the palliative drug that numbs this society into complacent bliss. He has a conversation with Mustapha Mond, the Controller. Mond asserts that society has had to eliminate individuality, suppress truth and beauty and feelings to maintain a stable and well-controlled social order. John responds: "But I don't want comfort, I want God, I want poetry, I want real danger, I want freedom, I want goodness, I want sin." Mustpha Mond responds: "You are claiming the right to be unhappy."[40] Mond remarks that no one in this society needs God any longer. Everything is stable and there is never any need to reach out for a God.

John retreats to a lighthouse where he punishes himself. However, he is soon discovered there and followed with cameras as if he is the star of a reality TV show. While punishing himself with self-flagellation he is filmed and cast in the new feature *The Savage of Surrey*. He is the biggest loser, a titillating spectacle, a great sensation that brings mocking laughter and public entertainment. Bernard Marx can relate to John the Savage because he has experienced his own difference from the masses of decanted people in the new world society:

> "You see," he said, mumbling with averted eyes, "I'm rather different from most people, I suppose. If one happens to be decanted different. . . . Yes, that's just it." The young man nodded. "If one's different, one's bound to be lonely. They're beastly to one. Do you know they shut me out of absolutely everything."[41]

The uniqueness of alienated characters is valued by idiosyncratic creative performers like David Bowie, or the band Rush. In their work, dystopia is confronted by imagination and uniqueness, a thorough rejection of the authoritarian, and an embrace of the artistic, scientific, and technological possibilities of the brave new world. "It's a brave new world and either we join it, or we become relics," Bowie once told a music critic. He spoke of his music and art as participating in "a wave of the future."[42] Perhaps creative and uncompromising rock music participates in that wave.

RUSH

Rush, with five albums in the 1970s, rebelled against convention and asserted their determination to maintain liberty from restraint. Rush's progressive rock never fit into neat rock music marketing categories. The music of Alex Lifeson (Alex Zivojinovich), Geddy Lee (Gary Weinrib), and Neil Peart is characterized by musical virtuosity, tempo changes, lengthy instrumental passages, transitions of drum fills and guitar riffs, and unexpected chord progressions. The high-pitched vocals of Geddy Lee pierce through loud bass runs, drums that shift into new time signatures, and shimmering guitar leads. The bass line and the kick drum must always match to hold the tempo together, even as time signatures shift. Geddy Lee's ability to sing while playing bass and keyboards is itself an extraordinary phenomenon. To sing while playing guitar may include some challenges, depending upon how intricate the guitar playing is. However, to sing lead vocals while playing bass is an accomplishment. The bass part generally lies under the melody and sometimes works against it and the bass must match the rhythm. Playing keyboards while maintaining the bass within the musical flights of the band adds a further element of virtuosity.

Science fiction imagination took flight in Rush's recordings. When an article in *Time* magazine about black holes appeared in 1975 it sparked lyricist Neil Peart's interest in science fiction and the result was Rush's "Cygnus X–1: The Voyage," a wide ranging, spacious tune that enchants listeners with its changing rhythms that may be likened to an operatic overture. Rush dedicated the album *Caress of Steel* (September 1975, Mercury) to Rod Serling, the creator of *The Twilight Zone*, who died in 1975. The album was filled with Rush's complex rhythms and lyrical fantasies. *Caress of Steel* emerged as an esoteric venture. Michael Moorcock's science fiction fantasy lay behind their song "Necromancer." The song tells of three travelers, no doubt the members of Rush, "men of Willowdale," who go to unknown places. This recording signaled Rush's new ventures in imagination. From Willowdale, a suburb of Toronto, they travelled across the United States and Canada with their music. "The Necromancer" is suggestive of the rest of the album. The songs that follow are imaginative musical journeys into science fiction inspired realms of thought. "The Fountain of Lamneth" is followed by "In the Valley" and "Didacts and Narpets." (Narpets is an inversion of letters for "parents" and didacts are teachers.) "No One at the Bridge" sends up a call for assistance, which is followed by "Panacea." and "Bacchus Plateau." The album concluded with "The Fountain." Rock critics did not embrace the album. However, on *Caress of Steel*, Rush's excursions into science fiction established a style, offered innovative musicianship, and asserted their creative freedom.

RUSH'S *2112*

Rush's *2112* (March/April 1, 1976, Mercury) appeared as a classic album of imagination. Their science fiction fantasy takes a listener into a place of dystopia and a rejection of establishment structures. Rush challenges the idea of an egalitarian society where individuality is consumed. The iconography of the album cover of computer circuits and man against star indicates human aspiration and a quest for freedom.[43] Reflecting upon the thoughtful concepts on *2112*, Deena Weinstein has called Rush's *2112* an example of the turn toward "serious rock" by rock acts like Rush, Pink Floyd, Bruce Springsteen, and others.[44]

For *2112*, Neil Peart devises a tale in which the priests of the Temple of Syrinx control a collectivist society. Echoes of dystopian fiction like Aldous Huxley's *Brave New World* or Yvgeny Zamyatin's *We* might be heard. The priests of Syrinx are not able to impede human creativity altogether, however. In Rush's story, the protagonist discovers a guitar left over from the twentieth century. He learns to play the instrument and offers his gift to the controllers, who fear and reject it. Naively, he believes that the controllers will be interested in his discovery. They are not pleased. The priests of the culture consider the guitar a threat and they destroy it and any chance this individual has for personal expression.

Whereas Ayn Rand's character in *Anthem* discovers electric light and this leads toward change, Peart's character's discovery of the electric guitar leads to its destruction and his dismissal because it is "not part of the plan." Rand's dissident questions collectivism and discovers a past technology that enables hope to be regained. However, in Peart's version, the guitar playing dissident does not flourish. He is a captive in a demeaning, soul-diminishing maze. He remains nameless and his dream fades. Peart's lyric is one of romantic pessimism rather than libertarian optimism.

The record immediately signals that a science fiction narrative in a context of progressive space music will present concerns about a dystopian future society. The overture to *2112* starts with high pitched electronic glissandos and sustained notes that rise over bass tones. The sounds evoke space in the same way that much of the genre of space music or science fiction film scores have often done: with sustained and echoed tones, slow tempos, high pitches, and low bass tones that convey a sense of the vastness of space. Rush's lyrics on *2112* present what Chris McDonald has called "a vision of society that is divided between a pessimistic portrayal of it as a conformist social order which the individual should resist and an optimistic view of it as an environment in which the exceptional stands out and flourishes."[45]

2112, like its title, is futuristic. A synthesized "overture" opens the album's second song, based upon Rand's *Anthem*. The discovery of electricity in Rand's novel is related to the electric guitar in Rush's song. A key figure on this album is the anonymous narrator's discovery of that guitar: a relic of the twentieth century.[46] The priests of "The Temple of Syrinx" represent music business executives and critics who did not always like what was coming from Rush. They insisted upon a commercial formula for the music produced for the public. Rush did not subscribe to those categories. The band asserted that they would be engaged in the discovery of musical expression on their own terms. For *2112* marked Rush as an album-oriented band: one not inclined toward producing short radio friendly singles. Mercury Records, which had recently been purchased by Polygram, did not view *2112* as a commercial album. However, the recording attracted and built Rush's following. Rush further developed as a touring act. The album sold an estimated 160,000 copies by June 1976. In October, it reached #61 on the *Billboard* charts. Across the years, the record has had platinum album sales.

Neil Peart's lyrics drew inspiration from Ayn Rand, who vigorously opposed communist totalitarianism by asserting "the virtue of selfishness" and a libertarian view of individual choice. Some listeners wondered why the band was creating lyrics that sounded like they had come from the novels of Ayn Rand. The reason for that was Neil Peart's conscientious reading of

Atlas Shrugged and *Anthem* (1938). He and Alex Lifeson and Geddy Lee had adopted a libertarian stance against all systems that would diminish individuality and autonomy. Neil Peart's lyrics contested the system or structure of Western material society and asserted themes of individualism. Critics who had not read Ayn Rand were tipped off to Peart's reference to her work when he added a mention of Ayn Rand in the album's liner notes, crediting her work. Critics began to note how the vigorous independence and libertarian stance in Ayn Rand's work appealed to the band.

Peart's embrace of the libertarian philosophy of Ayn Rand complicates any notion that rock's critiques of society are always from the left. Rand's philosophy was forged in distaste for the statist, communist left of the Soviet Union and any form of control that would violate personal autonomy. Yet, she would not unequivocally embrace the counterculture and its utopian dreams. She abhorred collectivity. Rand would see irrationality, subjectivism, and nihilism in some expressions of the counterculture and would fervently oppose the "new left" politics strand of counterculture. Philosophically, her emphasis was not on the "Geist" and Idealism of Hegel, a spiritual ideal of synthesis, but on reason and science. She saw in Hegelianism, as well as in the Marxist materialist inversion of it, the roots of totalitarian oppression. Any altruistic claims of the value of self-sacrifice and any calls for the individual to submit to the public good were anathema. The self ought to remain free and fiercely independent. (Of course, the egoism and lack of social obligation in Rand may raise questions about purpose and meaning in life, the value of consideration of others, and the merits of any individual's contributions to humanity.)

Peart's lyrics draw upon an assertion of individuality, non-conformity, and creativity that we also see in Rand's work. Ayn Rand's heroic fictional characters John Galt and Howard Roark are independent-minded, creative spirits who reflect Friedrich Nietzsche's notion of the Ubermensch, the far-reaching superman who transcends the masses. Rand does not see the tension in Nietzsche's Apollonian-Dionysian concept of art and music as a dichotomy. Rather, the principle of organization and the fire of creativity work in tandem. In her *Romantic Manifesto* (1969) Rand asserts the value of art in society, calling upon romantic art (not Romanticism as a philosophy) to reanimate the modern world. For Ayn Rand's utopia is one of creativity, freedom, and authentic individualism.

The anti-authoritarianism in Rand's thought likely appealed to Neil Peart, who created scenarios in which the creative soul opposes the bureaucratic, faceless authorities. Insofar as Rush participates in what Edward Macan has called rock's "romantic ethos of transcendence." They can be said to have drawn from the thought of Ayn Rand without being Randian.[47] That is, as Durrell Bowman observes, references to Rand's thought make up only a portion of Rush's overall catalog of lyrical statements. Rand's romantic realism has a place in Rush's work but attention to this ought not to be disproportionate. Certainly, the shadow of Ayn Rand lingers behind the fierce independence that Rush declares with their concept album. However, Rush explored conceptual worlds beyond *2112*.

Rush followed *2112* with a live album, *All the World's A Stage* (September 29, 1976), which sold well and became a gold album within two months. The band toured widely for seven months. By now, they had assumed outsider status: they were a concept album band in a music industry that remained largely focused upon producing hit singles. Their audience responded to themes of alienation and feeling disaffected and to Rush's music and stance as nonconformists. Their science fiction motifs suggested a struggle for freedom that connected well with their fan base.

A FAREWELL TO KINGS AND HEMISPHERES

The synthesizer sound grew more prominent on *A Farewell to Kings*. The sound was augmented by the bass pedals that Geddy Lee brought in so that he could accompany Alex Lifeson's guitar at live shows, while keeping himself free to either play bass or keyboards. Geddy Lee had gotten a Mini-Moog. Its sound complemented the science fiction aspects of this record. *A Farewell to Kings* opens with Rush's eleven-minute version of "Xanadu," drawn from Samuel Taylor Coleridge's opiate dream poem "Kublai Kahn." "Cinderella Man," filled with Alex Lifeson guitar solos, echoes the anti-establishment tones of Rush's previous work.

When Neil Peart read a *Time* magazine about black holes it moved him to write "Cygnus X–1: The Voyage." On *Hemispheres* (1978) the narrator passes through the black hole Cygnus X–1. Terry Brown, the recording's producer, spoke the introduction to Cygnus X–1. The song follows the journey of the spaceship *Rocinante*, named after Don Quixote's horse. Rush recorded it in South Wales at Rockfield Studios and brought the product for mixing to Advision Studios in London. "La Villa Strangiatto," on the *Hemispheres* album has a middle section in 7/8 time. The principal theme recedes into Alex Lifeson's guitar solo, when he moves into an arpeggio pattern after the lead peaks at about 5:14. Such musical transitions in the band's compositions increasingly called for Geddy Lee to work at the intersection of pre-recorded, processed material and the performance he created uniquely each night on bass and keyboards. Lee is primarily a bass guitar player rather than a keyboardist. However, beginning in 1976, we hear Rush's increasing use of synthesizers on their recordings. Five of the six songs on *Permanent Waves* (1980) and all seven songs on *Moving Pictures* (1981) incorporate synthesizers.[48]

One of Rush's signature songs, "YYZ," the third track from *Moving Pictures*, is a song filled with transition and asymmetrical meter. For the members of Rush "YYZ" is the aviation code for Toronto's Pearson International Airport. The song signals for them airports, travel, and homecoming to Toronto. The song opens in Morse code and soon guitar, bass, and drums unite in 5/4 time. However, a half-minute into the song a quick passage of sixteenth notes in 6/8 time creates a change. Bass and guitar play the melody in counterpoint out to about a minute and a half into the piece, at which point Peart's drum fills bring us into the next section which features solo guitar work by Lifeson. The song expresses the virtuosity of the band well, with features like a thirty-two-note tom fill by Peart and dazzling guitar and bass work by Lifeson and Lee.

PERMANENT WAVES

"The Spirit of Radio," the opening song on *Permanent Waves* (1980), affirms that music has cultural value and offers a comment on programmed radio airplay and record industry calculations. Record companies are more intent upon units sold and *Billboard* chart position than the enduring qualities of the art of music. The song lyric affirms that one likes to believe in music. However, Rush critiques the industry—its machinations, its concerts, promotions and money-making engine—and asserts its right to create music that has nothing to do with studio doctored cookie-cutter singles aimed at the pop charts. Throughout the 1980s Rush repeatedly emphasized the theme of awareness and the lyrics of their songs increasingly delved into human issues. Meanwhile, their lyrics continued to draw upon science fiction motifs and figures like robots and androids and their music suggested space and technology with synthesizers and a variety of effects.

Memorably, Geddy Lee's declares in Rush's song "Freewill," the second track on *Permanent Waves* (1980), that one must choose and exercise free will. A stubborn free will is what Rush persists in expressing. On *Permanent Waves*, the song "Natural Science" offers a reflection on the social impact of technology. We hear about causes that cannot see effects. The song suggests that the accomplishments of science and technology must be balanced with care when they are applied to human beings who have free will. *Permanent Waves* continued with the science and technology theme across several songs. With "Hyperspace" comes a driving 7/8 tempo, synthesizer and heavy bass, and high vocals in brief phrases. The lyrics of these songs suggest that science can be brought into humanistic relation with humanity if science is approached with integrity.

The album *Grace Under Pressure* (1984) features a Hugh Syme album cover design on which an android looks to the distance at a circuit board encompassed by liquid clouds. What might this figure be thinking, if indeed this robotic creature can think? Rush brought synthesizers, sequencers, guitar and keyboard effect boxes, samplers, and pre-recorded materials out of the studio and into their live performances. This led some critics to question this arrangement of technology and mixture of live and processed sounds.[49]

On *Grace Under Pressure*, Rush called attention to the human-electronics/robotics interface in "The Body Electric." Peart's lyric creates the story of an android that can feel and who has will. The song lyric is filled with computer imagery, as Durrell Bowman points out.[50] It refers to a "humanoid escapee," an "android on the run," "data overload," "memory banks unloading . . . bytes breaking" and a binary code that is sung during the song's chorus. In a *Twilight Zone* episode of that title, a grandmother-housekeeper is a robot. ("The Body Electric" appears to draw its title from a Ray Bradbury story, the title of which hearkens back to the poet Walt Whitman.) Rush's song explores the increasing interface between the human and the machine that poststructuralist critic Mark Poster has called "the mode of information." As Poster points out, there is in several Philip K. Dick stories a symbiotic merger between human and machine: "What may be happening is that human beings create computers and then computers create a new species of humans."[51] Poster focuses his concern on electronic mediated communication and language and its impact upon people and society. "Information has become a privileged term in our culture," he says, "each method of preserving and transmitting information profoundly intervenes in the network of relationship that constitute a society."[52] Poster points out: "The case of recorded rock music presents a quite different configuration of language. Many studio recordings of rock are from the outset structured for reproduction in the home."[53] What follows from this, he says, is a simulacrum: tracks that have been assembled into performances that exist only in their reproductions.

In the late 1980s, the references to science fiction, fantasy, and mythology began to drift away from Rush's records. Rush melded progressive rock, jazz fusion, and new wave/post-punk. Their song lyrics appeared as reflections on social problems and human issues like loneliness, ambition, vulnerability, war, and freedom. However, they continued to evoke the exotic landscapes of J.R.R. Tolkein's "Rivendell" and Samuel Taylor Coleridge's "Kublai Kahn" in "Xanadu" on *A Farewell to Kings* (1977). After 2010, Rush would turn back to science fiction themes.

CLOCKWORK ANGELS

Collaboration with science fiction writer Kevin J. Anderson led to *Clockwork Angels* (2012). Kevin J. Anderson's novel *Resurrection, Inc.* (1988) drew upon Rush's music and lyrics from their album *Grace Under Pressure* (1984). *The Saga of the Seven Suns* science fiction series interested Neil

Peart and Geddy Lee. With *Clockwork Angels*, based on a science fiction adventure novel, Peart took a new direction with the dystopian issues.

Clockwork Angels was released on June 12, 2012. The album cover, designed by Hugh Syme, showed a clock with alchemical symbols and the number 9:12, or 21:12 in twenty-four-hour time, recalling the band's *2112* recording. The story line for the concept album reflected the social dystopia of that previous album and developed a new scenario. The Kevin J. Anderson novelization appeared in February 2012.

The central character of *Clockwork Angels* is Owen Hardy, who grows up in a small town in a world controlled by the Watchmaker. Owen dreams of being an assistant in the apple orchard. He misses his girlfriend and is pulled aboard a train bound for the city in Albion, where the Watchmaker rules through alchemical creations of gold and manipulations of the time and the weather. All things need order and fall under his control. On the train, Owen has no money and he is given a loan by the Anarchist. (We hear of him in the fourth cut on the record, "The Anarchist.") The Anarchist faces off against the Watchmaker, who asserts that there is a perfect universe. Owen gets caught up in a plot that might remind one of the anarchism in Joseph Conrad's *The Secret Agent*. The anarchist implicates him in a bombing and Owen is on the run.

Clockwork Angels received Canada's Juno Award for best album of the year in 2013. It led Peart to explore writing "2113," as a sequel to *2112*. He imagined a new recording: *Clockwork Lives*.[54] *Clockwork Angels* is a reminder that science fiction imagination has figured significantly in Rush's journey. The imagination of Rush has embraced technology fervently, while warning against excesses of scientism or political control and asserting the dignity and rights of individuals to be as unique as they choose to be.

ECOLOGICAL AND POLITICAL CONCERNS

More recently, recording artists have drawn attention to the potential for ecological disaster. For example, in a recent recording, *Savage (Songs from a Broken World)*, Gary Numan presents a dystopian scenario that extends concerns about global warming. Numan raises the ethical question of whether we are not responsible for future generations and the welfare of the planet. Numan imagines a barren landscape and creates a dystopian fiction. "Ghost Nation," with its programmed synthesizers carries his science fiction sense through a "windswept hell." "My Name is Ruin" has synthesizers with a funk beat. "Bed of Thorns" feels mid-Eastern and "Broken" is like a busted hymn with a female singer vocalizing and a bright chorus. The rhythmically driven "The End of Things" with its upper-register melody lines is where the world "comes apart." Amid keyboard riffs, we are asked to consider "What God

Intended" and to look at a future world that is devastated by human mistakes and ecological neglect.[55]

Political challenges are also frequently a subject of dystopian lyrics and stories. A central feature of the songs of Rage Against the Machine, for example, have been their leftist, sociopolitical lyrics. In 1992, this immediately was evident in their debut album and reinforced by *Evil Empire* (1996) and *The Battle of Los Angeles* (1999). In the 1990s the band's rebellious political stance was no-nonsense. They opened for U2 in 1997, with concert proceeds going to relief organizations. They played at the 1999 iteration of Woodstock. An indirect connection between the band's music and science fiction occurred when "Wake Up" was on *The Matrix* film soundtrack and "Calm Like a Bomb" appeared in the sequel, *The Matrix Reloaded*. *Renegades* covered tunes by other bands. Zack de la Rocha left the band and, in 2000, they went their separate ways, but several band members soon joined with Chris Cornell of Soundgarden to form Audioslave. The band Audioslave recorded three albums and discontinued in 2007. Tom Morello played folk-acoustic gigs for several years as the Nightwatchman. Rage Against the Machine reunited at the Coachella Festival in April 2007. Morello, Tim Commerford, and Brad Wilk later formed Prophets of Rage in 2016. Rage Against the Machine's criticisms of government policy, challenges to capitalist inequities, and leftist politics came with some dystopian images and a call to activism. Their spirit recalled that of the imaginative romantic rebel who takes institutions to task for dehumanization. The mind forg'd manacles of blind reason are criticized by William Blake. Jean-Jacques Rousseau declared that man is born free but is everywhere in chains. Rock music asserts a Promethean break from the rocky cliff of modern mechanism into a renewal of imaginative fire and freedom.

NOTES

1. Thomas Kitts, *John Fogerty: An American Son*. New York and London: Routledge, 2016, p. 124. Bruce Miroff in *Rolling Stone* called "Who'll Stop the Rain" an anguished cry in which "the Old Testament becomes rock and roll." "Records: Travelin' Band" "Who'll Stop the Rain" CCR (Fantasy 637) *Rolling Stone* (February 21, 1970), cited by Thomas Kitts, p. 124. Kitts lists several other Fogerty songs, including "The Wall," "Walking in a Hurricane," "Long Dark Night," and "Premonition."

2. John Carey describes Wells as opposed to the masses and creating invasion scare fictions. He refers to Wyndham Lewis' similar discontent with the masses. One can see the same concerns in Ortega y Gasset's *The Revolt of the Masses*. John Carey, *The Intellectuals and the Masses: Pride and Prejudice Among the Literary Intelligensia, 1880–1939*. Chicago: Chicago Review Press, 2005.

3. William Irwin, *Black Sabbath and Philosophy: Mastering Reality*. Malden, MA: Wiley Blackwell, 2013, p. 7.

4. Irwin, p. 8.

5. George Orwell, "The Scientists Take Over," Review of C.S. Lewis *That Hideous Strength*. *Manchester Review* (August 16, 1945).

6. John Rodden, *George Orwell: The Politics of Literary Reputation*. New York: Oxford University Press, 1989, pp. 207–8.

7. Of a February 12, 1972, show at Imperial Hall *Melody Maker* wrote "Bowie and his band are nothing if not superb parodists." This appeared in "Caught in the Act," *Melody Maker* (February 19, 1972).

8. Bowie interview. Broadcast Interviews, 1977. See YouTube.com. This otherness defined Bowie's work, says Nicholas Pegg, who observes that "time, mortality, and oblivion . . . runs like a seam through Bowie's songwriting." Nicholas Pegg, *The Complete David Bowie*. London: Titan, 2011.

9. Gordon Coxkill, *Bowie on Bowie, Interviews and Encounters with David Bowie*. Ed. Sean Egan. Chicago: Chicago Review Press, 2015, p. 11.

10. James T. Jones, *Post Jungian Criticism: Theory and Practice*. Ed. James S. Baumlin et. al. Albany: State University of New York Press, 2004, p. 236.

11. Ellen Willis, "The Velvet Underground: I'll Let You Be in My Dream," *Situations* Vol. 5, No. 2, pp. 7–18. This essay appeared in the anthology *Stranded: Rock for a Desert Island*. Ed. Greil Marcus, New York: Knopf, 1979. See also Willis, *Out of the Vinyl Deeps*. Ed. Nona Willis Aronowitz. University of Minnesota, 2014.

12. See David Fricke, "Lou Reed: The Rolling Stone Interview," *Rolling Stone* (May 4, 1989). Willis suggests that Pete Townshend also represented this and "united elegance and defiant cruelty." Willis, "The Velvet Underground," p. 7.

13. Willis, "The Velvet Underground," p. 8.

14. Willis, "The Velvet Underground," p. 9. Velvet Underground song covers include: David Bowie's version of "I'm Waiting for the Man" in 1972 Ziggy Stardust shows, Mott the Hoople's version of Sweet Jane, REM "Femme Fatale" and "Pale Blue Eyes," Kurt Cobain, "Here She Comes" (1991 EP), The Feelies "What Goes On" on *Only Life*. Jeremy Gilbert sees in The Kinks "potential affinities" with the Velvet Underground. Jeremy Gilbert "White Light, White Heat: Jouissance Beyond Gender in the Velvet Underground," *Living Through Pop*. Ed. Andrew Blake. London: Routledge, 1999, p. 46. The Velvets are discussed by Ellen Willis. See *Out of the Vinyl Deeps,* "Walk on the Wild Side" by Lou Reed was produced by David Bowie. A contribution by Herbie Flowers, a session musician, was not credited. The recording included passages from jazz saxophonist Ronnie Ross.

15. See Bernardo Alexander Attias, "Authenticity and Artifice in Rock and Roll: And I Guess That I Just Don't Care," *Rock Music Studies* Vol. 3, Is. 2 (2016): 131–47. Attias begins his article on the Velvet Underground by noting that "Musicians, journalists, and academics often hold up the Velvet Underground as the paragon of authenticity in rock music." The *Rock Music Studies* issue on The Velvet Underground is a must-read for anyone who wants to better understand the band.

16. Richard Hell, *I Dreamed I Was A Very Clean Tramp: An Autobiography*. New York: HarperCollins, 2013.

17. Johnny Ramone (John Cummings) died in 2004 and is buried in Hollywood's Forever Cemetery.

18. Kirk Hammett of Metallica and Johnny Ramone both liked horror movies and rare horror movie collector posters. Charles M. Young, "The Last Days of Johnny Ramone," *Rolling Stone* (October 14, 2004). See also Melissa Locker, "Ork Records: The Hidden Side of New York Punk," (December 8, 2015). On October 30, 2015, compilation from Ork Records: First recordings included "Little Johnny Jewel" by Television, Richard Hell, Alex Chilton, The Erasers, The Feelies "Fa Ce La," "The Boy with Perpetual Nervousness" (1978), and "My Little Red Book" by Burt Bacharach and Hal David (Performance on December 14, 1976, at CBGBs.) Terry Ork with curls of hair and beard was "a cherubic individual," said Lenny Kaye. Ork Records fell apart in 1980.

19. Dave Thompson, *True Adventures on the Front Lines of Punk, 1976–1977*. Chicago: Chicago Review Press, 2009.

20. Critic Ellen Willis reflected on her ambivalence about female rock acts in the late 1970s. She regarded The Sex Pistols' anti-abortion stance in "Bodies" as more stimulating than women's music played at the time. See *Out of the Vinyl Deeps*. Ed. Nona Willis Aronowitz. Minneapolis: University of Minnesota Press, 2014.

21. For further reading, see Sean Egan, *The Clash: The Only Band That Mattered*. Lanham: Rowman and Littlefield, 2014.

22. Eric Abbey, *Garage Rock and Its Roots: Musical Rebels and the Drive for Individuality*. McFarland, 2006, pp. 4–5.

23. Abbey, p. 8. The title recalls Joe Strummer's statement: "We deal in junk, you know. We deal in . . . the rubbish bin." (xiv).

24. See Sigmund Freud, *Civilization and Its Discontents* (1929). Freud writes of "the urgencies of instinct and the restrictions of civilization."

25. Abbey, p. xvi; Konrad Lorenz, *On Aggression*. London: Methuen, 1963.

26. David Easley, "Riff Schemes, Form, and the Genre of Early American Hardcore Punk (1978–1983)," *MTO: A Journal of the Society for Music Theory* Vol. 21, No. 1 (March 2015): 1–2. Easley explores changes in pitch, fretboard motion, rhythmic grouping, and textures.

27. Steve Waksman, *This Ain't the Summer of Love: Conflict and Crossover in Metal and Punk*. Berkeley: University of California Press, 2009, p. 265. Rock welcomes trash, writes Steven Hamelman, noting that "punk rock celebrates trash and derives much of its power from a 'trash this' attitude." (p. 60). (He cites Joe Strummer's comment: "We deal in junk, you know" [p. 61].) Hamelman provides a series of comments from the press from 1955 to 1958 in which rock and roll was derided as "garbage" and "rubbish" (pp. 65–66). He cites rock critic Richard Meltzer's recognition of trash waste in rock (pp. 38–39). New wave figured strongly in Britain into the early 1980s. (Rhino Records has a new waves compilation that ends in 1985. A listener might wonder: Did new wave subside then?)

28. See Theo Cateforis, *Are We Not New Wave?* Ann Arbor: University of Michigan Press, 2011, p. 32.

29. Cateforis, p. 33.

30. The point has been made by Will Straw and pointed out by Theo Cateforis, p. 56.

31. Ben Ratliff, "Metallica Earns Top Billing of the Big Four," *New York Times* (September 15, 2011), commented that "metal in the 1980s was a boy's game built on aggression, not love." Metallica's story started out by their being "scrappy."

32. Aldous Huxley, *Brave New World*, pp. 226–27.

33. *Huxley's Brave New World: Essays*. Ed. David Garrett Izzo. Jefferson, NC: McFarland, 2008. Gavin Miller, "Political Repression and Sexual Freedom in *Brave New World* and *1984*," *Huxley's Brave New World: Essays*, pp. 17–25. Angelo Arciero, "Some Kind of *Brave New World*: Humans, Society and NAture in the Dystopian Interpretations of Huxley and Orwell," *Huxley's Brave New World: Essays*, pp. 46–61.

34. Aldous Huxley, Letter of May 18, 1931. *The Letters of Aldous Huxley*. Ed. Grover Smith, New York: Harper and Row, 1969, p. 348.

35. Huxley, *Brave New World*, p. 6.

36. Peter Firchow, *Huxley's Brave New World: Essays*. Ed. David Garrett Izzo. McFarland, 2008, p. 108.

37. Scott Peller, "Laboring for a Brave New World: Our Ford and the Epsilons," *Huxley's Brave New World: Essays*, p. 69.

38. Granville Hicks is referred to by Scott Peller, p. 219.

39. Huxley, *Brave New World*, p. 44.

40. Huxley, *Brave New World*, p. 246.

41. Huxley, *Brave New World*, p. 139.

42. David Bowie, *Bowie on Bowie: Interviews and Encounters with David Bowie*. Ed. Sean Egan. Chicago: Chicago Review Press, 2015, p. 167.

43. Timothy Smolko, "What Can This Device Be?" *Rush and Philosophy*. Ed. Durrell Bowman and Jim Berti. Chicago: Open Court, 2011, p. 228.

44. Deena Weinstein, *The Artistic Vision of Modern Society in Rush, Pink Floyd, and Bruce Springsteen*. Montreal: New World Perspectives, 1985.

45. Chris McDonald, "Open Secrets, Individualism, and Middle-Class Identity in the Songs of Rush," *Popular Music and Society* Vol. 31 (2008): 319.

46. Indeed, his story might have been different if he had found the tiniest guitar on earth in existence today. With experiments in nanotechnology, Cornell University scientists have made a guitar of crystalline silicon that is far smaller than a human hair. Played by an atom force

microscope it produces a high-pitched sound that the Priests of Syrinx would not have heard because they exceed the range of the human ear. See Michio Kaku, *Physics of the Impossible*. New York: Doubleday, 2008, p. 31.

47. Edward Macan, "Reply to Chris Matthew Sciabbara," *Journal of Ayn Rand Studies* Vol. 5, No. 1 (2003): 173–88.

48. Durrell Bowman, "More Than We Bargained For," *Rush and Philosophy: Heart and Mind United*. Ed. Durrell Bowman and Jim Burti. Chicago: Open Court, 2011, p. 170.

49. Durrell Bowman in *Rush and Philosophy* refers to Paul Theberge, *Any Sound You Can Imagine* and H. Stith Bennett, "Notation and Identity in Contemporary Popular Music," *Popular Music* Vol. 3 (1983): 231.

50. Bowman, *Rush and Philosophy*, p. 179.

51. Mark Poster, *The Mode of Information: Poststructuralism and the Social Context*. Chicago: University of Chicago and Cambridge: Polity, 1990, p. 4.

52. Poster, p. 7.

53. Poster, p. 9.

54. Neil Peart also wrote another memoir: *Far and Near: On Days Like These*. Toronto: ECW Press, October 2014.

55. There have been many songs concerning ecological problems from Marvin Gaye's "Mercy Me" to the present. Michael Jackson's "Earth Song" video in particular projects a nasty apocalyptic scenario.

Chapter Five

Rock Romanticism

Power Chords and the Visionary Company

Rock embodies the legacy of Romanticism. Creativity, emotion, rebellion, discovering the voice of the people: that's romantic. Romanticism may be presented as a worldview that affirms individual subjectivity, authenticity, imagination, and organicism in nature. As an ideology connected with artistic creation, romanticism values originality and opposes the alienation of the rationalized human in a mechanistic universe. The authentic is unique, nonstandard, something other than instrumental rationality. Indeed, the notion of authenticity in rock originates in Romanticism. The artist, true to his or her art, expresses fierce individuality and independence. Romanticism wishes to exceed the prosaic world of mankind. It seeks an alternative in dreams.

The relationship between Romanticism and rock music has been explored by several critics. They appear to agree that there is in Romanticism "a longing for unity" that is "focused on the subject."[1] Romanticism engages neo-classicism while being innovative, even transgressive, with form. This Romanticism is a response to culture, a response to political revolution, industrialism, global trade, and colonialism. At its center is imagination, which is held to be the highest faculty of the human mind, a dynamic through which we see and create the world. Samuel Taylor Coleridge defined the imagination as constitutive, creating reality, as well as receptive. It brings together and reconciles opposites. Coleridge wrote: "The Primary Imagination I hold to be a living power and prime agent of human perception and as repetition in the finite mind of the eternal act of creation in the infinite I Am."[2] Creative poetry and music arise from the unconscious. Fancy assembles and gathers associations of images and metaphors. Imagination transcends sensory experience and reshapes the world.

Several writers on rock have outlined characteristics of romanticism that might be found in rock: transcendence of boundaries (material and spirit), individuality in personal expression, social critique (as in Blake or Shelley), concern with experience and the self or internal emotional life, an interest in nature and the natural, curiosity about the Gothic and the mysterious, exotic, or Satanic; trust in the intuitive, an embrace of passion and rebellion, affirmation of imagination, wistful nostalgia, hope in the utopian, a critique of the rational or instrumental reason. Camille Paglia recognizes that Romantic characteristics of "energy, passion, rebellion, and demonism" live within rock music and rock musicians.[3] Rock lyrics also reflect William Wordsworth's attention to common people and agrarian culture, as in his poem "Michael," and his use of common diction, or ordinary and easily accessible daily language.

Throughout rock there is evidence of the contemporary romantic imagination. We see the rock rebel. We witness musical showmen from Liszt to Eddie Van Halen to the science fiction persona and expressions of David Bowie. The melancholy, angst, nostalgia, and self-destructiveness of Romanticism can also be found in rock and its loss of artists from Jimi Hendrix and Janis Joplin to Kurt Cobain. The word romanticism is being used broadly here, to embrace all these phenomena. It refers to the rock musician's capacity to use his or her emotional resources and tap into a sense of wonder. A.O. Lovejoy in "On the Discrimination of Romanticisms" (1924) provides a survey of how the term romanticism has been used. Rene Welleck (1949) and Morse Peckham (1951) also explored this question of definition.[4] Georg Lukacs' view was that Romanticism was "a critique of modernity, that is, of modern capitalist civilization, in the name of ideals and values drawn from the past."[5] We can see Rock participating in this critique.

What rock musicians have in common with the British romantics is their inheritance of a pose of rebellion against Enlightenment reason and an assertion of the powers of imagination. Romanticism is "the artist's struggle against past forms," observes Perry Meisel.[6] Romanticism emphasizes imagination, intuition, and emotion. Robert Pattison sees rock as "a mutant variety of Romanticism."[7] Lee Marshall connects Romanticism with authenticity. Philosopher Charles Taylor has referred to authenticity as a "child of the Romantic period."[8] The poetry of Percy Bysshe Shelley and William Blake may be viewed in connection with rock music's spirit of innovation and countercultural challenges to society. Romanticism connects art with feeling, an intense awareness and emotion, and self-expression. There is a wind of emotional intuitionism that supersedes rationalism. The nineteenth-century music critic E. T. A. Hoffmann once said of music: "It is the most romantic of the arts . . . for its sole subject is the infinite."[9] French poet Alfred de Musset called music "l'art c'est le sentment": an art of feeling.[10]

A Romanticism of ruins and melancholy appears in Gothic fiction and poetry and lies behind the production of fearful effects in heavy metal. The sublime is characterized as a feeling of awe, terror, or wonder that takes one beyond oneself. A powerful blast of amplified discord and the combustible energy of stage performance attempts to invigorate an audience with that ecstasy. From the histrionic showmanship of Franz Liszt in one era to the shamanic spell and drama of the rock front-man there is romanticism in performance. There is a dream of collective unity, hierophany, and transcendence. Imagination, in that moment, creates a world.

In the consideration of artistic imagination, Samuel Taylor Coleridge's *Biographia Literaria* provides a reference point for the crucial recognition of the powers and qualities of imagination. Elsewhere, Coleridge wrote: "the sense of musical delight, with the power of producing it, is a gift of imagination." In this passage, he is writing about sound in poetry. Yet, as composer Aaron Copland cites this comment by Coleridge, he says that to him "it seems even more true when applied to the musical delights of music." Music is "the freest, the most abstract, the least fettered of all the arts," Copland writes.[11] That is to say that in music itself there is apparently no narrative story line and there are no pictures. Copland writes that music "by its very nature invites imaginative treatment."[12] He explores the aspects of music that are open to creative influences of the imagination. In a section on "the imaginative listener," Copland recognizes that "listening is a talent."[13] To listen is to open oneself to a musical experience and then to evaluate that experience. The professional is "an initiate" who has "inner understanding" of music's mysteries, like a priest at the altar before the sacrament.[14] However, to be able to execute a passage of music is no guarantee of the ability to instinctively grasp it.[15]

Rock's musicians appear to have intuitively grasped the power of music. The period of the sixties (that is, about 1965 to about 1974), a turbulent time, saw the creation of imaginative expression from rock music artists whose rebellion and quest for transcendence parallels that of the French Revolutionary period during which Samuel Taylor Coleridge and William Wordsworth engaged in dreams of liberation and William Blake raised his protest against the "mind forged manacles" of institutions, instrumental reason, and impoverished vision. What literary critic Harold Bloom has called "the visionary company"—Blake, Coleridge, Wordsworth, Keats, Byron, Shelley—represented a creative challenge to Augustan neo-classical form and a call for reform of society that parallels the quest of consciousness in "the sixties" that was so deeply connected with rock music (Rolling Stones, The Who, Yardbirds, Cream, Traffic, and many others). The romantic quest for transcendence continued to take mythopoeic forms with progressive rock bands such as Rush, Genesis, Yes, and the heavy metal/progressive rock band Iron

Maiden. (Notably Rush and Iron Maiden have adapted Coleridge's "Kublai Kahn" and "The Rime of the Ancient Mariner," respectively.)

In the 1980s Robert Pattison linked rock music with romanticism, which, in its English and German forms, indeed countered an emphasis upon rationality with the reminder that we are also emotional, intuitive, feeling beings. However, we may qualify Pattison's approach to rock, which he called "the triumph of vulgarity." He contended that rock refuses to submit to measures of good taste. He recognized "various Romantic myths of which rock is composed" and considered rock as a world of thought.[16] However, how we view both rock and romanticism can be extended beyond these terms. For example, when Bruce Springsteen speaks of rock as a kind of salvation, he comes quite close to a notion held by the German romantics, from Novalis, Tieck, and Hoffmann to Schopenhauer, Wagner, and Nietzsche, that music was the most significant art, one deeply connected with what Schopenhauer called "the word soul" and that Nietzsche viewed as birthing the tragic drama. The Pattison book does not spend enough time recognizing how rock may be transformative in this sense.

The Promethean assertion in rock claims a fire in the human spirit that can transform things. It is this creative energy that the poet Percy Bysshe Shelley felt in the elements, in the majestic power of Mont Blanc and in the West Wind he invoked for inspiration. With a sharp wit and fierce verse, he protested the Peterloo Massacre, as Bob Dylan or Phil Ochs would later protest injustice through American folk music. Like Dylan writing against the "Masters of War," he rejected the authoritarian arrogance of Ozymandias and signaled the demise of all tyrants. If the answer was blowing in the wind, perhaps that answer would penetrate the heart and rouse a sense of indignation. Shelley believed in those profuse strains of unpremeditated art that could flow from the song of a skylark, or from the acid pen of the rebel poet. As his young wife to be, Mary, discovered in 1816, even Frankenstein began in the fires of inspiration. Rock, in its expressions of vigor, beauty, and horror seizes that same fire.

Rock has engaged with romanticism far more deeply than merely recycling the Promethean myth, the Garden of Eden myth, or the image of Milton's Satan. It has enlisted Gothicism, innovations with form, and a quest for transcendence—much like the romantics. The London based music critic Simon Frith, in his review of Pattison's book, *The Triumph of Vulgarity*, pointed out some of the shortcomings of his view. The romantic myths largely resided in what he called the "art school bands": The Rolling Stones, The Yardbirds, The Who, Cream, and Led Zeppelin. (Eric Clapton, Jimmy Page, Pete Townshend, and Keith Richards all attended art school at one time. John Lennon did also.) Simon Frith argued that Pattison's thesis that rock was black music, or the blues, meeting with white Romanticism failed to account for bohemian influences and sources of rock. Meanwhile, as a reviewer in *The Nation* (March 28, 1987) pointed out, in commenting upon rock music we cannot only "resituate [rock songs] on a high cultural terrain" in terms of traditional musicology. Rock is more than "an organic development of Western Romanticism expressed in the vulgar mode," as Pattison pointed out. Indeed, rock is this, in part, but it is also something more.[17]

Certainly, the German romanticism of Novalis, Hoffmann, Holderlin, or Nietzsche and the British romanticism of Coleridge, Blake, and Shelley are precursors for the rock attitude that music is liberating, that imagination is to be celebrated, and that rebellion against confining norms is an imperative. These poets and thinkers all sought to proclaim the power of imagination and dwelled in dark fantasies. They turned to the force of poetry and story. Rock music, likewise, in our age of science and technology, has combined these impulses with imaginative resources. Transcendence, which was so important to the romantics, is a significant feature of rock music as well. Imagination seeks a renewal of the world. Wordsworth, who once lamented that "the world is too much with us," hoped that he could hold the power of myth and hear Triton blow his wreathed horn. By valuing imagination and the mythopoeic in our world we can continue to "see" and to dream of human horizons. Rock music is an assertion of creativity against dominant expressions of rationalism. To voice this is to assert qualities of the human soul (intuition, feeling, compassion, imagination) against blind instrumental reason. In this sense rock-poets are, as Shelley wrote in his *Defense of Poetry*, the "unacknowledged legislators of the world." Rock provides a dream-world, a speculative wonder-world, or a way of critiquing present-day assumptions about what is "real." It offers a way of storytelling and image-making that stretches the musical and visual imaginations of rock music listeners. It is that expansive thinking—imagination and feeling, intuition and compassion, iconoclastic rebellion and innovation—that will contribute toward art, sensitivity, expanded consciousness, and transformation.

ROCK POETRY AND THE GHOST OF ARTHUR RIMBAUD

The lyrical talents of Bob Dylan, Joni Mitchell, Leonard Cohen, Paul Simon, and many other songwriters draw our attention to rock music's correspondences with poetry. Lingering behind them, in the distance of the past, are the Romantic poets, the Symbolists, the lyrical Modernists. In the lyrics of Jim Morrison, Patti Smith, and Bob Dylan one comes forward from the mist. More than one hundred years ago, amid the streets of Paris a young French poet Arthur Rimbaud produced the poignant lines of "The Drunken Boat" and the poems of *A Season in Hell*. At night he caroused with the poet Paul Verlaine, the two of them drinking absinthe, writing verse, and engaging in a sometimes tense relationship. The poet could not then know that he would inspire a generation of rock-poets with his visionary poetry. One might include Bob Dylan, Jim Morrison, and Patti Smith, along with Joni Mitchell, Paul Simon, and Leonard Cohen, among the visionary poets of rock. Dylan, Morrison, and Smith have all referenced the poetry of Arthur Rimbaud.

JIM MORRISON

Jim Morrison was one of rock's poet-lyricists. David Dalton calls Jim Morrison the last of the pop utopians. Wallace Fowlie compares Jim Morrison with Arthur Rimbaud. Fowlie's background in French and in Rimbaud scholarship allows him to examine the influence of Rimbaud on Morrison's lyrics and poetry. He points to Morrison's recognition of Rimbaud's orientation which Rimbaud expressed in a letter to Paul Demeny: "The poet makes himself into a visionary by a long derangement of the senses." (*un long dereglement de tons les sens*) "I say that one must be a seer, make oneself a seer. The poet makes himself a ser by a long, prodigious, and rational disordering of the senses."[18] Rimbaud created his poetry while in his teens and twenties. After his poetry in *Season in Hell* he left poetry behind. Rimbaud engaged in a not particularly successful decade of work in business in Africa.

Jim Morrison had in his possession a copy of Wallace Fowlie's translation of Arthur Rimbaud's poetry. Fowlie recognizes that Morrison was like a poet who sang his lyrics. He was introduced to The Doors by a student who suggested to him a book by Jerry Hopkins and Danny Sugarman, *No One Here Gets Out Alive*. Fowlie began hearing in the poems by Jim Morrison the influence of Rimbaud. He discusses "Oraison du soir" (Evening Prayer) and he looks at Morrison's poems that were collected in *Lords and New Creatures* and in *An American Prayer*.

In *Lords and New Creatures*, Jim Morrison points out that shamans were once esteemed as channels who were between earth and spirit and exercised powers. They entered this liminal state through chant, dance, and drugs. Native American traditions that he was aware of indicate the shaman's ability to move across time and space: to break on through to the other side, as Morrison put it. The rock concert, likewise, is a ritual in which the singer-front man might enter a shamanic trance and produce revelatory art. In Morrison's view, this can be a ritual toward something "cleaner, freer." To interviewers, Jim Morrison described the need to "purify the elements and find a new seed of life." There could be a movement from disorder toward transformation. Morrison said, "hopefully, you emerge and marry all these dualisms and opposites."[19] The notion is much like that of William Blake, who worked with contraries in many of his poems. Morrison also references Blake's "Auguries of Innocence."

PATTI SMITH

Patti Smith made her mark as a poet. She was involved with spoken word and performance art. Her lyric for "Baby, Ice Dog" was recorded by Blue Oyster Cult in 1973. "Career of Evil" followed on Blue Oyster Cult's third album, *Secret Treaties* (1974). The revenge of Vera Gemini appeared on *Agents of Fortune* (1976). "Shooting Shark" was recorded later for a 1983 Blue Oyster Cult release. The Patti Smith Group made a significant impact between 1975 and 1980, fostering the new wave/punk influence throughout popular music. "Because the Night," written and sung with Bruce Springsteen, was a radio airplay hit. The song appeared in her album *Easter* (1978). She stopped recording in 1979, married Fred Smith of the MC5, and retired to Detroit. She remained a thoughtful poet and returned to recording while in her forties.

More recently, Patti Smith has bought Rimbaud's childhood house in Roche. The French visionary poet was often on her mind as she crafted her poems and created the lyrics for *Horses* (December 1975). Her book *Just Kids* received the National Book Award and was followed by *M Train*. She has produced "My Blakean Year" and *Auguries of Innocence* (2005), recalling the poetry of William Blake.

BOB DYLAN

Bob Dylan links the Romantic and Symbolist traditions in literature, in which the poetry of Arthur Rimbaud may be placed, with the blues and the folk ballad traditions. The Nobel Prize committee has recognized the literary character of his inventiveness. He has sometimes been called a poet, although song lyrics are always written in connection with music. Certainly, his tune "Bob Dylan's Dream," which appeared on *The Freewheelin' Bob Dylan* (1963), indicated early on that Bob Dylan dreamed and imagined. However, not many of his listeners dreamed he would one day be recognized with such a literary award. Florence Dore points out that the award to Dylan didn't break down a barrier but rather acknowledged a connection that had been developing across years. Poet David Orr, responding to the award in the *New York Times* (March 24, 2017), considered how lyrics are like poems and how they are different. Poet Charlotte Pence reminds us that Gordon Ball, a scholar of Allen Ginsberg and the Beat Generation, has advocated for Dylan for many years. She affirms that songs are literature and song-poets' "words shape and move us." Christopher Ricks approaches Dylan as a poet and sees well-structured verse, although he recognizes that Dylan when singing his lyrics is "playing his timing against his rhyming."[20] Dylan is not, in conventional terms, a poet. He is a lyricist-musician and performer who once called himself a "song and dance man." Dylan is involved in performance literature says Betsy Bowden. He is a musician who engages in oral presentation, with vocal inflection, punctuation, and improvisation. As Perry Meisel points out, considering Bob Dylan and Kurt Cobain, "It is their . . . Romanticism in a combination of media that defines their achievement." It is in music, singing and language, vocal stress and accent, in which we discover an originality that is not in the "lyric form alone."[21] The award to Bob Dylan reminds us of connections between music and the literary and that culture studies calls for critical reflection on the objects of pop culture. This includes reflection on the rock song and how it emerges from the shaping force of the imagination.

Bob Dylan mentions Arthur Rimbaud in *Chronicles*. "I came across one of his letters called 'je est un autre' which translates into 'I is somebody else.' When I read those words the bells went off. It made perfect sense."[22] Dylan writes that he wishes someone had brought that idea to him sooner. His song "You're Going to Make Me Lonesome When You Go" has a line that recalls poets Arthur Rimbaud and Paul Verlaine. It seems that Dylan absorbed Rimbaud's near surrealist visions and symbolist inversions and transformations.

One can detect a bit of Rimbaud and a strain of poets like Ginsberg, Corso, and Ferlinghetti in *Another Side of Bob Dylan* (1964), his fourth album. It is acoustic. Coupe describes this album as "beat in ethos."[23] Dylan called it "vision music."[24] The recording included "My Back Pages" and "Chimes of Freedom." Coupe observes that the Beats expressed a kind of "religious reverence."[25] Dylan, who called himself a song and dance man at this time, is linked with the poet John Keats, who sought through mystery and expressed the notion of negative capability.[26] Referring to Andy Gillan's article on "Chimes," Coupe see this album as Dylan's "move away from straight protest songs to more allusive images."[27] Andy Gillan wrote: "It's his own Tempest, a compelling account of a visionary epiphany experienced in an electric storm rendered in a hyper-vivid poetic style heavily influenced by the French symbolist poet Arthur Rimbaud."[28]

Of course, Bob Dylan was first associated with the protest song. Dylan produced "The Death of Emmet Till" in April 1962, opposing racism. "Only a Pawn in Their Game" was written in 1963 and "The Lonesome Death of Hattie Carroll" in 1963, argued that William Zantzinger, who beat Hattie Carroll, her with a cane, got off too lightly in his sentencing. *Freewheelin'* includes protest songs: "With God on Our Side," "Hard Rain's A'Gonna Fall," "Blowing in the Wind," "Masters of War," "It's Alright Ma," and "Oxford Town." The song "Oxford Town" tells the story of the Mississippi call for troops when James Meredith was to enter the desegregated school. "Masters of War" directs a seething critique of the men who buy and sell the guns and profit from war and the military industrial complex. We hear "The Girl from North Country" and "Don't Think Twice It's Alright." Dylan's reference to a hard rain was immediately interpreted as a reference to the

Cuban Missile Crisis and nuclear devastation, although he wrote the song before October 1962.

In 1964 the Civil Rights movement showed some results as President Johnson focused on the Civil Rights Act, the Voting Rights Act, and the war on poverty. Meanwhile, more military assistance was being sent to South Vietnam. Dylan had declared that "The Times They Are A' Changin'." Dylan's self-invention can be seen on *Another Side of Bob Dylan* as he moves into a new manner of expression, one richer in imagery. In 1964, Johnny Cash recorded "It Ain't Me Babe." In 1965, the Turtles recorded "It Ain't Me Babe" and it became a hit. The Byrds were recording "All I Really Want to Do," "My Back Pages," "Chimes of Freedom," and "Mr. Tambourine Man." Dylan toured England in Spring 1965. (He was interviewed and filmed for D.A. Pennebaker's *Don't Look Back*, a film released in 1967.) At the Newport Folk Festival in July 1965, Dylan went electric.

Highway 61 Revisited recognized the great American highway traveled by blues players and other migrating to the cities of the north. The record unfolded with some stream of consciousness lyrics and was energized by electric guitars. *Highway 61* brings new textures. We hear the hit "Like A Rolling Stone" with its depiction of a fallen society's child facing hard times and "the mystery tramp," lost and staring into eyes that are a vacuum. The C-F-G pattern is filled with the organ sound, accented by a light electric guitar touch, and moved along steadily across several verses by the percussion section. In "Subterranean Homesick Blues" Dylan delivers a rap-like lyric that rollicks along. "Tombstone Blues" with its lengthy lyric casts a solemn note. "Maggie's Farm" cries out the speaker's insistence that he won't be pinned down into that drudgery on the farm any more. Dylan provides the long, tongue-in-cheek title "It Takes a Lot to Laugh, It Takes a Train to Cry" and ends side one on "The Ballad of a Thin Man," where even the president must stand naked. Side two includes the surrealistic titled "Queen Jane Approximately," the visionary and surrealistic "Desolation Row," with its many verses, and "Just Like Tom Thumb's Blues."

With *Blonde on Blonde*, Dylan shifted toward a surrealistic, expressionistic lyric-style. Dylan's surrealist lyrics broke with social realism. "Sad Eyed Lady of the Lowlands" remained centered in traditional lyric. However, word-play entered songs like "Absolutely Sweet Marie."[29] There is a dreamy distortion of images. In "Visions of Johanna," the speaker tells of the visions that kept him up past the dawn.

During Dylan's hiatus he played songs with The Band (Rick Danko, Richard Manuel, Robbie Robertson, Garth Hudson, Levon Helm) and they produced *The Basement Tapes* (March 1967). In March 1967 Columbia Records released Bob Dylan's *Greatest Hits* (Volume One) with its blue cover and Rowland Scherman's portrait of Dylan, photographed in profile with his tumble of hair in the bright light. "Rainy Day Women #12 and 35" opens this record with his declaration that everybody must get stoned. The record announces Dylan now situated in what is clearly a folk-rock era. "Blowing in the Wind," "The Times They Are a Changing," and "It Ain't Me Babe" represent the folk-acoustic Dylan. The remainder of the record is laced with electric guitar, organ, harmonica, and folk-rock arrangements. "Like a Rolling Stone" ends side one. "Mr. Tambourine Man" begins side two. We hear the electric Dylan putting down a fair-weather friend in "Positively 4th Street." The record ends with "Just Like A Woman." Dylan's *John Wesley Harding*, which followed, was a story-oriented record. His lyrics refer to characters (a ragman, the preacher, the rain-man, Mona, Ruthie).

In her essay on Bob Dylan, "Before the Flood," Ellen Willis asserted that "Dylan's break with the topical song was inevitable." This new-Dylan became "self-consciously poetic, adopting a neo-Beat style, loaded with images." He was "more aesthete than activist" yet "scornful of the social order."[30] Despite her respect for Dylan's work, perhaps Willis would not have voted for Dylan as a Nobel Prize recipient. She wrote: "As poetry these songs were overrated, *Howl* had said it all much better—and they were unmusical near chants declaimed to a monotonous guitar strum."[31] Willis remarks that during his retreat from music following his motorcycle accident Dylan "needed time to replenish his imagination."[32] He was continually involved in "escaping identity," with "self-annihilation" and trading personas with a "mask hidden by other masks."[33] To close this section, let us not forget Bob Dylan's wit and sly humor, or that of some of his fellow songwriters.

Dylan's wry observations of society were followed by other songwriters who engaged in quirky lyrics. Warren Zevon provided rock and pop with satirical humor and cynicism with "Desperados Under the Eaves" (1976), "Lawyers, Guns and Money," "Werewolves of London" (1978), and "Join Me in L.A." "Excitable Boy" (1978) is about a perverse murderous character. Zevon also wrote ballads of heartache. Zevon's werewolf meets film noir macabre. He breaks through L.A. Hollywood façade and creates grotesques, like *The Day of the Locust* by Nathanael West. In "Johnny Strikes Up the Band" he refers to Johnny Rotten of The Sex Pistols. In his quirky, iconoclastic way, Zevon ventured a moral critique of society. Randy Newman gave us the unreliable narrator and urban life brought Tom Waits rough-edged songs about drunks and loners. Jackson Browne saw that individually and collectively people were *Running on Empty* (1978). Frank Zappa expressed creative freedom and individuality. He opposed social conditioning by institutions or media. He rejected "plastic" and critiqued society. Zappa invites interpretation.[34] On *Just Another Band from L.A.* there is stream of consciousness, a live performance from UCLA, Howard Kaylan and Mark Volman including falsetto vocals, a news wire. In Zappa's song there are quotations, the Air Force theme, Johnny Carson on the *Tonight Show*, "Over the Rainbow" from *The Wizard of Oz*, and Kaylan calls for Toto. Elsewhere he draws upon a grab-bag of similarly eclectic sources. On *Absolutely Free*, Zappa quotes Igor Stravinsky's *The Firebird* and *Rite of Spring* on "Amnesia Vivace." In "Invocation and Ritual Dance of the Young Pumpkin" he quotes from Gustav Holst's *The Planets*, "Jupiter: The Bringer of Jollity." Zappa also drew upon Edgard Varese's techniques in *Ionization* and other compositions. He underscored the reality that the creative rock musician is a romantic rebel, an iconoclast, a critic, and a force of inspiration and imagination.

ROMANTIC POETRY AND ROCK

Romantic poetry is about the expression of a singer-poet's individual and unmistakably unique consciousness. This expression generally emerges in the lyric poem, a form that intensely projects an emotion. The lyric poem is the focused sigh, laugh, or cry of consciousness. The ode, from the Greek *aidein*, or "chant," is the expression of some exalted tribute. The elegy is the darker tribute of mourning. The lyric sometimes plays with rhyme and rhythm, alliteration, assonance, parallelism, and antithesis. It has the integrity of form and yet suggests a spontaneity of voice and expression. The lyric does this, in part, through its innate musicality, its tendency to dwell in sound.

The dimension of poetry which is its sound system can be referred to as *melos*. Romantic poetry, from Blake and Robert Burns to Keats and Byron, makes intentional uses of sound. The ear listens for the "music" possible in language. Romantic poetry thus creates a bridge between vowels and consonants, stressed and unstressed syllables, or rhythmic arrangements and what the poem is saying. The romantic poet, in part, recollects memory through sound. Further, as John Minahan notes, "The self-image of the Romantic poet is a singer."[35] If one listens to the singer-songwriters who became prominent during the late 1960s and early 1970s—James Taylor, Joni Mitchell, Paul Simon, Jackson Browne—one will hear their careful attention to vowel sounds and to the rhythms and patterns of their song lyrics.

The attitude of the Romantic poet toward music in relation to poetry is generally quite different from that of his predecessors of the Augustan period. When Alexander Pope wrote that "the sound must seem an echo to the sense" he privileged the verbal meaning of the poem as supported by its sound. Typically, Augustan poets did not at all seek the dissolving of sense into sound, as we hear in John Lennon's "goo-goo-ga-joob" or the la-la's of Stevie Wonder's "My Cherie Amour." John Dryden did write his verses for St. Cecilia's Day, celebrating the patron saint of music, but generally his verses were didactic. Pope rejected poems that "ring round the same unvary'd Chimes/ With sure Returns of still expected Rhymes."[36]

Rock musicians, like the Romantics, are willing to imagine that their music will "say" something, unlike the Augustan writers who found music ambiguous and lacking definition. Samuel Johnson, erroneously, claimed that listening to music did not involve thinking. The philosophers Kant and Hegel likewise privileged reason and regarded music as a lesser art because of its lack of referential content. Some of the British Romantic poets share in this attitude. Shelley, for example, esteemed poetry but found music devoid of "ideas." He believed that sound pushes a poem's movement and shape. But for all his innovations and attention to sound in his poetry, Shelley felt that the word's referential content is where "ideas" were available. Music, he observed, does not have ideas of this sort. Evidently, rhythmic variation, harmonic changes, and structural ideas, or melodic motifs and musical "themes" in music did not count as "ideas" for Shelley. But then, he was a poet, not a composer.

Rock makes it clear that neither poetry or music is all pleasant and to be "musical" in poetry (or in rock) is not the necessarily same thing as to "sound nice." Rather, *melos* is something besides mellifluous. Jagged, uneven, challenging poetry may be more "musical" at times than smooth, end stopped rhyming Hallmark card verse. Metrical regularity is not more "musical" than syncopation and enjambment. It is equally true that, particularly in contemporary music, meaningful and interesting musical sound may be best expressed in atonality, or polyrhythms, or devices which add a complexity to the piece. Rock is not at all hesitant to employ dissonance.

Obviously, the arts of music and poetry come together in songs, in opera (and "rock-operas" like The Who's *Tommy*), and in the music-drama. They meet in word-music, as uses of sound. Yet, to sing is to create different effects with words rather than to speak them. Mick Jagger brings attitude and inflection and phrasing to make a song his own. Jagger's lyrics pay attention to the sound patterns that Keith Richards has created. Music is something different than poetry and rock's composers organize sound differently than poets do. The particular "feel" of Charlie Watts' drums and the texture and tone of the Stones guitar sound makes this a Rolling Stones song.

Rock music gives us a tonal system. A piece of music is set in a certain key signature. It moves according to tonal patterns. We can't really find "key" changes in poetry, although these might be suggested by shifts in tone. There are no minor thirds in poetry. Perhaps we can suggest tempo changes, or different tonal colors, but usually in poetry these are secondary devices to support the primary content. In music, the sounds are the primary thing. As James Anderson Winn has noted, poetry has to have content that can say something. Music does not have to have this particular rational or logical appeal. Music, instead, may suggest emotion. Musical structures may underscore our own psychological experiences of journey, movement into difference or dissonance, and return, Winn points out. They may suggest tension, loss of familiarity, and then recovery of "home." Language points to things; it is referential. Music, in contrast, may be vague, holding implicit meanings. Music has what musicologist Lawrence Kramer has called a "unique suggestiveness."[37]

The ringing clocks on Pink Floyd's *The Dark Side of the Moon* album may remind us that music dwells in time. Wordsworth remembers a time when he felt intimations of immortality and he yearns for the vision and sensibility he feels he has lost. Wordsworth speaks of experience "recollected in tranquility." As John Minahan points out, in John Keats's poetry "music is associated either with the past or with the present's liability to become the past."[38] One is in "the act of returning, or of trying to return," as we see in Coleridge's speaker's wish for return to the fount of inspiration in his poem *Kubali Kahn*. Romantic time has a pattern, or what Paul de Man calls "the rhetoric of temporality." Minahan makes much of how this Romantic sense of time reflects the pattern of music, saying: "The Romantics manifest this view of time as duration—as growth, change, dynamism, birth, decay."[39] The Romantic poem thus reflects the pattern present in much Romantic music. This is much like the monomyth pattern of call to adventure, exploration, and tribulation and return that mythologist Joseph Campbell observes. It is something we may hear in the grand concepts of journey in progressive rock.

When we listen to music we engage in recollection and anticipation as the music moves forward, goes somewhere new, or recapitulates where we have been. Music comes to us "now" in time and passes. Our pleasure of music may come in this movement in us of anticipation and resolution or surprise as we listen, as theorist Leonard Meyer suggested back in 1956. The Romantic lyric reflects this pattern. One begins inspired by experience. This moves the poet out of ordinary experience into heightened experience. He or she returns to "a different, past-inspired experience."[40] There is memory, or "return with a difference." The spontaneous overflow of powerful feelings is recollected in a moment of quiet and life is cast as a renewal.

Indeed, there is a similar triadic movement in the philosophy of G.F.W. Hegel, another contemporary of these Romantic poets: thesis-antithesis-synthesis. As M.H. Abrams has noted, there is in Romantic poetry a paradigm of unity-separation-reunification. This too might remind us of Joseph Campbell's mythic scheme in *The Hero of a Thousand Faces*. Rock engages in musical adventurousness. Rock's rebellion is antithesis—a counter to the cultural thesis of norm and convention. The adventurous rock song, infused by imagination, takes us through changes and seeks resolution. This scheme is present in Hegelian philosophy, Beethoven's symphonies, and Wordsworth's poetry.

As rock music listeners, we recollect what we have heard. We remember, or bring together again ideas, memories, in our thinking. Our lives are something like a song cycle, a spiral of movements, a series of new ventures, and recollections. Romantic poetry embraces music in this relation between language, sound, time, memory, and consciousness. Wordsworth, for example, finds the delight and pleasure of poetry in recollection. Hegelian philosophy, likewise, contemplates the movement of the Absolute Spirit in time and the dialectic of the mind that inevitably participates in this unfolding dynamic. History (including rock history) is, in a sense, memory. Romantic poetry makes the memory of experience explicit.[41] Music merges with poetry as a matter of time and consciousness: it is the spirit coming home again, returning with a difference.

So, are Bob Dylan's lyrics poetry, or something else? In our encounter with a poem, unless we are listening to a reading of it, we can generally refer back to the printed page on which it appears. The performance of music—which is something other than the musical notation of a score—exists once in time as we listen to it. We now can revisit this music through recordings. That was not an option for people who read the Romantic poets in the late eighteenth century or early nineteenth century. If Dylan is in some way their heir, he is a most spontaneous one: ever changing his phrasing in his performances of his work. The times are not the only thing that is a-changing. As an artist, Dylan's song-voice, his reworkings of blues and ballads, is marked by the creativity of Keats's negative capability. Knowledgeable of traditions, he is ever open to change.

Percy Bysshe Shelley writes that Intellectual Beauty is "Like hues and harmonies of evening. . . . Like memory of music fled."[42] Indeed, in Shelley's time anyone listening to music had to rely upon memory to grasp the flow of music emerging, transforming, and passing. Notes change, combine, shift in time in patterns unfolding like the light of dawn or the twilight of evening. When words meet with music, they may tend to enter this "twilight zone" in which there is a kind of dissolve at work. Words are filled out by the music, perhaps, like a sunset sky that fills with a kind of radiance. Even so, they are drained of definiteness; they have a less certain referentiality as they combine with sound, tone, and rhythm.

Typically, Romanticism has focused upon the purely instrumental: music without words. E.T.A. Hoffmann, in his review of Beethoven's Fifth Symphony, wrote: "music discloses to man an unknown realm, a world that has nothing to do with the outer sensual world surrounding him, a world which he leaves behind all feeling ascertainable by concepts in order to devote himself to the inexpressible."[43] Philosopher Soren Kierkegaard, in *Either/Or* (1843), referred to listening to Mozart's *Don Giovanni* as a positive loss of reason, for which he was grateful.[44]

In Hoffmann's fiction, he writes of the composer: "Kreisler stood there shaken to the depths, unable to utter a word. He had always been obsessed with the idea that madness lay in wait for him like a wild beast slavering for prey, and one day would suddenly tear him to pieces." Kreisler comments on music: "so much lies in the mischief my notes create.... They often come to life and jump up from the white pages like little black many tailed imps. They whirl me along in their senseless spinning."[45]

CREATIVITY, THE UNCONSCIOUS, ALTERED STATES OF CONSCIOUSNESS AND DREAMS

Romanticism is deeply concerned with imagination, creativity, and expression. This creative thinking is free associative, analogical, divergent thinking. It can be spontaneous, receptive, and deal in images. Psychologist James Hillman refers to the value of "a poetic basis of mind ... a psychology that starts neither in the physiology of the brain, or in the structure of language, or the organization of society, nor the analysis of behavior, but in the imagination."[46] That is to begin a music criticism "within the processes of imagination," while taking other factors into consideration, may be a valuable route to new perspectives, as Hubbs points out.[47] This creativity ought to include some elements of feeling and play. Dreams have also fascinated the romantic poets, from Coleridge's "Kublai Kahn" to Keats' "La Belle Dame sans Merci."

Popular music has often brought radio listeners many songs about dreams. We've heard Supertramp's "Dreamer," Aerosmith's "Dream On," Eurythmics "Sweet Dreams Are Made of This," Fleetwood Mac's "Dreams," The Everly Brothers "All I Have to Do Is Dream," and The Moody Blues "Your Wildest Dreams," among many others. About sixty of Ray Davies' songs refer to dreams, Thomas Kitts points out.[48] Kitts mentions "David Watts" on *Something Else*, "Oklahoma USA," "Predictable," "Dreams," "Lavender Hill," "Misty Water," and "I Go to Sleep," among others. Kitts observes that often Ray Davies' dreamers seek escape. In "Lavender Hill" the speaker seeks a pastoral distance where clouds embrace the landscape and there is sunshine, and birdsong fills the air. This is an imaginary place in which he can step into eternity or into make-believe.[49]

Thomas Kitts has observed that Ray Davies, in 1967, unconsciously tapped into the English Romantic tradition and found his strongest artistic "impulse."[50] He points to a turn in Ray Davies' songwriting from the vigorous outward energy of "You Really Got Me" and "All Day and All of the Night" to a more "reflective ... personal" Romanticism that is characterized by "Waterloo Sunset" and "Autumn Almanac."[51] With "A Well-Respected Man" in 1965 Davies turned toward satire and to English folk and music hall traditions. His satirical voice came through on *Face to Face* (1966), which included "Dandy," "Session Man," "Rainy Day in June," "A House in the Country," "Holiday in Waikiki," "Most Exclusive Residence for Sale." The hit song "Sunny Afternoon" sounds cheery but it is ironic and has a music hall tone and attitude about it that is interlaced with social critique.[52] Davies also created the hits "Tired of Waiting for You," "Lola," and "A Dedicated Follower of Fashion."

Several of Ray Davies' songs proclaim resistance to conformity and announce opposition to a constricting culture. Davies presents creative, rebellious figures like the transvestite Lola and sounds defiance in songs like "I'm Not Like Everybody Else."[53] From social critique to music hall theatricality, the songs of Ray Davies convey the kind of passion we may read in the sharp satires of Jonathan Swift, or the romantic rebellion of Blake and Shelley.

Rock music intersects with emotion, mood, passion, and fantasy. Creative musical thinking deals in polyvalent possibilities. Meaning comes to us in metaphors and symbols. This associative or connotative thinking invites our interpretations. Lyrics that tap into the mythopoetic consciousness may be interpreted through archetypal psychology, which explores figures arising from the unconscious in dreams.[54] For psychologist Carl Jung, within the collective unconscious are archetypes or primordial images that may be expressed in images, symbols, or metaphors. The personal unconscious includes memories and repressed contents, whereas the collective unconscious is grounded in a more universal foundation of mind.[55]

The explorers of consciousness sought transcendence: an awareness of expansive spirit beyond one-dimensional technological consciousness. This parallels the Romantic's quest for new form and a return to feeling beyond the containments of Enlightenment reason. There is a reaffirmation of imagination, intuition, feeling, and bodily experience, a recognition that a person is not only rational intellect. This realization of human potential includes a reacquaintance with mythic perspectives, an overcoming of the reductionist logic of positivist science that would narrow our sense of the human. The cost of a one-dimensional techno-consciousness is alienation, critics like Carl Jung, Mircea Eliade, or Theodore Roszak claimed.[56]

Drummer Mickey Hart of the Grateful Dead has explored mythic perspectives and the role of the unconscious in music making. Along with his many years of creating music with the Grateful Dead, he has investigated Native American shamanic and Tibetan approaches to music and has studied the drumming of the Nigerian Obatwaji and the Brazilian drummer Airto.[57] Even musicians not quite as eclectic in their tastes discover their musical personalities and taste moments of peak experience in music performance. Some, like those interviewed by Jenny Boyd in *Musicians in Tune*, have recognized moments of mystery and wonder in musical experiences.

A rock musician learns the codes and gestures of the field. He or she develops patterns. Style consists of the idiosyncratic revisiting and repetition of certain patterns. Vladimir Nabokov once wrote that "style constitutes an intrinsic component or characteristic of the author's personality."[58] One's art becomes a way of life, a way of seeing, and a way of being. Uniquely, idiosyncratically the rock musician enters the creative process.

Graham Wallas outlined the stages of the creative process as Preparation, Incubation, Illumination (the a-ha moments), Verification (sending one's art out into the field). He recognized long training in an art, development of skills, unconscious practices, and the working out of ideas. Later psychologists have recognized that most brain centers for music and visual art are in the right hemisphere. Others have reminded us of the interactions of brain hemispheres. As Norbert Jausovev observes: "It seems that creative thinking requires broader cooperation between brain areas."[59]

There are moments when the creative rock musician moves beyond ordinary experience. William James once wrote: "Our normal waking consciousness, rational consciousness as we call it, is but one special type of consciousness, whilst all about it, parted from the filmiest of screens, there lies potential forms of consciousness entirely different."[60] Psychologist Charles Tart has observed that normal consciousness is a "tool" for everyday purposes in the social and physical environment. To speak of altered consciousness is to assume that this steady and stable state of our everyday consciousness is the norm, our "consensus state."[61]

Leonard Bernstein was once asked if listeners might be able to get back to the stage the composer was in when he wrote a composition. "I guess it's conceivable. That's a mystical idea. I think that's more mystical than anything I've said."[62] He knew of the stories that Schumann, Tartini, and Stravinsky heard music in dreams. Rachmaninoff's piano concerto in C minor was dedicated to hypnotherapist Nikolai Dahl.

The rock musician plays on waves of emotion and glimpses possibilities provided by imagination. This becomes apparent in the context of a band when musicians are in tune with each other. When trumpeter-neuroscientist Bill Benzon addresses this experience in his book *Beethoven's Anvil* (2001), he speaks of musicking together and of neurological linkages between the players. The psychologist Robert Ornstein speaks of consciousness as relationship. This suggests that musicians are not only locked in as ego but engage in a movement beyond self. In *Music and Trance* (1985), Gilbert Rouget asserts that music directly induces trance states. Trance in ritual is "context-dependent." For Rouget a conjunction of emotion and imagination contributes to trance.[63] However, Rouget finds that "no rhythmic system is specifically related to trance."[64] The comparative mythologist Mircea Eliade points to incantation.

Charles Tart notes that transpersonal consciousness appears to imply experiences that go beyond the individual brain/body. Physicalist, monistic views are dominant in science, he affirms.[65] Principal attention is given to observational data. Other psychologists suggest that altered states of consciousness can be distinguished from REM dreams. Considering "general characteristics of altered states of consciousness," Dittrich accounts for alterations in thinking, a disturbed sense of time, loss of control, change in emotional expression and body image, perceptual distortions, change in meaning or significance, a sense of the ineffable, and feelings of rejuvenation. One experiences an oceanic sense of boundlessness. There is what he refers to as visionary re-structuralization, a reduction of vigilance, and auditive alteration.[66] Art historian James Elkins (2008) has offered the claim that "the border between intuition and calculation cannot be clearly defined."[67] Rock guitarist Carlos Santana speaks of these moments as religious experiences.[68]

The artist welcomes the "a-ha" discovery, forges a new path, and does not merely accept the status-quo. Rock musicians create music by inundating themselves with music. They develop a knowledge of rock music, often of many kinds of music, which assists them in the ideational process. They repeat riffs, play variations, develop chord patterns. They engage in divergent thinking and creative ways of seeing. They tap into feeling, inventing music, dreaming images, connecting with emotions. Rock as popular art, the people's music, thrives on creativity. Rock will continue to thrive as long as bands continue to innovate and embody romantic rebellion.

NOTES

1. See James Rovira's list, *Rock and Romanticism: Blake, Wordsworth and Romanticism from Dylan to U2*. Lanham: Lexington, 2018, p. 6. In his study of Ray Davies, Thomas Kitts makes some comparisons to Wordsworth poems, p. 89. Works connecting rock with romanticism include Robert Pattison's *The Triumph of Vulgarity*, the essays in James Rovira's edited volumes, and essays such as John P. McCombe, "Not Only Sleeping: The Beatles and a Neo-Romantic Aesthetic of Indolence," *Mosaic* Vol. 44, No. 2 (2011): 137–52. Tristanne Connelly, "He Took a Face from the Ancient Gallery: Blake and Jim Morrison," *Blake 2.0: William Blake in Twentieth Century Art, Music, and Culture*. Ed. Steve Clark, Iristanne Connolly, and Jason Whittaker. New York: Palgrave Macmillan, 2012, p. 230–47. David Fallon, "Hear the Drunken Archangel Sing: Blakean Notes in 1990s Pop Music," *Blake 2.0*, p. 248–62. William Blake is referred to by ELP, The Doors, Bob Dylan, Patti Smith, and U2. Blake was an artist who reconnected song with poetry and visual art. One may find additional essays in *Blake 2.0*. James Rovira's continuing work on rock and romanticism will next include an edited collection on David Bowie and Romanticism. Previous books include Luke Walker's essay on Bob Dylan's turn to Blake. Douglas T. Root points to iconoclasts like Kurt Cobain as parallel with Blake (xix). Both were non-imitative. Both engaged in "deliberate dissociation from their predecessors." Appearing in both was an anti-industrial disillusionment, a reaction to urban blight and desire to escape from it. Lisa Crafton focuses on themes of social protest, erotic/spiritual love. Following Blake, we may consider how mind forg'd manacles inhibit creativity and freedom and the importance of imaginative vision. Gary Tandy makes the case for a nostalgic vision of paradise lost/regained in Jackson Browne's songs. Tandy describes how Browne alternates revolutionary and utopian themes. See James Rovira's introduction (xx) where he connects nostalgia and the perspective of the Romantic poet William Wordsworth.

2. Samuel Taylor Coleridge, Chapter 13, *Biographia Literaria*. (1817) Edinburgh: Edinburgh University Press, 2014. Contemporary brain science gives us a materialist approach to imagination. In his time, Coleridge recognized the value of the empiricist David Hartley's focus on the senses and associations: a view that had emerged with John Locke and David Hume. He attempted to reconcile the thought of Hartley, after whom he named his son, with the epistemology of Immanuel Kant.

3. Thomas Kitts, *Ray Davies: Not Like Everybody Else*. London and New York: Routledge, 2008, p. 89. Camille Paglia, *Sex, Art and American Culture*. New York: Vintage, 1992, p. 20.

4. Rovira, p. 3. The focus here is on worldview and characteristics of Romanticism that we find in rock. In *Rock and Romanticism*, edited by James Rovira, the first six essays are correlated with William Blake. These essays include reflections on Dylan and The Beats, Mick Jagger's use of Shelley's "Adonais" in his park tribute to Brian Jones Martha Redbone, and Leonard Cohen. Three other essays turn to William Wordsworth. We also read "'Swimming Against the Stream': Rush's Romantic Critique of Their Modern Age" by David S. Hogsette (pp. 111–26) and on "'When the Light that's Lost within Us Reaches the Sky': Jackson Browne's Romantic Vision" by Gary L. Ton (pp. 95–110) in Rovira's *Rock and Romanticism*.

5. James Rovira, *Rock and Romanticism: Post-Punk, Goth and Metal as Dark Romanticism*. New York: Palgrave, 2016, p. 4.

6. Perry Meisel. *The Cowboy and the Dandy*. New York and Oxford: Oxford University Press, 1999, p. 132. Perry Meisel discusses music artists cogently throughout his book, but his analysis, density of language, and jargon may be a bit difficult for some readers.

7. Robert Pattison, *The Triumph of Vulgarity*. Oxford and New York: Oxford University Press, 1987, p. 187. Little that is "musical" appears in Pattison's book, where he sees rock as "a mutant variety of Romanticism" (p. 187) and presents pantheism and vulgarity as a base for rock's social power.

8. Lee Marshall, *Bootlegging: Romanticism and Copyright in the Music Industry*. London Sage Productions, 2005, p. 56; Charles Taylor, *Reconciling the Solitudes*. Montreal: McGill-Queens, 1993, p. 250. In another interesting book, Craig Shufton looks at lyrics and poems but nothing musicological. Craig Shufton's *Hey Nietzsche Leave the Kids Alone: The Romantic Movement, Rock and Roll, and the End of Civilisation as We Know It* (Sydney: ABC Books, 2009). In *Entertain Us: The Rise and Fall of Alternative Rock in the Nineties* (New York: HarperCollins, 2012), Shufton considers bands from Sonic Youth to Motorhead and Stone Temple Pilots to Smashing Pumpkins. He looks at nu-metal, neo-punk, riotgirl, Nirvana, Pearl Jam, and grunge's commercial breakthrough in 1991 to the rise of alternative rock bands.

9. Oliver Strunk, *Source Readings in Music History* (1950). Vol. 6, The Nineteenth Century. Ed. Ruth Solie, Leo Treitler. New York: W.W. Norton, 1997, p. 775.

10. Alfred de Musset, "Un Mot sur l'art modern" (1833) *Oeuvres Complete En Prose*. Paris: Maurice Allen, 1951, p. 898.

11. Aaron Copland, *Music and Imagination*. Cambridge: Harvard University Press, 1952, p. 7.

12. Ibid.

13. Copland, p. 8.

14. Copland, p. 7.

15. Copland, p. 9.

16. Pattison, Introduction, *The Triumph of Vulgarity*.

17. Simon Frith review of *The Triumph of Vulgarity* in *The Nation* (March 28, 1987).

18. Albert Camus once called Rimbaud "our greatest poet of revolt." This comment is cited by Wallace Fowlie, p. 9. Fowlie translated *Rimbaud: Selected Letters*, 1966. His papers are at Duke University in Durham, North Carolina.

19. See interview with Jerry Hopkins and Danny Sugerman in *No One Here Gets Out Alive*. New York: Warner, 1995, p. 143.

20. David Orr, "After Dylan's Nobel: What Makes a Poet a Poet?" *The New York Times* (March 24, 2017); Charlotte Pence (www.upmississippi.blogspot.com); Christopher Ricks, *Dylan's Vision of Sin*. New York: Echo/Harper, 2005, p. 19. Also see Charlotte Pence, *The Poetics of American Song Lyrics*. Jackson: University of Mississippi Press, 2011.

21. Betsy Bowden, *Performed Literature: Words and Music of Bob Dylan*. Lanham: University Press of America, 1982, rpt. 2001; Perry Meisel, *The Myth of Popular Culture*. New York: John Wiley and Sons, 2009, p. 15.

22. Bob Dylan, *Chronicles, Volume 1*.

23. Laurence Coupe, *Beat Sounds, Beat Vision: The Spirit of the Beats and Popular Song*. Manchester: Manchester University Press, 2007, p. 87. Lynn M. Zott, *The Beat Generation*.

Gale Critical Companion. Detroit: Gale-Thompson, 2003. See Coupe's essay "Waiting for the End: Ginsberg, Dylan and the Poetry of Apocalypse" *English Review* (September 1998).

24. Dylan is quoted in *Bob Dylan in his Own Words*. Ed. Barry Miles, London: Omnibus Press, 1978, pp. 48–53.

25. Coupe, p. 118.

26. Coupe, 87–88; *Bob Dylan in his Own Words*, p. 73

27. Coupe, 88.

28. Andy Gillan is cited by Laurence Coupe, pp. 87–88. Coupe links Dylan's "Visions of Johanna" with William Blake's *Songs of Experience* (p. 114). Robert Shelton looks at Dylan's reference to William Blake in "Gates of Eden," *No Direction Home: The Life and Music of Bob Dylan*. New York: Penguin, 1987, p. 276. "Mr. Tambourine" is considered visionary.

29. Donald Brown, *Bob Dylan: American Troubadour*. Lanham: Rowman and Littlefield, 2016. Brown comments on this word-play and "verbal effects" (p. 55–56). Brown points out when a song "invites an allegorical reading" (p. 47).

30. Ellen Willis, "Before the Flood," *Out of the Vinyl Deeps*. Ed. Nona Willis Aronowitz. Minneapolis: University of Minnesota Press, 2014, p. 9. Willis essay "Dylan" appeared in *Cheetah*, 1967.

31. Willis, p. 10.

32. Willis, pp. 3–4.

33. Willis, p. 5.

34. Alex Di Blasi and Victoria Willis, *Geek Rock*. Lanham: Lexington, 2014, pp. 26–29.

35. John Minahan, *Word Like a Bell: John Keats, Music and the Romantic Poet*. Kent State: Kent State University Press, 1992, p. 90.

36. Alexander Pope, *An Essay on Man*, lines 348–49.

37. Lawrence Kramer, "Music, Metaphor, Metaphysics." *Musical Times* Vol. 45, Is. 1888 (Autumn 2004): 5–18. See also Kromer's *Music and Poetry: The Nineteenth Century and After*. Berkeley: University of California Press, 1984.

38. Minahan, p.11.

39. Minahan p.10.

40. Minahan, p. 15.

41. Minahan, p. 21.

42. Percy Bysshe Shelley, "Hymn to Intellectual Beauty."

43. E.T.A. Hoffmann, Review of Ludwig van Beethoven Fifth Symphony, 1810. HW 1.532/ HMW 236.

44. Soren Kierkegaard, *Either/Or*. Trans. David Swenson and Lillian M. Swenson. Princeton: Princeton University Press, 1959.

45. E.T.A. Hoffmann, (HW 2.1, 369). In Romanticism, music and poetry has sometimes carried associations with madness (Schumann, Kleist, Nietzsche, Holderlin, Nerval). Jean Paul Richter, Clemens Brentano, Ludwig Tieck, Novalis, and Hoffmann all made connections between music and madness. In Hoffmann's "Heilig Cacile" four brothers are driven insane when they hear an oratorio at Mass. This is a legacy of the Greek myth of the Sirens and that of Orpheus, facing the furies and shredded by the maenads. The passionate artist has been associated with suffering (Van Gogh, Tchaikovski). See Frederick Burwick, "Romantic Madness: Holderlin, Nerval, Clare," *Cultural Interactions in the Romantic Age*. Ed. Gregory Maertz. New York: SUNY Press, 1998. John T. Hamilton, *Music, Madness, and the Unworking of Language*. New York: Columbia University Press, 2008.

46. James Hillman, *A Blue Fire*. Ed. Thomas Moore. New York: Harper, 1997. See also the 1987 edition of Hillman's book.

47. Nadine Hubbs, "The Imagination of Pop-Rock Criticism," *Expression in Pop Rock Music: A Collection of Critical and Analytical Essays*. Ed. Walter Everett. London: Routledge, 2007, pp. 3–4. Hubbs also notes that those who live most intimately with music may find the ways of analyzing music somewhat "inimical" to their appreciation and experience of it. Rather, their listening is aesthetic, holistic, and intuitive.

48. Thomas Kitts, *Ray Davies: Not Like Everybody Else*. New York and London: Routledge, 2008, p. 93.

49. Kitts, p. 4.

50. Kitts, p. 84. Thomas Kitts, Kitts recognizes that Michael Kraus (p. 202) and Russ Wetzstean (p. 75) make a similar point. See Michael J. Kraus, "The Greatest Rock Star of the Century: Ray Davies, Romanticism, and the Art of Being English," *Popular Music and Society* Vol. 29, No. 2 (2006): 202; Ross Wetzstean, "Theater: Dedicated Follower," Review of *20th Century Man. Village Voice* (February 27, 1996): 75.

51. Kitts, p. 83. "Waterloo Sunset" was released in the United Kingdom May 5, 1967, at the same time as The Beatles' "All You Need is Love." The song was released in the United States on July 26, 1967, and did not move on the US charts.

52. Kitts, p. 73. See Kitts' discussion pp. 72–75.

53. Kitts, p. 97. Kitts takes note of the angry young man Jimmy Porter of John Osborne's *Look Back in Anger*, which had a significant impact on the British theater in the 1950s, p. 100.

54. Carl Jung, *Analytical Psychology*, 1925 Seminars. Princeton: Princeton University Press, 1925; James Hillman, *The Dream and the Underworld*. New York: Harper and Row, 1979.

55. A book by Jenny Boyd and Holly George-Warren, *Musicians in Tune: Seventy-Five Musicians Discuss the Creative Process* (Fireside, 1992), explores rock music creativity with reference to the Jungian collective unconscious through a series of interviews with rock musicians. The book has been reissued under the title *It's Not Only Rock n' Roll: Iconic Musicians Reveal the Source of Their Creativity* (John Blake, 2014).

56. In 1933, psychologist Carl Jung published a book titled *Modern Man in Search of a Soul* (Harcourt, 1933). Helton Godwin Baynes wrote in an introduction to that volume of people who held the optimistic view that "the western world stands on the verge of a spiritual rebirth" (vii). Perhaps . . . but the world also soon stood on the edge of the Second World War. The issue of alienation would arise.

57. Mickey Hart, *Drumming at the Edge of Magic: A Journey into the Spirit of Percussion*. Novato, CA: Grateful Dead Books, 1990.

58. Vladimir Nabokov is cited in Norman Holland, *Literature and the Brain*. Gainsville, FL: PsyArt Foundation, 2009, p. 275.

59. Colin Martindale, "Biological Bases for Creativity," *Handbook of Creativity*. Ed. Robert J. Sternberg. Cambridge and New York: Cambridge University Press, 1999, pp. 257–93. Norbert Jausovec, "Working Memory Theory, Training Intelligence," *Brain and Cognition* Vol. 79, No. 2. (2012): 205–6. "Neuropsychological Bases of Creativity," *Advances in Psychology Research* Vol. 15. Ed. Frankl H. Columbus and Serge Shohov. Huntington NY: Nova Science Publishers, 2002, pp. 193–219.

60. William James, *Varieties of Religious Experience*. Cambridge: Harvard University Press, 1902, p. 228.

61. Charles Tart, *Transpersonal Psychologies*. Garden City: Doubleday, 1975, p. 3.

62. Evan Harris Walker, *The Physics of Consciousness*. New York: Perseus, 2000. Also see Evan Harris Walker, "Quantum Theory of Psi Phenomena," *Psychoenergetic Systems* Vol. 3 (1979): 259–99.

63. Rouget, *Music and Trance: A Theory of the Relations Between Music and Possession*. Chicago: University of Chicago Press, 1985, p. 326.

64. Rouget, p. 317.

65. Tart, p. 202.

66. Arnold M. Ludwig, "Altered States of Consciousness," *Archives of General Psychology* Vol. 15, No. 3 (1966): 225–34; Adolph Dittrich, "Construction of a Questionnaire (APZ) for Assessing Abnormal Mental States," *Zeitschrift fur Kliniske Psychologie und Psychotherapie (Journal for Clinical Psychology and Psychotherapy)* Vol. 23, No.1 (1975): 12–20, rpt. 1996, p. 1. See *Wiley-Blackwell Handbook of Transpersonal Psychology*. Ed. Charles Tart. Wiley-Blackwell, 2013.

67. James Elkins, *Six Stories from the End of Representation*. Palo Alto: Stanford University Press, 2008, pp. 99–100.

68. See Chris Heath, "The Epic Life of Carlos Santana," *Rolling Stone* (March 16, 2000). Also see www.hollowverse.com, www.christiantoday.com, and www.elevatedexistence.com.

Chapter Six

Paperback Writers

Rock Music and Fiction

The rock music imagination tells stories. We hear stories often in songs. We also read stories about the artists, the performances, the fans, the record companies. Rock music biographies and histories are plentiful. So are essay collections that delve into the corners of rock music production and reception. Narrative recalls and creates rock history. We take events and make a story out of them. The verbal structure or form of a text conveys history to us. This acts as a model through which we peer into history and the lives of rock music performers. One recalls, arranges, and chronicles the story of rock: including things, excluding other things, emphasizing some things and not others. The story may come to us as romance, as irony and satire, as tragedy, or with a comic twist. Songs and stories become texts, inscribing memory.

Rock music has been part of life and culture since the 1950s. Rock music experience across these years has been portrayed in fiction and film. Fiction set in the context of rock music offers us a window into life and contemporary culture. Participant observers like Greil Marcus have recognized rock as part of human experience: "Rock 'n roll was and is and will be a basic part of experience, of the growing up years of the present college or non-student generation. It will continue to be so for the generations that will follow," Marcus writes. In *Mystery Train* (1975) Marcus observed that rock had become the national popular music of America. (This was a decade before the emergence of hip-hop. Rock, at this point, presumably included the precursors of the varieties of metal and alternative which subsequently emerged.) Rock expressed the "transcendence of untrammeled authenticity, of passion, truth, and love."[1] Fiction often attempts to capture that authenticity and passion.

By the 1960s, rock music had become a means of communication, a discourse, and a mass art. It had become a subject for fictional creation and storytelling. Meanwhile, recordings became cultural texts, familiar reference points. Songs were historical artifacts to be read, as Theodore Gracyk has pointed out. Rock was defined by the primacy of the recording as text. Today we can see that "musical works are woven into a constructed narrative" to "make sense" of rock music history, as John Encarnaceo has observed.[2] Recordings provide an archival record for that narrative history. Meanwhile, within those songs often are stories, images, and voicings of life experience.

We tell stories because it is natural to do so. Narrative form has been consistently present in rock music. Songwriters construct and give us narratives. (Thus, many songs can be analyzed through the techniques of narratology, although this has not been frequently done.) Rock sings love songs and tells stories about the human condition and the lives of modern men and women. Classic archetypal story-forms are repeated in rock music's journey and quest narratives. They are employed by heavy metal bands that tell stories of heroes battling and overcoming the monster. We have seen the storytelling instinct employed frequently in rock music. Pete Townshend created stories for The Who's "rock-opera" *Tommy* and he called his solo concept album *White City: A Novel*. David Bowie became a series of personas, or characters, offering musical narratives like "Space Oddity." Bruce Springsteen has spent his career telling stories in songs, recalling the garage, the factory, the neighborhood, the turnpike, and the city. He has created a cast of characters (Rosalita, Sandy, Hazy Davey, Spanish Johnny, the soldier in Iraq who sees only devils and dust, the small-time criminal who wants to bum a ride from Eddie for a meeting across the river, to name a few), kids on the beach, dreamers circling mansions of glory in their cars. Ray Davies' storytelling has included "A Dedicated Follower of Fashion," "Lola," and "20th Century Man." In April 1998, he participated in a VH-1 cable television series called The Storyteller that included performances and discussions about his songs. (The series also aired similar performances and talks by Jackson Browne and Elvis Costello.) It is particular songs that form rock texts, observes Theodore Gracyk (1996).[3] The concept album reflects the thematic gathering and storytelling movement of a novel.

John Lennon never wrote a novel, but he gave us stories. At the beginning of "Girl" his vocal comes to us questioning whether anyone will listen to his story. "A Day in the Life" unfolds as a story of the narrator's experience. "She's Leaving Home" gives us the story of a runaway, told from various viewpoints. "Paperback Writer" expresses the hope of a dreamer who wants to be a writer of stories. He tells us his story of "a dirty man" with a "clinging wife" who doesn't understand him. Beatles' songs express states of mind, attitudes, dispositions. However, they might also tell stories, as in "Norwegian Wood" or "Eleanor Rigby," for example. That writerly aspect of The Beatles was present in John Lennon's *In His Own Write* and *A Spaniard in the Works* (1964–1965), which included vignettes and nonsense verse. In "Paperback Writer" we hear about a story that is based on a novel by a man named Lear. Edward Lear and Lewis Carroll lie in the background of Lennon's playful wit. The word-play of "I Am the Walrus" loosely recalls Lewis Carroll's *Alice in Wonderland* and his poem "Jabberwocky." Lennon's wordplay includes puns. In "Lady Madonna" stockings "run." The carnivalesque appears throughout "For the Benefit of Mr. Kite" on *Sergeant Pepper's Lonely-Hearts Club Band*. Paul McCartney joined Lennon to contribute stories throughout The Beatles' catalogue. They created first person narratives for Ringo Starr to sing about living in a yellow submarine and getting by with a little help from his friends. They created characters: Billy Shears, Polythene Pam, Rocky Raccoon, Bungalow Bill, lovely Rita the meter maid, Eleanor Rigby, and JoJo and Sweet Loretta Modern. They were nostalgic about the hustle and bustle on "Penny Lane." *Sergeant Pepper's Lonely-Hearts Club Band* suggests a band and audience that become a community. The album concludes with the story "A Day in the Life." Next, we are rolling up for *The Magical Mystery Tour*. *The White Album* splices together a medley of vignettes, fragments, phrases, and songs.[4]

The stories conveyed by songs may reflect life, or they may be simply fantastic. For a few moments as we listen to Elton John we are traveling with Daniel on a plane. Robert Plant helps us to picture a lady who is sure all that glitters is gold, a lady who is discovering a stairway to heaven. Reality is suspended on that stairway for a time. The willing suspension of disbelief is the poetic faith by which we suspend reality and involve ourselves with music or with a story, allowing ourselves to be absorbed and transported. How will a listener relate to this music? What are his or her expectations, or schemas, by which the listener will approach and participate in this listening experience? We give attention to the patterns and the coherence of a musical language. We may find authenticity in the distinctive style of the artist. A creative artist like John Lennon, Frank Zappa, or David Bowie surprises us with what the psychologist William James called "sullies for wit and humor" and "flashes of poetry and eloquence." Their divergent thinking glides off the beaten track into new combinations of words and sounds, "abrupt cross-cuts and transitions," "associations of analogy" amid a "cauldron of ideas." This is rock creativity: the imprint of a style on songs, stories, images, puns, and performances. Songs emerge from the idiosyncratic uniqueness of the artist and "their genesis is sudden and spontaneous."[5]

Rock and folk/rock artists have given narrative shape to the dreams and concerns of culture by producing story-songs and fictional characters. Bob Dylan's *Blood on the Tracks* includes the story song "Lily, Rosemary, and the Jack of Hearts." "Jeremy" by Pearl Jam addresses the story of a troubled teen who is bullied and commits suicide. There are Jim Steinman's story songs for Meat Loaf like "Paradise by the Dashboard Light." Bob Seger recalls "Hollywood Nights" and the passions of youthful sex in "Night Moves." Billy Joel's Piano Man character tells the story of playing piano in a bar among a Saturday night clientele. Jim Croce, in "Operator," creates a narrator who makes a phone call to a woman he misses, who is now with someone named Ray and who no longer cares for him. Harry Chapin tells stories of a father who is never available for his children and a disc jockey who has fallen on hard times. Bruce Springsteen tells the story of changes in a hometown. The family farm is auctioned in John Mellencamp's "Rain on the Scarecrow." The Temptations tells us that "Papa Was a Rolling Stone." The Eagles, in "Lyin' Eyes," tell the story of a woman having an affair. Carly Simon declares that she has transcended naivete and the allure of an egotist in "You're So Vain." Heart's "Magic Man" seduces a girl and her mother calls her to come home. Nickelback looks at old photographs and recalls friends, high school, and past experiences. Iron Maiden draws upon Samuel Taylor Coleridge's haunting tale of *The Rime of the Ancient Mariner*. Outlaws are chased by a Dallas, Texas, detective in "Take the Money and Run." In Metallica songs a "Sandman" is hiding in the bedroom; a soldier recalls the loss of limbs in war. Neil Young begins *Zuma* (1975) with "Cortez the Killer," featuring the conquistador Hernan Cortez. Folksinger Gordon Lightfoot sang the story of "The Wreck of the Edmund Fitzgerald." Steely Dan told stories in oblique lyrics to jazz inflected tunes. One could point to many more examples.

Storytelling has been central to human communities as far back as the telling of ancient myths and the origins of recorded history. Music, ritual, and communal gathering were intertwined with the telling of the epics of the ancient world. The rock concert audience may tap into this primal collective experience of song, story, and theater. Meanwhile, musical progressions and dynamics may create a story of their own.

Some musicologists contend that we can find the quest narrative in rock music, not only in lyrics but in music compositions themselves. Countering claims that absolute music—music without words—is just music, a self-referential system, they have asked whether instrumental music can tell stories and represent something non-musical. Might musical patterns be related to narrative forms? Instrumental music does not carry with it lexical or semantic meanings of verbal signifiers. However, a musical composition may appear to unfold in a manner that suggests the monomyth of the heroic journey. We may first hear the "home" ground of the tonic and then hear how the musical line departs from it into new territory. The music may travel on an adventure and then return to "home." Music is non-linguistic and on rock albums such a process is usually surrounded with imagery and given definition through a lyric. Robert Walser observes that there are difficulties when "oral modes" like music are analyzed by "literal modes" like sequential, logical narrative.[6] Lawrence Kramer points out that "music is something like an embodied critique of discursive authority."[7] He adds that narrative "effects are hard to produce in music" and that "music enters the narrative situation only in relation to textuality, even when the music overtly lacks text."[8] Kramer refers to Carolyn Abbate's caution that "the analogy between music and narrative . . . may be used unthinkingly to elude secret convictions that music has no meaning."[9] Meanwhile, "literary theories of narrative suggest ways in which music cannot narrate, or how our metaphor of narration collapses and lies empty in strange folds and corners."[10] Even so, Susan McClary uses feminist models of narrativity to argue that "music since the Seventeenth Century has been regularly engaged in the cultural work of constructing gender identities and the ideological work of enforcing them."[11] McClary suggests that music may unfold a narrative.

Following McClary's considerations of music and narrative, John Encarnaceo writes in his essay "Musical Structure as Narrative in Rock," about an atmosphere or "state of mind" that may be expressed in music without an intelligible lyric. He observes that Nirvana's "Smells Like Teen Spirit" is evocative but makes "little literal sense." While Bob Dylan's lyrics are often significant, it is his timbre and phrasing that also communicate. Encarnaceo adds that rock artist biographies and other constructed narratives may "give greater understanding to this or that album" and help us to "make sense" of the history of popular music.[12] Citing Susan McClary's essay "Conventional Wisdom" (2000), Encarnaceo argues that the twelve-bar blues is a "quest narrative in miniature" in which gesture, groove, and timbre are all significant.[13]

Expression in rock music occurs always within music, within time, and in a performance.

The musicologist can tell us that there are twelve diatonic scales. He or she will point out that pentatonic scales are also prominent in rock, such as in Deep Purple's "Smoke on the Water." The story of a gambling house, the casino at Montreux, burning down after a Frank Zappa concert is told in a musical setting of power chords and harmonic changes, from the memorable riff through variation in vocal phrasing. The Temptations "My Girl" unfolds in major five-tone pentatonic. The Eagles' "Witchy Woman" portrays the witchy with a falsetto cry atop the chorus vocals in a minor five-tone pentatonic, with E flat and B flat in the scale.

In each of these cases, the story and attitude of the song is conveyed by the music, the vocal delivery, instrumental and production values, and a memorable hook. The lyric engages the listener in a story, with imagery, a play of rhymes, and a narrative. However, the feel of the song and its groove arises from the play of rhythmic elements: tempo, pulse, attack, and the creation of rhythmic texture. Vocals contribute colors to the song, extending and riding on vowels (singing "smo-ke on the wa-ter"). Rhythms and guitars and vocal edge cut into something visceral and the story engages our thought as the music draws us in.

Ancient music was often described according to the mode of the music. If we apply that to rock, we have The Who's "The Kids Are Alright" in Ionian (C-F-G in the verses to D minor G F C in the choruses, or I-IV-V-I and ii-v-iv-i). Jefferson Airplane's "Somebody to Love" comes to us in Dorian. Nirvana's "Smells Like Teen Spirit" moves along in Aeolian. "Nights in White Satin" by The Moody Blues rests upon E minor chords, in an Aeolian scale in the introduction and the verse. The vocal revolves around the note of B in the melody. Chicago's "25 or 6 to 4" is also Aeolian and moves along a bass line and descending chord pattern of A minor, G, F. (We find a similar A minor-G-F pattern in "While My Guitar Gently Weeps," the conclusion of "Stairway to Heaven," and "All Along the Watchtower.") Elton John and Bernie Taupin's "Sorry Seems to Be the Hardest Word" begins with a minor tonic triad in G minor. It uses the G in an Aeolian scale and F sharp in its final cadence. The Beatles "Norwegian Wood" uses a Mixolodian scale and can be compared with an Indian raga. Lydian and Phrygian seldom appear in popular rock, although Phrygian may appear in heavy metal.[14]

Rock frequently makes use of I-IV-V-I, in which there are five half-steps from I to IV and two half steps back to I. We also hear the I-VI-IV-V progression which begins with a major triad on the tonic. Then this progression moves to the sixth tone, a minor chord. Next there is movement to the major on the fourth tone and this pattern ends on the fifth tone. This is the C-A minor-F-G that repeats in numerous songs from the 1950s.

The musicologist can point out that "Back in the High Life Again" by Stevie Winwood has verses and a chorus that both begin in D major. "I Wouldn't Want to Be Like You" by the Alan Parsons Group has C as its tonic and moves to C minor in the introduction. (The tonal scale is C Eb F G Bb C for the vocal melody.) That alone will not give us the tone and texture, the attitude and expressiveness of the rock performer. When a musicologist like Walter Everett or John Covach analyzes songs like these, we are reminded that rock is not only three chords: those familiar triads. It is more about dynamics and cadence and variations. That standard or typical harmonic progression is often treated with variations. The Allman Brothers' "Ramblin' Man" travels on a G chord with a blues feel, while telling a story of wandering. Yet, oh the wonders of those winding lead guitar lines. Bruce Hornsby's piano riff in "On the Western Skyline" moves from verse to chorus on the root chord of G. [GABCDE] Yet, oh, the piano playing. Bob Seger celebrates "Old Time Rock and Roll" for its impact on the soul. The chords B and E conclude each verse. (This is the I [the E] and the V [the B].) Yet, oh, the raspy, edgy delivery of the vocal. The sounds or tonality is different for different instrumentalists. These are voicings that a guitarist creates and shapes. They become gestures, or repetitive lateral motions, riff schemes, unique stylings.

Those intangibles of style and performance underscore what should be obvious to rock music listeners: a formalist analysis of rock only gives us one angle on rock music composition. It may miss "the central question of how music articulates from within its very structure social and cultural meaning," writes John Shepherd.[15] It may miss the imagination and personality that an individual artist breathes into his or her music. And so, we need to turn also to other approaches. Aspects of popular music performance including "social, psychological, visual, gestural, ritual, technical, historical, economic and linguistic aspects relevant to the genre, style, and listening attitude connected (re)performance and listening attitude connected with the sound event being studied," observes Philip Tagg.[16] For Robert Walser, "musical details and structures are intelligible only as traces, provocations and enactments of power relationships."[17] Songs convey energy, tensions, movement. Like stories, they point to experience; they take us on journeys.

How has fiction writing attempted to capture the rock lifestyle, rock music's impact upon daily life, or the rise and fall of would-be rock stars? The narratives of songs and the images of rock have become part of our popular culture in film, television, and advertisements. Rock has been the stuff of dreams, the hopes of the local band, the passion of audiences. It has fueled the imagination and become the source of stories.

ROCK IN FICTION

What do novels that are set within a framework of rock culture say about our lives and our culture today? Philip Roth once wrote: "Literature requires a habit of mind that has disappeared. It requires silence, some form of isolation, and sustained concentration in the presence of an enigmatic thing."[18] For those who take the time to read fiction, it too can affect our listening to rock and inform our sense of rock's place in contemporary culture.

Great Jones Street

In Don De Lillo's *Great Jones Street*, Bucky Wunderlick runs for cover on the lower West Side of Manhattan to get away from the music business. He drifts and withdraws, holding an "apocalyptic vision."[19] The rock star is pursued by members of Happy Valley, a rural cult, who arrive in the city. Bucky withdraws from them, but they invade his privacy. David Cowart writes: "I do not think De Lillo wants his readers to accept Bucky Wunderlick and his profession uncritically."[20] This is rock music business that ought to be scrutinized. Cowart suggests that Bucky is troubled and that readers will approach this character differently: "The reader enamored of popular music will perhaps see in Bucky a heroic figure; the reader who sees rock as insipid will project a possibly imaginary antihero contempt on Bucky."[21] Rock critic Anthony De Curtis sees a self-consuming character baffled by a materialistic world: "What De Lillo depicts is a society in which there are no meaningful alternatives . . . all is cash nexus and commodities."[22]

Bucky Wunderlick is caught in a world without depth and substance. One may see his situation as that of the struggle of the romantic artist in a setting that applauds popular art when it is commercially successful and otherwise ignores or marginalizes creative artists. The society creates media heroes, surrounds them with empty adulation, and then tosses them aside. Cowart observes: "De Lillo ultimately characterizes America as the land where business rapacity and mass desire" prevail. From a perspective critiquing the rock medium, the critic suggests that the novel may view contemporary America as a place "where rock concerts un-dam, channel, and warp into a hysteria a host of powerful if inchoate passions." Rock, it may be argued, is "committed to depthlessness . . . indifferent to history" and may be a popular music form which "embodies the most puerile tendencies in American society." From this viewpoint, rock is like Peter Pan, attempting to hold perpetually to lost or fading youth. "In the land of perpetual youth, rock fuels an unceasing celebration of adolescent innocence, adolescent idealism, adolescent . . . energy, confusion, appetite."[23] Yet, surely, rock is something more than this. Bucky has not merely outgrown rock. He is disillusioned by the world. He has yet to find access to a new sense of meaning.

In *Understanding Don De Lillo*, literary critic Henry Veggian points out that the writer mixes media, to "ask readers to consider familiar objects and emotions in new ways."[24] This is a novel about language. The story's plot concerns a drug that affects the human brain's ability to organize words. He points to Florence Dore's thesis that the rock novel as a subgenre in fiction, emerging as a mature form after 2000, provides a way for the novel to comment on life in the twenty-first century and to re-enliven "private experience." *Great Jones Street* is a precursor to this genre and it focuses in on the lack of privacy in modern life. Dore and Veggian recall Ian Watt's *The Rise of the Novel*, in which Watt addresses the private orientation of the modern novel.[25] They also point out neo-Marxist critic Georg Lukacs' view that the novel "confirms the inner life of the subject."[26]

Bucky Wunderlick is the reluctant rock star. He is our narrator who is in semi-monastic seclusion, in retreat from society. His management, his fans, and a sycophantic public want to make him public. They want to shine the spotlight on him, put him onstage, and gain wealth or vicarious acknowledgment through him.[27]

In his textual analysis, Veggian observes that the surface of De Lillo's novel present "a casual style": vernacular with the use of some music industry slang. He writes that "Symbolic ordering of sentences is idiosyncratic at times, with the occasional inverted sentence . . . suggesting an urban, ethnic linguistic scene." The modern detective genre is mixed with the "psychedelic jargon of the counterculture." Globke, Wunderlick's manager, is a "philosopher of bad taste."[28]

The sale of the drug "product" may parallel the sale of Bucky's records. This drug was allegedly developed by the government to affect the verbal-cognitive area of the left hemisphere of the brain: the region where words are kept.[29] The Happy Valley commune stole the drug from a Long Island laboratory and brought it to Bucky's apartment in at Great Jones Street in Greenwich Village. Happy Valley wants to sell this product for as much money as they can possibly make from it. Bucky continues to try to retain his privacy. His record company concedes to the released of his Mountain Tapes. "Don't think of it as a performance. Think of it as an appearance."[30] Watney, a retired British rocker, and Bohack from the Happy Valley commune appear. (The Mountain Tapes of his unreleased songs also appear after chapter 20.) Hanes, meanwhile, tries to sneak out the product and to shop it. He travels extensively to try to sell it but his efforts fail. Dr. Pepper is pharmacist underground and he is sought out by those who are trying to sell the drug. Dr. Pepper, like the others, seeks the product: to synthesize it and sell it to the global market. But who is Dr. Pepper? Is he a chemical analyst or a buyer? Hanes will return it. Bucky doesn't want it.

It has been revealed publicly where Bucky will be recording—and so his privacy is blown. His attempt at self-expression is all managed by others, orchestrated by those who would make a profit from his work. There is a suggestion that Bucky is now "sinking into history."[31] Is this what happens to rock performers?

In a last chapter, Bucky wanders through lower Manhattan. For some time, he is with Sandy, a girl of the commune who originally bought the product. Then he is alone. Bucky has wanted to be alone. Yet, he has been our narrator and we have seen his predicament—and perhaps some reflection of the broader culture—through his words, his experiences.

De Lillo told Anthony De Curtis that he approaches ideas as they come to him. De Curtis views the novel through the decline model: that sense of loss of sixties vitality and seventies disillusion. He says that Bucky's retreat "would seem to suggest the movement of American society from the political upheavals and turmoil of the late sixties to the dreadful cynicism, deep alienation, and desperate privatism of the seventies."[32]

The Commitments

Roddy Doyle's *The Commitments* presents an Irish band to uncover the voices of marginalized youths who are economically and educationally disadvantaged. Hailing from a working-class suburb of Dublin, Barrytown, they love rock music and express their restlessness through their music. Jimmy Rabbitte, Jr. attempts to create a band that draws upon African American R&B/soul music. The band's sound, like their experience, is raw and unaffected. The narrative is a play of voices. As literary critic Mikhail Bakhtin has observed, novels are characterized by polyphony and heteroglossia. In this novel, we have an interaction of colloquial language with the sounds and texts of soul. The narrative is interrupted by these voices and fragments of conversation.

In *Reading Contemporary Irish Fiction*, Liam Hartz points out that *The Commitments* is about "the advent of a globalized, post-modern Irish culture." It is a novel that brings a recognition that "disparate culture forces" are affecting young people and are "now molding the mindsets of working-class urban youth."[33] The story is filled with a play of accents and speech patterns of working-class Dublin. The punctuation jumps out at us, with its use of capitalization and exclamation marks, as if its characters are braking through grammatical conventions in an effort to assert themselves and to be heard. There are dashes, perhaps suggesting the movement of music. Hartz views these marks as resembling musical notation. He points out that we are given words as sounds: "righ" "anymore" scarleh" and phrases—"pricking around," "Puked me ring," or slang—"ride," "geen," "goff.") The novel's characters speak a rough vernacular filled with the habitual use of expletives. Language flows somewhere between sound and word, between orality and textuality.

The narrator is a participant in this band. The voice that we meet is one that reflects these band members and their socioeconomic milieu. Their verbal and musical expression is grounded in their subcultural context. The narrator asserts: "Your music should be abou' where you're from an' the sort o' people yeh come from."[34] He is connected with this place and has absorbed the habits of speech of his locale. When he speaks his mind, it is in the tones and rhythms of his place. Outspan, Derek, and Jimmy bring together African-American soul, which was partly a response to the denigration of blacks, with the history of the Irish peasantry positioned as outcasts in the United Kingdom. In this sense, the novel implicitly suggests rock and soul as akin to Ireland's history of subversive responses to British colonial domination and imperialistic hegemony. Linguistically, the word-play and breaking of grammatical form or convention is likewise a transgression of standards. Writing on the author, Paddy Doyle, Wheeler and Newman contended that "It's about overcoming the legacy of colonization and it's also there to shock people out of their respectable middle-class positions."[35] Rock music has given these youths a place to gather and a vehicle through which to express their voices. Or, as Irish bass player Phil Lynott of Thin Lizzy pointed out back in the 1970s: the boys are back in town.

Garden State

In Rick Moody's *Garden State* three young people in Haledon, New Jersey, start a band. While he may have been listening to The Feelies, who hail from Haledon, the fictional group he imagines is not at all like them. In 1976, Glenn Mercer, Bill Million, Dave Weckerman, Vinny and Keith De Nunzio were in Bill's basement playing "Fa Ce La" and drinking Heinekens. In Moody's story we read: "All over Haledon kids were coming apart." They weren't—or at least they were coming apart in Haledon no more than anywhere else. Glenn and Bill had created their energetic, almost tinny guitar-driven sound with a sure sense of the Velvet Underground. They were thoughtful, intense, and creative. Meeting the De Nunzio brothers at Mr. D's, on the edge of Elmwood Park and Saddle Brook, they launched into the first of several lineups and set their sights on CBGB's and Max's in New York City.

In Moody's novel, Lane, who tries drugs, slips off a roof at any April Fool's party. Bass guitarist Scarlett dwells upon disappointment. Alice tries to maintain a relationship with Dennis, who is Lane's half-brother. In *Garden State*, Lane has just gotten out of a state mental hospital. Alice Smail used to be in a band called Critical Mass with Scarlett, who now has a place over an exterminator's office and has to work as a carpet salesperson. "Desolate lives. Desolate landscape," writes a *Kirkus Review* writer about the characters in Moody's novel.[36]

Moody listened to a slightly later incarnation of The Feelies as he wrote his novel. While living in Hoboken, Moody listened to *The Good Earth*. He pictured a New Jersey of industrial decay and decline where his characters were alienated and adrift, like smoke from refineries over the Turnpike. By then, Vinny De Nunzio had left to work with Richard Lloyd of Television and with Richard Hell. Keith, who renamed himself Clayton, much to his parents' chagrin, also went on to other things after The Feelies' first album, *Crazy Rhythms*. Drummer Anton Fier moved on and the band added bassist Brenda Sauter. Stan Demeski became The Feelies long-term drummer. The Feelies practiced rock minimalism, with fierce rhythmic guitars chiming at near-impossible speed. In a sense, they helped define indie-rock, as they were listened to by REM and other bands.[37] Glenn intoned oblique lyrics. If this was singing, it was all about phrasing. It was guitars and speed and intensity. In 1976 they changed from calling themselves The Outkids to The Feelies. The band's name referred to Aldous Huxley's novel, in which people could feel sensations as they watched the movies. Yet, it was never clear whether anyone in the band had read the novel.[38]

Janet Burroway at Florida State University observes that Rick Moody has been likened to John Cheever for having "the same knack about whimsy careening into keen lament." She suggests that he is a chronicler of the middle class for the millennium."[39] Dale Peck in the *New Republic* (July 1, 2002) excoriated Rick Moody as "the worst writer of his generation." Peck, an accomplished young adult author, wrote: "I have stared and stared at pages and pages of Moody's prose and they remain as meaningless to me as the Korean characters that paper the wall of a local restaurant." He added that he recognized that Korean language does mean something "but I am not convinced that Moody's books are about anything at all." He concluded that Moody makes his characters "suffer to solicit your pity." For Peck the stories did not ring true.[40]

Fortress of Solitude

In Jonathan Lethem's *Fortress of Solitude* (2003) fabulism meets realism. Lethem mixes genres, writing with an approach to scenes and characters that is traditional, while veering off into creative romps through language and postmodern fragmentation and fabulism. "I'm heading toward a fantastic which is grained like realism, which everywhere makes feints of realism" Lethem said in a 2001 interview.[41] In this novel, we get more R&B than rock. However, since music is everywhere in this novel it is also relevant for a consideration of all forms of popular music. Dylan Ebdus is in Brooklyn in the 1970s. At home, Dylan finds Abraham, his father, distant. In the neighborhood, he feels like an outsider. Mingus Rude is his friend. Mingus is the son of a soul singer, Marcus Rude, Junior. His mother ran off with a neighborhood developer's nephew. Dylan and Mingus both love R&B and comic books. They listen together to 1970s R&B records. Mingus says that his father has a large record collection: "all of them cuts them DJ's can't even find."[42] They are each named after influential musicians: Bob Dylan and Charles Mingus, respectively. Arthur Lamb is Dylan's only white friend and he adopts the artifice of black style. Meanwhile, Isabel Vendle reflects gentrification of their old neighborhood. It appears that she fears minorities and wants an all-white neighborhood which she can then have renamed. Dylan and Mingus get a magical ring from a homeless man. Marilla, a friend, sings pop songs in the street.[43]

Dylan trades his mother's CCR albums for The Clash's second album, in a move from sixties idealism toward punk disillusionment. Meanwhile, his friendship with Mingus unfolds amid their musical tastes. Those tastes begin changing and there is separation between them. Dylan Ebdus has migrated from funk, soul, and R&B to punk rock and The Clash.[44]

In the second part of the novel we see Dylan's liner notes to the reissue of Barrett Rude Junior's *Greatest Hits* album. ("For what it's worth, the man's still alive."[45]) Dylan is now a music journalist. Booted out of college and back in Brooklyn, he uses the magical ring to free Mingus Rude who has been in jail. In the third part, Dylan works at a Berkeley radio station where all of the disc jockeys become like another family for him. He lives with his African American girlfriend Abby, who finds him "moody." He has become a serious record collector and he is writing liner notes.[46]

The novel appears to reflect upon popular music and nostalgia. Evan Hughes writes that Lethem conveys "a reverie and nostalgia" of a "youthful world-view" and that his writing is "jazzy, loose, even exuberant."[47] Matthew Luter observes that in Lethem's novel "New York is symbolic cultural space." Brooklyn is "a kind of under-city" and "a place in flux." For Luter, *Fortress* is a coming of age novel. Ultimately, "Dylan has far more interest in reproducing the past than in building a new future."[48] James Peacock sees in Dylan Edbus a music writer busy at work even while Mingus is stuck in prison. This contrast, he suggests, underscores the racial elements in the novel. Luter disagrees with that assessment, seeing those boundaries overcome by their friendship and mutual interests. He sees an early kind of hip-hop culture beginning in the Brooklyn neighborhood. He points out that Dick Hebdidge, in his study of subcultures, observed: "Youth subcultures . . . particularly punk, articulate their political standpoints implicitly by appropriating and recontextualizing signifiers that had been theretofore largely apolitical." Luter points out that Dylan realized that "punk has already begun to splinter into subcategories."[49] Gabe has bought a leather jacket to imitate The Ramones. People who see him misinterpret the semiotics of this. ("Hey, you think you're tough?" "I'm just wearing it. It doesn't mean anything.") "This was a problem of codes," Lethem's narrator says, "the self-loathing ironies of punk was not sufficiently conveyed yet to the Puerto-Rican gang quadrant of the universe."[50]

Taking a different approach, Matt Godbey asserts that the novel is part of a body of works that may be called the fiction of gentrification. This is related to the urban redevelopment of cities.[51] The relationship between Dylan Ebdus and Mingus Rude "personalizes and intensifies insoluble questions of race, class, authentication and memory which bedevil the gentrifying process."[52] Godbey recognizes: "Lethem's passion for music has long been evident in the essays on his website." He points out that the successor to *Fortress* is "a full-blown rock and roll novel."[53]

You Don't Love Me

In *You Don't Love Me* the band is instructed to play quietly by a promoter, Jules Harvey. No one is paying attention. The band's lead singer, Matthew, works at the zoo. In a subplot, a kangaroo named Shelf is kidnapped. The novel is analyzed by James Peacock, who recognizes in it "a hypermediated reality culture."[54] He notes that as the band performs the reader is placed in the audience. The reader sees and "discovers" the band: Bedwin, Lucinda, Denise, Matthew. Lethem writes: "Without footlights to provide underlighting, the band appears mysteriously remote."[55] They hear the song "The Houseguest," which we are told "a performer with a series of false faces to wear, urgent charades to put across."[56] Listeners can barely grasp the words. Yet, the music connects with the audience. The second song, "Monster Eyes," is also attempting to communicate something that listeners interpret. We read: "this song is about you and me and the dangerous way we feel sometimes. It's about all of us. But most of all it's about me each listener thinks."[57] In the critic's view, Lethem is advancing a "romantic, emancipatory notion of rock music."[58]

A Visit from the Goon Squad

Jennifer Egan's *A Visit from the Goon Squad* is a story told by several narrators. Each of them is a point of view protagonist who hands off the narrative to the next one. In his review in *The New York Times*, "To Their Own Beat," Will Blythe pointed out that this is a novel that is not easily addressed in a summary. It is rather a "freely flung" series of interlinked stories with "a madness to her method." How loose can she be with these connections while maintaining coherence, he asks.[59]

The novel begins with the image of Sasha in a public restroom where she sees a wallet that has been left outside a bathroom stall. She takes the wallet. Within a few pages we learn that she is a habitual kleptomaniac. Maybe she should stop stealing, she thinks, and give her attention to the music and the friends she had when she first arrived in New York. She might even "find a band to manage."[60] There is panic in the voice of the woman who thinks she lost her wallet. Sasha assumed that the wallet belonged to a New York City resident. She had no idea that this woman was from out of town, or that the wallet held a plane ticket. She realizes that she has disrupted this woman's life.

Bennie Salazar, the music manager, believes that a deal must be accomplished. He thinks he now must start "pulling the plug on Stop/Go" a band with members who are sisters. He signed them to a three-record deal with the view that they could sound like Cindi Lauper meets Chrissie Hynde and appeal to a young audience. Now they are at the age of thirty and a teen audience is less likely to respond to them. "The vocals are buried under seven layers of guitar," says Collette.[61] Yet, Benny is caught up in memories, like a needle caught in the groove of a vinyl record. He is "caught in a loop from twenty years ago."[62] He remembers Westchester and a spot behind a nunnery where he once heard the nuns singing, making a "spooky sweet sound."[63] Sow's Ear Records has moved into an old coffee factory in Tribeca. The industry is changing. Bennie wonders what it was about the Stop/Go sisters and their music that once interested him so much.

Bennie's son Chris has grown up around rock groups. We are told that he is "part of the post-piracy generation, for whom things like copyright and creative ownership did not exist."[64] Bennie believes that the downloaders and file sharers ("the dismantlers who murdered the music business") were of a generation before his son: people who are adults now. Bennie concludes that he and his son ought to just appreciate the music that they both enjoy, like Pearl Jam. They visit the Stop/Go sisters and Sasha, greeting Chris at the door calls him Crisco. He sees the sisters: their hair pulled back and their eyes "glistening."[65]

Bennie is enchanted again by the music as they record at home. There is a perfume scent "like apricots" in the room. We read: "Then the sisters began to sing. Oh, the raw, almost threadbare sound of their voices mixed with the clash of instruments."[66] What is he to do? He joins in, playing a cowbell. Bennie once played bass guitar for the Flaming Dildos. Scotty played the steel lap guitar that he had built. Now Bennie is caught up again in music. We read: "The sisters were screaming, the tiny room imploding from their sound."[67] Time has gone by: some twenty years. Two years ago, the girl-band Stop/Go sounded different. In the music business, Sasha says, "five years is five hundred years."[68]

On his ride back home with his son on the Henry Hudson Parkway onto the West Side Highway, Bennie plays The Who, the Stooges, and San Francisco Bay area bands from the sixties. He remembers that years ago Scotty had a guitar "in the shape of a gold flame." We are back with him in San Francisco with Alice's arms around him, the music "flooding out" through the apartment. The music runs from Blondie's "Heart of Glass" to Iggy Pop's "The Passenger."[69] In Chapter Three, "Ask Me If I Care," Bennie has bootleg recordings of The Stranglers and The Nuns. It is the late 1970s and the San Francisco hippie scene is surely in demise. Bennie marries Stephanie. Bennie signs the singing nuns, kisses Mother Superior, and loses the deal. He tries to resurrect a musician's career. Jules comes across as a parody of a music management figure.

Critics have observed that Jennifer Egan considers the impact of time on her character's lives. Time, of course, is central to music. We listen to the unfolding of a song, or a symphony, in time. Memory is involved when a song resonates with past experiences. As we listen, we absorb musical phrases; we anticipate their return. In Egan's novel, some forty years of rock music comes to us across thirteen chapters.

In *The Washington Post* (June 16, 2010) Ron Charles noted that the story is a "symphony of boomer life" that is "scrambled through time." The novel ought to come with a CD. These stories, he writes, are achieved with "technical bravado" and "tender sympathy." The novel gives us "a story about growing up and growing old in a culture corroded by technology and marketing." Charles observes that the youthful ideals and dreams of characters are juxtaposed with their adult selves. So how did these older flabby adults caught up in the rat race come to this?[70]

Meanwhile, Celia McGee in the *Chicago Tribune* compared the novel to a circling vinyl record of personal history. To her the novel felt like a series of short stories or songs "only gradually and implicitly interlocking." She writes: "Egan is a canny handler of the remix."[71] So, in what sense is *A Visit from the Goon Squad* something like a concept album, a "narrative constellation," as Carolyn Kellogg referred to it in the *L.A. Times* (June 6, 2010)? Kellogg observes that Sasha has "fallen out of sync with the music business." Yet, surely that is something that it is easy to do—especially for a baby boomer like Bennie. "Sasha and Bennie are pushed to the margins," Kellogg observes. Amid flashbacks, the novel tugs in different directions across time. If we follow Kellogg's observation that the novel provides "a nearly pitch perfect understanding of American culture" might it also suggest a modulation of our culture's tone and "tune" in the digital age? We read of the impact of the digital remix on the sound of records: "The problem was precision, perfection, the problem was digitization, which sucked the life out of everything."[72]

More Rock Fiction Snapshots

The wide cultural influence of rock music is apparent in several other novels. One sees titles like *The Day the Music Died, Guitar Girl, Along the Watchtower, How to Kill a Rock Star*, [Tiffanie Di Bartola] and *Don't Sleep with Your Drummer* [Jen Sincero]. Stephanie Kuehnert gives us *Ballads of Suburbia* (2009) and *I Wanna Be Your Joey Ramone* (2008).

Dana Spiotta in *Stone Arabia* (2013) portrays musician Nik Worth's life. He has recorded many never released albums and is a rock star in his own mind. Nik's sister is the narrator who imagines his career that never was. The story explores obsession and the creation of self in relation to rock. What is rock music if there is no audience?

Master of Reality (2008) by John Darnielle appears in the 33 and 1/3 series. In this novella the narrator is a teen in a psych ward who argues to get back his Black Sabbath cassette of the album *Masters of Reality*.

Live from Medicine Park (2017) by Constance Squires is set in an Oklahoma town where Lena Wells is a rock star from the 1970s now in hiding. This is a story about fame, money, and broken families. Can Lena Wells make a comeback? A documentary film maker intends to create a film about her effort.

In *Hard Rain* (1988), Peter Abrahams gives us a creepy guy who goes by the knick-name of Bo Dai who re-enters American life deranged after his overseas experience of capture and torture in Vietnam. There is an aura of Woodstock and mystery suspense throughout this novel.

In Tom Perrotta's *The Wishbones* (1997) a man proposes to one woman and falls in love with another. Dave Raymond is a guitarist for this five-member wedding band. He lives at home with his parents, drives for a courier service, and plays with the band. Stan is their drummer. Buzzy plays bass. Artie is their manager and he plays saxophone. Ian is a singer-keyboard player who wrote a musical he called "Grassy Knoll," based on the Kennedy assassination. At a band showcase an elderly singer topples over and dies. Phil falls on his face, "his arms wide like Al Jolson's." The band plays Dylan's "Knocking on Heaven's Door." Deeply affected by this, Dave Raymond proposes to Julie Muller, whom he has known since high school. However, he is attracted to a bridesmaid, Gretchen, that he meets on a wedding band gig. Gretchen attends a poetry reading. The Wishbones play in a setting of neo-Nazi skinheads. They play at a Wednesday night showcase at the Cranwood Ramada. This reflects competent but tedious bands like Reunion that played regularly at Ramada Inns in Northern New Jersey but never created or performed any material of their own.[73] There are only a few cars in the parking lot. The array of talent is absurd: Phil Hart and his Heartstring Orchestra play "Celebration" by Kool and the Gang. Older men from the big band era wear blue uniforms and play Madonna's "Like a Virgin." This underscores that the New Jersey suburbs are a place where people listen to cover songs: hit songs that they have heard often on the radio. The novel treats the experiences of this band with dark comedy. *Publishers Weekly* said that *The Wishbones* provided "incisive humor and pop music riffs" that "make this late coming of age novel" fresh and lively. *Kirkus Reviews* called the novel "funny and charming."[74]

Please Step Back (2009) by Ben Greenman is a work of fiction by a rock critic, reviewer, and a biographer of Prince. He has been a New Yorker editor and likes the music of Sly and the Family Stone, Curtis Mayfield, and Marvin Gaye. Robert Franklin (Rock Foxx) is drawn into the sound of Otis Redding and the style of Ray Charles. He reflects on the "unrealized hopes and dreams of the turbulent sixties," observed a writer for *Publishers Weekly*. This is "a haunting vision of a man, music, and a culture driven by the author's undeniable passion for his subject."[75] What becomes of Rock Foxx as they become "darker, edgier, angrier"?

Never Mind Nirvana (2000) is a novel by Mark Lindquist that is set in Seattle's grunge scene. Lindquist uses a Nirvana album title for his novel. His protagonist is someone who was involved in the scene who has become a prosecutor. Critics pointed out that Lindquist, with this novel, gets the details of Seattle right but not much else.

In Tara Kelly's *Amplified* (2011), Jasmine, booted out of her house, runs off to Santa Cruz to be a musician. Three young guys share a place with an ocean view and Jasmine aims to be in the band, called C-Side. Yet, what is she to do if she has stage fright? Can she show them she has the chops to play every song well? Drea, Justin, and Naomi are outsiders who band together in Kelly's *Harmonic Feedback* (2010), a young adult novel.

Haruki Murakami's *Norwegian Wood* (1987) makes use of the title of The Beatles' song but does not deal much with rock music. Naoko says this is her favorite song. She is a friend of Kizuki, who is close to the protagonist-narrator, Toru Watanabe.

In Stephanie Kuehnert's *Ballads of Suburbia* (2009) Kara McNaughton keeps a notebook as she observes Oak Park, Illinois, outside of Chicago. She calls the stories she collects "ballads" and they are about dark events in the suburbs. She writes *I Wanna Be Your Joey Ramone* (2008). Emily's mother Louisa went on the road on the rock circuit and abandoned her. She is now a fan of The Clash, Patti Smith, The Dead Kennedys, and The Ramones. She starts and band and wants to write a song that would prompt her mother to return.

This Is Memorial Device (2017) by music journalist Dave Keeshan explores the post-punk scenes in Scotland in the 1980s. Memorial Device is the name of the local indie band, who represent a world filled with indie bands. Their idols are Iggy Pop, Johnny Thunders, and the voices of punk rock. The story is presented as an oral history through interviews and monologues which contribute many voices to the mix. This novel is about a locale; it is a series of stories born in a place, Airdrie, a mined borderland almost lost between Edinburgh and Glasgow. Ross Raymond is the fictional editor who calls them "the greatest rock group of the modern age or at least of Airdrie." In Katherine Park lies a shrine to rock critic Lester Bangs, maintained by Ross Raymond and Richard Curtis in 1982. In chapter two Ross Raymond interviews band member Big Patty Pierce in the park. Richard Curtis and Patty Pierce play in Memorial Device with Lucas Black and Remy Farr. The novel uses the word "hallucinated" in the title. Indeed, it is a hallucinated time. We hear a character say that there came a time when everything felt at sea and then describe beginning to lose consciousness and seeing only shapes. This is a punk music scene of hanger-ons, where the music scene "fostered belief."

Rock fosters belief. It becomes a zone where people find connection and belonging. It is a context for memorialization. The rock story is a recollection of experience, an elaboration of the human spirit in space and time. In this fictional world of make-believe indie-rock is a borderland, an underground where otherwise stifled voices can be heard. Rock creates edgy girl-bands, aging, lost managers, and determined daydreamers. Some pop music, in contrast, fosters wedding bands in New Jersey with no special skills to break into the business of recorded music: Tom Perrotta's humorous account of cover bands and gigs for money and drinks at the bar. Rock is a story of aspiration, a story of ascendancy and decline—Buddy Wunderlicks and rough-edged youths from Barrytown. Fiction pays tribute to rock imagination and wonder, to the spark of high heeled boys and the gymnastic strut of Mick Jagger. It uses rock as a context in which to tell stories. Rock, which is embedded in popular culture, is an atmosphere, a pulse of life, a distinct, living memory for these writers and their readers. Sound, imagery, and volume spark imagination. Rock music evokes emotion, generates characters, tells stories. Even as hip-hop, dance, or pop music dominates the charts, rock now lives in legend, in memory, in dozens of young indie bands with new sounds and stories.

NOTES

1. Greil Marcus, *Mystery Train: Images of America in Rock and Roll Music*. New York: E.P. Dutton, 1975, p. 119.

2. Theodore Gracyk, *Rhythm and Noise: An Aesthetics of Rock*. Durham: Duke University Press, 1996, pp. viii–x; John Encarnaceo, "Musical Structures as Narrative in Rock," *Portal: Journal of Multidisciplinary International Studies* Vol. 8, Is. 1 (January 2011): 1–15.

3. Theodore Gracyk, *Rhythm and Noise: An Aesthetics of Rock*. Durham: Duke University Press, 1996.

4. Erin Torkelson Weber analyzes narratives about The Beatles in *The Beatles and the Historians: An Analysis of Writings About the Fab Four*. Jefferson, NC: McFarland, 2016. The author takes an historiographical approach and seeks to broaden analysis of The Beatles across generations and across gender. She encourages analysis beyond personal encounters or nostalgia and encourages new perspectives in scholarly inquiry and writing about The Beatles.

5. William James, "Great Men, Great Thoughts and the Environment," *Atlantic Monthly* 46 (October 1880): 441–59.

6. Robert Walser, *Running with the Devil: Power, Gender and Madness in Heavy Metal Music*. Middletown: Wesleyan University Press, 1993, p. 39.

7. Lawrence Kramer, *Classical Music and Postmodern Knowledge*. Berkeley: University of California Press, 1996, p. 144.

8. Kramer, p. 145.

9. Kramer, p. 222.

10. Kramer, p. 228. See Carolyn Abbate, "What the Sorcerer Said," *Nineteenth Century Music* Vol. 12, No. 3 (Spring 1989): 221–30.

11. See Susan McClary, *Feminine Endings: Music, Gender and Sexuality*. Minneapolis: University of Minnesota Press, 1991, p. 149. See especially, pp. 3–79.

12. John Encarnaceo, "Musical Structure as Narrative in Rock," *Portal, Journal of Multidisciplinary International Studies* Vol. 8, No. 1 (January 2011).

13. Susan McClary, *Conventional Wisdom: The Content of Musical Form*. Berkeley: University of California Press, 2000. Susan McClary and Robert Walser, "Start Making Sense! Musicology Wrestles with Rock." *On the Record: Pop, Rock, and the Written Word*. Ed. Simon Frith and Andrew Goodwin. New York: Pantheon, 1990, pp. 277–92. John Covach looks at how Yes, *Close to the Edge* structurally connects art music with 1970s rock. In one of his many interesting essays, "Progressive Rock Close to the Edge and the Boundaries of Style," *Understanding Rock: Essays on Music Analysis*. Ed. John Covach and Graeme Boone. Oxford: Oxford University Press, 1997. Later in chapter five of *Undertsanding Rock*, "Swallowed by a Song: Paul Simon's Crisis of Chromaticism," Walter Everett views Paul Simon's chromaticism in contrast with his earlier and later diatonic work.

14. Ken Stephenson, *What to Listen for In Rock: A Stylistic Analysis*. New Haven: Yale University Press, 2002. John Covach, *What's That Sound: An Introduction to Rock and Its History*. New York: W.W. Norton, 2006. Walter Everett's analysis of Stephen Stills' "Suite: Judy Blue Eyes" in *The Foundations of Rock* is also a fine example of song analysis. Walter

Everett, *The Foundations of Rock: From "Blue Suede Shoes" to "Suite: Judy Blue Eyes."* New York and Oxford: Oxford University Press, 2008.

15. John Shepherd, *Tin Pan Alley*. New York and London: Routledge, Kegan Paul, 1982, p. 142.

16. Philip Tagg, "Analyzing Popular Music: Theory, Method and Practice," *Popular Music* Vol. 2 (1987): 35–65, p. 40.

17. Walser, *Running with the Devil*, p. 30.

18. Philip Roth interviewed by David Remnick, *The New Yorker* (May 8, 2000): 76–89.

19. David Cowart, "Don De Lillo: The Physics of Great Jones Street," p. 134. The essay also appears as "Pharmaceutical Philomela, Great Jones Street" in *Don De Lillo: The Physics of Language*. Athens: University of Georgia Press, 2002.

20. Cowart, p. 35.

21. Ibid.

22. Anthony De Curtis is cited in Cowart, p. 36.

23. Cowart, p. 37.

24. Henry Veggian, *Understanding Don De Lillo*. Columbia: University of South Carolina Press, 2015, p. 27. See Henry Veggian, "Jargon and Genre: *Americana, End Zone*, and *Great Jones Street*," (pp. 26–53) in *Understanding Don De Lillo*.

25. Ian Watt, *The Rise of the Novel*. London: Chatto and Windus, 1957. See Chapter Six, "Private Experience and the Novel," pp.174–207.

26. Veggian, p. 47. In his aesthetics, Lukacs emphasized "inwardness" and held that literature was the effort of the soul struggling with a difficult reality. While he reflected on the existential condition of the modern person, Lukacs turned toward Marxism and would argue that existentialism's focus on the individual would isolate the person from the social relationships and economic forces that played a strong role in his or her life. Literature could only be relevant as a kind of realism that takes into account the historical events and context of the time in which it is written.

27. In an interview with Tom Le Clair, cited by Henry Veggian, Don De Lillo remarked: "I think rock music is a music of loneliness and isolation." There is a reference to the music of The Doors that was used in *Apocalypse Now* in which we see a man in a room with "a half-shattered mind." There is noise, excess, electricity in contrast with Vietnam and "a certain tension is drawn out of the hero's silence, his withdrawal" (cited, p. 48).

28. Veggian, p. 12.

29. Don De Lillo, *Great Jones Street*. Boston and New York: Houghton Mifflin, 1973, p. 228.

30. De Lillo, *Great Jones Street*, p. 198.

31. De Lillo, *Great Jones Street*, p. 264.

32. Anthony De Curtis, "Matters of Fact and Fiction: Interview with Don De Lillo," *Rolling Stone* (November 17, 1988). Rpt. "An Outsider in This Society," *Introducing Don De Lillo*. Ed. Fran Lentricchia. Durham: Duke University Press, 1991.

33. Liam Harte, *Reading the Contemporary Irish Novel, 1987–2007*. UK: Wiley-Blackwell, 2014, p. 31.

34. Roddy Doyle, *The Commitments*. New York: Vintage, 1987, p. 33.

35. Doyle, p. 57.

36. "Garden State, Rick Moody," *Kirkus Reviews* (April 20, 1992).

37. Peter Buck of R.E.M. was Feelies producer of *The Good Earth*.

38. Bill and Glenn talked with Moody for "Blurt," Steven Rosen, "Earth Summit: The Feelies vs. Rick Moody." In *Washington Square Review*, Moody pointed out that literature and music both deal with sound: "They are about sound and for me they are related." *Washington Square Review*, Issue 37 (Spring 2016). It always seemed to me that Glenn and Bill knew exactly what they wanted musically and worked to accomplish it. In Moody's novel the band members are in their teens. We had all turned eighteen when we played the New Jersey dive bars. I did a brief solo set before them at a biker bar in Teaneck before I went off to college. During the Winter break I heard "Fa Ce La," "Forces at Work," "The Boy Next Door," and "Original Love" many times.

39. Janet Burroway, "Books, Toxic Dreams," *New York Times* (April 27, 1997).

40. Dale Peck, *New Republic* (July 1, 2002). Peck is a fine writer, particularly of young adult fiction. Perhaps he might have been a bit less harsh regarding Rick Moody's fiction, but he had his opinion.

41. Interview with Jonathan Lethem pp. 44–45.

42. Jonathan Lethem, *Fortress of Solitude*. Garden City: Doubleday, 2003, p. 204. Matthew Luter notes that Dylan and Mingus have been master appropriators. p. 62. Matthew Luter, *Understanding Jonathan Lethem*. Columbia: University of South Carolina Press, 2015.

43. For pop songs, see *Fortress of Solitude*, pp. 7, 45, 66, 77, 91, 161.

44. Typifying this transition is a punk rock band's ironic version at CBGB's of Aretha Franklin's song "Respect." Luter points out the "racial ambivalence" in Dylan's music listening. p. 65.

45. Lethem, *Fortress of Solitude*, p. 306.

46. Dylan, in this phase, appears to parallel the narrator in Nick Hornsby's *High Fidelity*. Matthew Luter recalls that there was in the 1990s "an upswing of interest in all things retro" (p.74). The quotation of the Talking Heads lyric from *Fear of Music* underscores Dylan's movement toward punk played by white musicians. Lethem wrote for the 33 1/3 series about this album.

47. Evan Hughes, *Literary Brooklyn: The Writers of Brooklyn and the Story of American City Life*. New York: Holt, 2011, p. 252, note 3.

48. Luter, pp. 51, 75.

49. Luter cites James Peacock: "Peacock implies there that pop representations and subcultural styles within youth culture are apolitical, or at least they lack the urgency of more serious adult political interventions." p. 62. James Peacock, *Jonathan Lethem*. Manchester: Manchester University Press, 2012. Luter refers to Dick Hebdige's sociological study, *Subculture: The Meaning of Style*, 1978, p. 63.

50. Lethem, *Fortress of Solitude*, p. 230.

51. Matt Godbey, "Gentrification, Authenticity and White Middle Class in Jonathan Lethem's *Fortress of Solitude*," *Arizona Quarterly* Vol. 64, No. 1 (Spring 2008):132.

52. Godbey, p. 116.

53. Ibid.

54. Peacock, p. 145.

55. Lethem, *You Don't Love Me*. New York: Vintage, 2007. pp. 39, 104.

56. Lethem, *You Don't Love Me*, p. 105.

57. Lethem, *You Don't Love Me*, p. 110.

58. Peacock, p. 146.

59. Will Blythe, "To Their Own Beat," *New York Times* (July 8, 2010).

60. Jennifer Egan, *A Visit to the Goon Squad*. New York: Alfred A. Knopf, 2010, p. 6.

61. Egan, p. 45.

62. Egan, p. 16.

63. Ibid.

64. Egan, p. 21.

65. Ibid.

66. Egan, p. 23.

67. Ibid.

68. Ibid.

69. Egan, p. 42.

70. Ron Charles, *The Washington Post* (June 16, 2010). He writes: "How did time, that punishing goon squad, creep over us and leave us with these flabby bodies, these remote spouses, these children we love but can't reach?"

71. Celia McGee, *Chicago Tribune* (June 14, 2010).

72. Carolyn Kellogg, *Los Angeles Times* (June 6, 2010).

73. Perhaps the fictional town in this novel is a combination of Cranford and Westwood or Wildwood, New Jersey.

74. *Publishers Weekly* (May 1, 1997); *Kirkus Reviews* (March 15, 1997).

75. *Publishers Weekly* (April 20, 2009).

Chapter Seven

Human Rights, Community, and Global Rock

When John Lennon sang "Imagine" he offered a utopian vision, a hope for the future that one day people might overcome conflict and "live as one." As we look back on more than a half-century of rock music history, we can see the imaginative contribution that rock music has made to our world. We can see rock not only as a commercial enterprise but as an expression of human concern. Sometimes rock musicians have expressed their commitment to making our world a more humane and caring place. Rock is a vehicle for social imagination and has the potential to create imagined community. It has become a platform, a means of drawing attention to human needs through concerts, like those for Bangladesh (1971), African relief (1985), and post-9/11 New York (2001).

An ethic of relationship, a regard for emotions and imagination, is often found in artists of romantic inclination. They are the dreamers. The hope that John Lennon advocates—to "join us"—is an invitation to community and the challenge to imagine a better world and to work toward it. This imagined community faces a world of nations, a landscape of realpolitik and religious and political divisions, in which songs and benefit concerts change little in practical terms. Yet, "Imagine" evokes a hope, an ethics of care. Rock, even as a commercial enterprise, has at times shown values of care and compassion. In a world dominated by conflict, preoccupied with economic gain, barely restrained by law, rock still suggests something imaginative and communal. In this section we will explore rock music's potential to benefit humanity. We will look at rock's outreach through benefit concerts on a global scale, such as Live Aid, at women in rock who represent a call to dignity, equality, and care, and at two of the "classic" rock acts that have had sustained impact from the 1970s and 1980s to the present: Bruce Springsteen and U2. These artists represent the importance of rock imagination and the spirit of community.

Creative imagination includes playfulness, enjoyment, and discovery of what is new to us. Rock music, while commercial, is playful, imaginative, theatrical, and emotive. The art of rock music engages with its own history and with culture in combinatorial and associative play, connecting dreams with facts. Within the economic realities of rock production and performance, the spontaneity, play, and freedom of rock crosses generations to bring novelty. Even while hip-hop/rap and pop music forms today dominate the charts there is indeed something rumbling in rock music. Yet another wave of an emergent rock culture is percolating.

In 1981, Stephen Holden wrote in *Rolling Stone*: "In fact, there is a new rock culture emerging. Internationalist rather than American in spirit, it's more hard-headed than utopian in its response to the cold realities of today's hipped computer world in which human life seems increasingly perilous and cheap." Holden wrote that there was a new generation of rock "consumers . . . weaned on the still potent myths of the sixties" who wondered what it was like to see Hendrix, The Doors, or The Rolling Stones in their prime. These listeners that he encountered were born in the mid-1960s. Holden writes: "They had grown up nostalgic for a past they've only experienced second hand." In his view, they were looking back rather than "looking forward to a rock culture of their own."[1] However, that rock culture was soon to appear as heavy metal took hold and was followed by grunge and alternative. The irrepressible rock imagination emerged in new forms and sounds.

Rock imagination today meets with a convergent world, one that Marshall MacLuhan once referred to as a "global village" in his book *Explorations of Communication* (1960). There is in this world an interaction of cultures, a shared media-experience, a technological expansion. Through digital media distribution, concerts, film, and airplay, rock provides images, narratives, and ideals, not only of Western commercial advantage but also of human hope and values that transcend materiality. Rock is a medium for dialogue, a resource for communitarian developments, a voice for imagined possibilities within the historically and culturally situated imaginations of individuals around the world.

ROCKIN' IN THE FREE WORLD

The Live Aid concert in 1985 was eagerly anticipated. The day before the show Bob Geldof, the events' organizer, was quoted by the *New York Times*, remarking on the complexity of the endeavor. "The logistics of this thing are staggering," he said. "What this is all about [is] to raise a lot of money to feed people."[2] Producers indicated that the target audience for Live Aid was the baby boom generation. "This show was designed to be most appreciated by a forty-year-old," said Michael C. Mitchell of Worldwide Sport and Entertainment, the company that produced the Live Aid concert telecast. He added that "individual performers with roots in the 1960s in general and Woodstock in particular" were sought for the concert.[3] The passage of time from those days of their youthful prime was thrown "into clear relief" the *New York Times* writer noted. Greil Marcus, quoted in the article, said: "I think it's great if the money raised does save lives." However, he added that the concert appeared like "an enormous orgy of self-satisfaction and self-congratulation."[4]

The New York Times reported that the countries chosen for immediate famine relief aid were Ethiopia, the Sudan, Burkina Faso, Mali, Chad, and Niger.[5] The Georgetown University unit at The Center for Immigration Policy and Refugee Assistance would screen proposals for spending the $70 million raised from the Live Aid concert. Reverend Harold Bradley, the organization's director met with Bob Geldof, who wanted to see the proceeds from the concerts spent within six months. In addition to the money directed toward famine relief, there would be funding for well-digging and water supply and reforestation.

Soon Geldof was organizing another benefit extravaganza. It would be Live 8, a concert to raise awareness about poverty, the Associated Press reported. This would be not a concert for charity but for political justice, Geldof said. It was announced that there would be performances by U2, Sting, Bon Jovi, Madonna, Dave Matthews, Lauren Hill, Crosby, Stills, and Nash, Stevie Wonder, Coldplay, Mariah Carey, Elton John, REM, and others. Live 8 sought to influence the G8 leaders to respond to African debt aid. Some criticized the event, pointing to its lack of African acts. Geldof argued that only recognizable popular music acts would draw money and audiences. Others questioned whether there would be any substantive political response to the effort.[6]

In January 2004, Bob Geldof spoke with British Prime Minister Tony Blair regarding the people at risk of starvation on the African continent. A Commission for Africa was formed. Blair invited Geldof and sixteen other commissioners to address Africa's need for change. Could African nations provide relief for their people and avoid corruption? The African Progress Panel would study problems in 2012, including the need for jobs, justice, and equality.

Bob Geldof of the Boomtown Rats, a band within the punk rock movement, is an advisor to the One campaign founded by Bono of U2. He was designated as an honorary knight as Man of Peace in Britain by Elizabeth II in 2005. He rejected the Freedom of Dublin City award when that city considered also honoring Myanmar leader Aung San Suo Kyi. Issues of genocide caused that to be revoked. In 2013, Geldof received the Freedom of the City of London honor.[7]

With "Do They Know It's Christmas?" (1984). Bob Geldof and Midge Ure focused upon Ethiopian famine. Live 8 itself did not change any of the structures upon which disparity of wealth or deprivation occurs. In 2005 Geldof organized to pressure the Group of 8 to increase aid to Africa and to produce fair trade agreements. Not much in terms of policy was achieved. Live Earth 2007 was formed to encourage activism among rock's listeners. Produced by Kevin Wall, this event made reference to Al Gore's concern with global warming and was aimed at the Kyoto Protocol.[8]

Jonathan D. Cohen argues that "We went from be here now to remember when" and that countercultural style was co-opted, "reducing everything countercultural, including rock, to hollow gestures and advertising semiotics."[9] John Strausbough argues similarly in *Rock Till You Drop* (2001). However, his argument becomes strained and disparaging. Strausbough may be right to argue against bands that call themselves Little Feat or Jefferson Starship that are made up of perhaps one original member surrounded by replacements who are well-studied musicians, or bands that include "none of the talents that originally made those names so recognizable."[10] However, his critique dissolves as he criticizes Fleetwood Mac as "just Abba with a decent drummer" or contends that The Who without Keith Moon is busy "creaking off another graybeard summer tour." He criticizes Crosby, Stills and Nash but has no crystal ball to see into the future to the fine solo work that has emerged from each of them since 2001.[11]

Rock music is now part of the global imagination. Rock has become a way in which people across the globe express their hopes and dreams. Lane Crothers has called rock and roll "the music of America's suburban youth—especially middle-class whites."[12] However, rock has always existed in working class communities. It has drawn from black R&B roots. It extends well beyond the baby boom generation or middle-class white communities and has expanded out to the world. Rock expresses dreams, anxieties, and fears, hopes, and feelings throughout the world.

Some critics have called "world music" a marketing tool and a commercial strategy. Others see it as an expression of global imagination.[13] Paul Simon, with *Graceland*, created Western interest in South African music. Was this creative interaction and fusion? Or, as some critics contend, was this a type of colonizing? Paul Simon had long been exploring music of other cultures, at least from the time he set the Peruvian melody for "Vaya Con Dios." Simon was an explorer of new sounds from his first solo albums, to the drum and horn parts for "Late in the Evening," to the Brazilian sounds of *Rhythm of the Saints*.

Globalization is a word like modernity: a word which is imprecise and can enlist a variety of interpretations. Is this an expansion of commercial networks, business interests, and global reach of corporate enterprise? Material culture transmitted by communications? A dirty word that means outsourcing of jobs and loss of work and human hands-on activity to automation? A blurring of cultures and national boundaries? In this convergent world cultures are crossing and interacting. There are satellite communications, the Internet, air travel, linked economics. There is a collapsing of geography, of time and space. How people experience time has changed. There is nationalism and populism as a reaction. There is a struggle to define the imagined community of nations. What is rock music's position and role in this communication, this exchange of cultures, and this search for community?

Rock is being put to a variety of uses. In Chemnitz in Eastern Germany, at the beginning of September 2018, 50,000 people assembled for a concert against the far right and in opposition to racism. The band Kraftlub led this effort. Their front-man Carpin Die Toten Hosen insisted that the concert was not about right or left but about decency. This was a pro-diversity concert and was presented as a response to far-right violence one week earlier. Such expressions of concern oppose violence and hatred in the world. They offer an alternative to the evil-intent that slashed out on September 11, 2001, and sent shock waves through the world. To that tragic event, rock musicians and the rock audience responded with compassion.

MUSIC POST 9/11

The effort to utilize music to bring people together in a common cause can be seen in the post-9/11 concerts. The response in rock, country, rap, and world music is documented in *Music in the Post-9/11 World,* edited by Jonathan Ritter and J. Martin Daughtry (New York: Routledge, 2007.) This work is described by J. Martin Daughtry as "a reflection on the historical moment in which this volume was produced and the place of musical scholarship in the post 9/11 world."[14] It appears to hold the hope that this world of ours is not only engaged in a "clash of civilizations," as Samuel Huntington (1996) has remarked but also bears potential for a global dialogue. It appears to be a premise of this book that the increasing proximity of economies and ideologies we sometimes call globalization calls for a reinvestigation and reanimation of the traditional role of the humanities: to further humanize our world with critical multiculturalism as we listen to each other and share our music and our lives. While these contributors observe our contemporary encounter with the use of music in nationalistic contexts that may be potentially divisive, their essays also move one to recognize the hope that music might act as a vehicle for healing in our world. Just as the "America: A Tribute to Heroes" concert was, as Kip Pegley and Susan Fast note in their essay, "an attempt to reconfigure an imagined community that had been distorted by the trauma," this book suggests that it was also a possibility for enhancing "community" through a reflective dialogue on music and cultural media. Conscious of music's "ability to channel powerful emotions," Pegley and Fast remind us that musical tributes and recollections could be found in every major media event in America: the World Series, the Super Bowl, the Olympics, and the Academy Awards among them. "America: A tribute to Heroes" is described as an event on 35 cable television networks and 8,000 radio stations that "through the power of celebrity, music and gesture . . . attempted to forge a unified American community." "America: A Tribute to Heroes" was an attempt to foreground community. Pegley and Fast point out that this image of unified American community was reinforced by metaphors for community like the appearance of singer/songwriters like Neil Young or Bruce Springsteen with vocal choirs.[15]

In *Music in the Post 9/11 World* Reebee Garofalo points out that music's social role after 9/11 emerged with the "gentle patriotism" of the "America: A Tribute to Heroes" broadcast and continued with the "Concert for New York City." The latter, he observes, carried amid assertions of confidence a theme of revenge that was amplified by Bon Jovi's song "Wanted Dead or Alive" and The Who's "Won't Get Fooled Again." Garofalo adds that "artists who would have been identified with an oppositional stance in a previous era adopted new positions in response to a new political reality."[16] (Of course, time shows some of this to have been temporary and of the moment.) Next turning to country music, he expresses the view that corporate radio stifled dissent. Garofalo contends that "the restrictive and at times partisan practices of corporate radio were not the only reasons behind the lack of protest music on the national airwaves."[17] He probes whether the Patriot Act "created a climate of intolerance for opposing viewpoints and caused many artists to censor themselves." Garofalo asserts that there was "suppression and marginalization of voices resistant to dominant ideologies" in popular music in 2001–2003. Garofalo recognizes that "many artists interested in protesting the war turned to the Internet, often posting protest songs as MP3's available for free download." Garofalo notes "hints of . . . dissatisfaction within the rap community" and recognizes rap and hip-hop "as the site of the most provocative political commentary in an otherwise timid and muted post 9/11 environment."[18] Garofalo reflects on Bruce Springsteen's *The Rising*. Bryan Garman comments that Bruce Springsteen's *The Rising* dealt with "the politics of fear, fame and faith," his Christian themes, and his hope for moral and spiritual renewal.

SPRINGSTEEN AND COMMUNITY

Bruce Springsteen is a participatory performer who is always in dialogue with his audience. With "Spirit in the Night," he dances into a crowd. With "Tenth Avenue Freeze Out," he slides to the edge of the stage, as if to touch the audience. The boundaries of performer-audience seem to dissolve. Springsteen reaches across space, geography, class, race, and gender. His song is a happening, a passion open to change. Like a match, it is filled with possibility. It just has to strike something. In "The Rising," all becomes voices chiming in to the flow together. A song comes alive when it is performed. It is then open to the moment in which it is given voice. That difference, that improvised novelty, is like the breakthrough of a cool rain, or the sudden wash of a warm ray of sun. What is breathtaking is what happens spontaneously. It's that echo across the stage from someone else in the band who suddenly knows—you don't know how—just where all of this is going. The pulse, the rasp, the sigh, the exclamation point: that is music!

In the 1970s, Springsteen declared that music is a kind of momentary salvation. The theme of "escape" on *Born to Run* gestured toward a hope that cannot be subdued, the promise of an American dream, even if one wonders if and how that dream is possible. The first line of "Born to Run" pulses rhythmically, placing that long i and e of "night" and "we" against the tight, short "e" of "sweat" and the alliterative "streets" with its long "e." The "r's" rumble into "runaway American dream." The lyric is working the "uh" of runaway and "American" and maybe the place is "ugh," or the strain of trying to break out is "ugh." But we are moving like pistons at this point, out to that long "e" vowel of "dream." We are in motion and we have an idea: what is this dream? Can this dream be fulfilled?

The second line springs to life with the "i" of "night" "ride," "suicide" and there is the balance of line lengths and the parallel structure: "by day we"/"at night we." A stark contrast of images all bump into each other. Those symbols of "glory," the mansions, cast shadows on a world of vehicles going in circles: cars that are as much a death trap as a means of freedom. One can see the teens circling, taking that shore road out to where the big houses keep watch over the ocean. Two lanes can take us anywhere. We are "Born to Run" and dream, libido, blood are fuel. These machines have revved up into life. They are risk, reach, aspiration: "stepping out over the line." The speaker aches for escape from a place that tears at the very fiber of a man or woman: a place they have got to get out of. And they will, with determination, with these engines, with this possibility. But this night is dark; it hangs like a dark cloud, a fog of fumes, and from behind a half-cracked window pane a radio plays. We're pulling out of here to win. The last lines of "Born to Run" are punctuated—one-two-three: a trinity of punches ("tramps like us"). They are given with, affirmation, with a note of destiny.

On record we hear versions of "Born to Run." Structurally, the song is in AABA form. The ragged, impossible roller coaster ride energy of the tempo seems to be the point. The lyrics and music both build toward a critical point of breaking out. In the studio Springsteen and the E Street Band clearly worked toward something like a live sound. They were making a record. This is an art in itself, full of calculations, calibrations, and textures. When we listen, we hear a layering of guitars and the sure rhythm section. The album's songs seem guided by Roy Bittan's piano, or at least centered in the movement of piano chords. The sound is characterized by—indeed deeply marked by—Clarence Clemons's saxophone. Whatever speaks in Springsteen's lyric lives and moves within this setting. The verbal is inseparable from music and performance. "Born to Run" has the layering of a dozen guitar tracks, a fullness of keyboards, the driving rhythm section and signature sax, and touches of bell-like glockenspiel.

The second verse offers a direct address to "Wendy." Her name is echoed with assonance in the word "let" and "me" balances "be" amid the internal off-rhyme of "in" and "friend." The singer's offer to guard her dreams and visions connects with the sexual "velvet rims" and "engines." There is a request, a plea, the sound of reassurance and dedication, all wrapped up in this line and in this embrace. Engine and flesh are fused in this sharp metaphor into passionate romantic abandonment. That want aspires to know what is wild, to know what is real.

The music itself provides this energy that breaks out from futility. We are brought to that moment with vivid imagery. In the song's bridge, our gaze rises with a picture of the horizon of the amusement park and the vivid image of kids huddled on the misty beach. One sees the distant curve of the park: rides above, beach below, where the kids "huddle." With a declaration, then comes the "everlasting kiss": like a firecracker, an exclamation point! We hear a drum hit, vocal punctuation, and we're off, and an explosive saxophone solo says the rest.

A count of four builds momentum that thrusts us back into the final verse. The highway's jammed with broken heroes. Everybody out on the road has "no place left to hide." The declaration of love is made "with all the madness in my soul." The dream of "someday" flashes again and we arrive at that trinity of punches—"tramps like us"—that brings us back to the title and a conclusion where words dissolve into sound.

The album *Darkness on the Edge of Town* is connected by constant references to work and the working life. It discloses an America of working men and women who survive with dreams sometimes shadowed by the circumstances of daily reality. The search for America, for integrity, continues: "I want to find out what I got." There is an effort like that of Sisyphus, the character in an ancient myth who rolls a rock up a hill only to have it roll back down again. In Albert Camus' retelling, it is Sisyphus' integrity in this "absurd" situation that counts. He is like the working man, who gets up and goes to work each day, whose monotonous pattern of labor sometimes feels futile. These are the jobs and the people Springsteen writes about: common Americans with uncommon spirits. They are anonymous to the world at large, but loved by their families, connecting with their friends, working alongside their co-workers.

Darkness on the Edge of Town is not only about escape. It is about facing the music, confronting the obstacles. Stark, pounding, propulsive, this album faces life. The lyrics repeatedly anchor in commitment and resolve. "Badlands" begins the album with its insistence on believing in love, hope, and faith in spite of it all. The music of "Adam Raised a Cain" pounds with the spare, solid drive of the music on a night at CBGB's in 1976–1978: Patti Smith or Television is onstage and a mirror along the right wall catches your reflection as you look at them. The album, as Robert Hilburn once observed, is "moodier" than the previous recording. The wide horizon of *Born to Run* appears to have contracted. Yet, the desire to escape, to flee monotony and limitation, is met with the determination to work with what one has and to find a realistic way to break out. Hope endures. Where the screen door once slammed, the narrator now works all day in his daddy's garage and by night chases some mirage. Now he is going to "take charge." As Dave Marsh pointed out in his August 1978 *Rolling Stone* cover article, the "darkness" is not "grim;" it is relentless. The working man endures relentless struggle. The sounds being thrashed out are its complement.[19]

After two pickup drumbeats on the tom-toms and a final roll, "Promised Land" launches on a harmonica. The song begins with an image of empty vastness and dryness: a poisonous highway twisting into the distance. Paid for his work, after picking up his money, the speaker is wandering out over the county line, "killing time." He has been working all day in a garage and night is that space where he chases a mirage. The verse lands on the assertion that he is going to take charge. The carpe diem poet seeks to seize the day, to pull life out of the jaws of death, or, as Springsteen puts it, to "take one moment into my hands." Roy Bittan's piano provides an interlude and Danny Federici's organ playing joins over the top. Gary Tallent does a descending bass run that moves into Springsteen's lyrical guitar lead. This climbs into a saxophone solo, which returns to the hook phrase, with the harmonica. All of this gives us some listening space.

We listen to the phrase from the harmonica: a folk instrument, portable, easily held and carried in the pocket of a traveler. It is like a little orchestra, tuned to a key. In *The Grapes of Wrath*, a story filled with dreams of the Promised Land, John Steinbeck writes of the harmonica, the guitar, and the fiddle.[20] "Promised Land" is filled out by the harmonica sounding its central riff. The wind blows from human breath. While the twister would blow away dreams, the human breath asserts, "I believe in." This self-reliance and assertion stands at the center of the song.

The character in Springsteen's song asserts that he has tried to live justly, dutifully going to work each day. He recognizes that he has struggled, and that struggle is vividly described in lines that are as much reality as hyperbole: eyes going blind and blood running cold. The pent-up energy and frustration that he feels is set to detonate. In the next verse, a dark cloud is rising and the speaker is heading out into the storm. A "twister" is coming that will "blow away" life. What is a man rooted to, grounded against such forces? A metaphor is at work here. The twister is a symbol. The repetition three times of "blow away," with its parallel structure, is an assertion against what would blow away the promise. One would expect the "twister" to do this blowing away. Yet, it is the speaker taking charge against the elements who will "blow away" the resistance to the dreams and those things that break the heart. Guitars are pulled back with Bittan's piano and Tallent's bass over Max Weinberg's drums leading the way. We land on the doubled vocals of the chorus, ending three times on the affirmation of a belief in the Promised Land. The harmonica that closes the song is assertive, jubilant.

Increasingly, after *Darkness on the Edge of Town*, Springsteen's songs open out on a world of uncommon common folks. In the albums after *Darkness on the Edge of Town*, *The River*, and *Nebraska*, there is less "flight" and an increasing confrontation with the world. Facing the music—or the world with his music—Springsteen's lyrical world increasingly adopts the voice of characters who live here and who have a variety of stories. The first-person narratives tell us these stories, as the landscape broadens. We are in the heartland. *Darkness on the Edge of Town* begins with "Badlands" and "trouble in the heartlands." Dave Marsh, Springsteen's biographer, captures a central theme: "Believe in yourself and the world will work better."[21]

This heartland of America is typified by families like the Joad family of John Steinbeck's *The Grapes of Wrath*. In Steinbeck's novel (1939) and the John Ford film (1940), this Oklahoma family is an exemplar of this striving of hard work, resilience, and conviction in the midst of systems and institutions that are often unresponsive, divorced from the breath and blood of lives. This family soon sees that there are other families who are just like them, who, beset by circumstances, struggle, seek a "promised land," and hold on to their integrity in the teeth of adversity. Springsteen characters, likewise, are extraordinary while ordinary and common. Digging down into folk traditions, on *The Ghost of Tom Joad*, *Nebraska*, *Devils and Dust*, Springsteen gives us something visceral, sturdy, and enduring about many of these characters. They are at the core and the variety of America and "the American dream" can be explored by listening to these imagined voices. We are drawn to feel for these people, even as some characters fail, or the dream seems to fail.

Springsteen moves across American life through a variety of voices and styles. Songs from *Nebraska*, or *Devils and Dust*, have a dark, storytelling quality. Many unfold in ballad patterns, rest on guitar chords, and are mixed in a way that draws attention to the vocal and to the story. Built on folk forms, these song patterns reflect those of anonymous ancestors who have sung of their lives from the days of settlement down through Woody Guthrie and Pete Seeger. Springsteen stands in line with this tradition. As much as he is a repository of rock music's legacy, he also grasps the earthy, enduring elements of the people's music, the unique songs, voices, and issues of these lives.

This orientation toward people's music and community was well-matched to the pain and need that arose from the tragic events of September 11, 2001. 9/11 brought the American people some deeply unsettling issues. Springsteen's song "The Rising" begins by focusing our attention on the spoken-sung voice of a first-person narrator. Going through the darkness, he "can't see nothing." From underneath, comes a pulse, and then the gated drums' deep, echoing reverb. We are given images: "Mary" in the garden, holding pictures of her children. In the presence of one who offers care, "lay your hands in mine" becomes "your blood mixed with mine": an intimate union of sympathy. You can hear this song move into that large group chorus to the point where words are not necessary and melt into "la-la-la." The song has been interpreted as being voiced by a character who encounters his dying, who thinks of his family, of those he loves. Its title may be interpreted as metaphorical or symbolic of hope, resurrection, or union. Inevitably, that depends upon what the listener, within a community of interpreters, brings to the song.

In Springsteen's repetition of "sky"—of black, of darkness, sorrow, love, tears, mercy—the parallel structure here is Whitman-like. The vocal in the foreground points to "the sky." This is matched by Springsteen's own background vocal, affirming "dream of love" over and over, between the lines. The bank of guitars, mixed back, emerges with overdrive-fuzz, amid overtones, and matches the "la-la" chorus. The song gathers intensity and the drums lead us back into the chorus: voices in unison. This joining in unity seems central to the song: a mixing of blood, breath, and spirit. The song reflects something like the mystic's movement from the darkness of *via negativa* toward illumination and unitive vision, resurrection, and hope. One hears synthesizer chords and a single reverbed guitar chord plays, accenting the end of the phrase. The rest is all mixed back. The voice rests on top of this and leads the chorus. We hear long extended notes of the guitar lead with overdrive and effect on the guitar. We hear the repetition, like a mantra: "Come on up for the rising."

Springsteen songs like this are characterized by their dynamics: shifts in timbre and tempo, pitch, rhythm, and volume. There are peaks and valleys, pacing and inflection. It's like the ocean at Asbury Park that rolls to a crest, crashes, and subsides. The roller coaster at the amusement park hits its peak, accelerates, and whirling down, makes its turn in a breathless blaze of glory.

The Springsteen lyric often moves toward affirmation. It recognizes the sharp sting of human pain and struggle. For people who move out on highways that get jammed everywhere, pain becomes a universal experience. Hungry hearts have dreams. What is jammed in these lives, trying to break free? Who are these broken heroes? How is this their last chance? Where will this affirmation of passion and life take them? This is the *carpe diem* of the poets—Jonson, Marvell, Herrick. "Someday" is up ahead: that horizon where they can "walk in the sun." But life is now, immediate: so, they must seize it. What might it mean to be born to run? One runs *from*—as to escape—but one also runs *toward* something. Hope works against life's resistance. Entropy will not, cannot, subdue the vital spirit.

WOMEN IN ROCK

In 2009, Melissa Etheridge's performance of Springsteen's "Born to Run" at the Kennedy Center brought the house down. It was yet another sign that the female rock performer had arrived. In the 1980s more female voices began to appear as solo artists in rock music. Even so, the distinction between presumably authentic-male rock and female-pop hovered over this new female creativity. Women have argued against neglect of their voices in Western societies from the prophetic call of Cassandra in Aeschylus' *Agamemnon* and Euripedes' *The Trojan Women* to the strident cries of the "me too" movement. It is difficult for a female songwriter to be taken seriously, said Lady Gaga at the 2018 Golden Globe Awards. NPR writes that "Women Are the Fabric of 21st Century Pop" (July 30, 2018). However, is that also true of rock, which determinedly expresses itself a bit outside of today's mainstream pop? As rock music moves on into the 2020s, will it continue to provide us with the voices of female rock musicians and maintain a creative space for their perspectives?

If one looks back to halcyon days, Grace Slick, Janis Joplin, and Patti Smith can be cited as being within the rock pantheon. The Wilson sisters of Heart, Joni Mitchell, Laura Nyro, Joan Jett, Suzi Quatro, Linda Ronstadt, Bonnie Raitt, Chrissie Hynde of The Pretenders, Deborah Harry of Blondie, and Pat Benatar had also made an impact. In R&B Aretha Franklin and many Motown acts from The Supremes to Martha and the Vandellas have also achieved similar Rock and Roll Hall of Fame recognition. In the 1980s, Madonna and Cindi Lauper were breakthrough pop performers regarded as pop. In those years into the 1990s the walls appeared to come down further with the emergence of Sinead O'Connor, Alannis Morrisette, Melissa Etheridge, Liz Phair, Kim Gordon of Sonic Youth, Gwen Stefani, Lucinda Williams, Courtney Love, Amy Winehouse, P.J. Harvey, Belinda Carlisle, Aimee Mann, Fiona Apple, Sheryl Crow, and others. However, in 2016 Helen Reddington was writing about *The Lost Women of Rock Music* and Judy Berman wrote in *The Village Voice*: "In the Age of Pop Feminism

Women Still Have to Scratch Their Names Into the Musical Record" (July 22, 2016).[22]

There has been at times a wall of alienation or marginalization facing the female rock performer, as feminist critics have pointed out. Feminist rock music critics like Norma Coates, Kristin J. Lieb, Mimi Schippers, Sheila Whiteley, Joanne Gottlieb and Gayle Wald, Deborah Harding and Emily Nett have pointed to misogyny in rock and have argued against neglect and exploitation of women in rock. In 1971 Marian Meade asked: "Does Rock Degrade Women?" (March 14, 1971), and answered in the affirmative. She pointed out that rock posited the Aquarian utopia but Woodstock had few female performers and (in 1971) a female rock band was perceived as "weird."

Witnessing the rise of the female performer in 2000, classical music scholar Susan McClary remained skeptical, observing that *Rolling Stone* and other popular rock publications "still tend to write about them in 'gee whiz' articles that marvel at the sheer existence of such creatures, rather like the proverbial dancing dog."[23] Kristin Lieb, who cites McClary's comment, demonstrates how pop music branding and star-making pop imagery have reinforced gender stereotypes and limitations. Like Marian Meade in 1971, Mimi Schippers, in 2002, contended that in moving toward masculinist commercial directions rock does not live up to its countercultural image.[24] Helen Davies in 2001 claimed that the British press tended to exclude women in rock and she claimed that "all of rock is homosocial." Norma Coates argued that masculinist discourse pervades rock. Jenny Garber pointed to some of the lost women of punk rock and rock subcultures.[25] These feminist critics have claimed that many writers on rock have employed gender categories to argue that pop is consumerist and "feminine." Roots rock without adornment has been favored. Yet, the rebellious image of Janis Joplin, the power chord songs of Joan Jett, the roots blues of Bonnie Raitt all appear to fit well with this notion of rock "authenticity." The rebellious, transgressive stance of rock's women is sometimes signaled by their dressing in leather or in plain street clothes as well as by their music.[26]

Even that seems not enough to satisfy those who adhere to the dichotomy spelled out by Norma Coates, who has seen females shaped as "pop" artists. "In this schema, rock is metonymic with 'authenticity' while pop is metonymic with artifice," she writes. Thus, authentic becomes masculine and inauthentic becomes feminine. "The two are set up in binary relation to each other."[27] A rock performer like Melissa Etheridge is pulled into the category of pop and "made over as pop stars once they achieve crossover level of sales," observes Kristin Lieb in her introduction.[28] Only 15 percent of the contributions to key albums given attention in the 33 1/3 book series involve women, Judy Berman pointed out in 2016 ("In the Age of Pop Feminism," *Village Voice*, July 22, 2016). Memoirs have been penned by Patti Smith,

Kim Gordon, Carrie Brownstein, Viv Albertine, Carly Simon, Kristina Hersch, Chrissie Hynde. NYU has a Riot Grrrl archive and Berman points to a trend in 2016 of female band reunions. Rock can be a feminist means of activism. However, from the thirty-six interviews in Mavis Bayton's "How Women Became Rock Musicians" in 1989 to the interviews in Kristin Lieb's 2013 book on the music industry, the same concerns about women having to overcome obstacles persist.

Rock poetess Patti Smith, in May 2005, told the British publication *The Guardian*, that she turned to art, poetry, and music while feeing a sense of disconnection or feeling alien: "What I wanted to do in rock n'roll was merge poetry with sonic-scapes."[29] Patti Smith's fusion of rock and Rimbaud was central to the development of new wave/punk in the mid-1970s. On *Horses*, in her androgynous "raggedy glory," said the *Guardian*, her fusion of Rimbaud and rock marked a pivotal movement in the mid to late 1970s that continues to be memorable and influential.[30] That sense of feeling alien and finding mutual connection with others appears to have been crucial to her art.

The interviews conducted by Kristin J. Lieb in 2006–2007 with industry professionals indicate that female performers may continue to be shaped by pop machinery that constructs them in roles as objects of desire. In her sociological pop culture/mass communication study she foregrounds female performers "framed by media professionals and received by fans" amid industry dynamics. She points out that we may approach this phenomenon through critical theory, as in the Frankfurt school's criticism of capitalism's manufactured desires.[31] Or we may ask if consumers of popular music might resist the persuasions of culture industries. We can approach audiences through symbolic interactionism and consider the interplay of cultural symbols, the influences of peers, or other social factors. We also have to look at the signs and myths surrounding the female pop star, such as, female equals beauty, youth, sexual allure, in relation to pop production.

The increasing attention to women in rock since 1990 is likewise addressed by Jenny Garber in "Girls and Subcultures." There she comments on the perception of females as consumers of pop music and men as purchasers of rock music. Garber repeats the claim that has been made that females in American culture are closer to consumerism and consequently are more inclined toward pop music than rock.[32] Several female rock acts resist this, although they clearly have entered the pop category. Among the alternative rock independent music bands, Riot Grrrl has received some critical attention from critics like Gayle Wald, who has identified shifting identifications and attitudes. Wald cites No Doubt's "I'm Just a Girl" and the song's use of Jamaican ska and cultivation of a "girl" identity. She describes how Gwen Stefani appropriates "girlhood" and plays with the codes of gender and a good girl/bad girl dichotomy. Stefani and No Doubt employ this "in a rhetorical or sarcastic manner," she observes.[33]

Rock's women have often chosen rebellious and transgressive stances. Some, like Joan Jett, will dress in leather, suggesting urban toughness. Others adopt imagery that underscores that they are experimental, Dionysian, edgy, and bold. They express a dark Eros, an urban savvy, and the soul-power of Hera, Kali, or other poetic figures. They break through bias, chauvinism, and limited viewpoints with their art. Joan Jett, Pat Benatar, Chrissy Hynde, Melissa Etheridge, all commercially popular, have maintained their rock edge. Christine McVie and Stevie Nicks of Fleetwood Mac brought "Rhiannon" to the pop charts in the 1970s and Lady Gaga, in her various guises, has appealed to the image of Venus. In the 1980s, pop music idol Madonna was applauded, derided, and faced stereotypes and dismissal as "a mindless doll fulfilling male fantasies" as Susan Mc Clary observed.[34] This is a perspective that McClary rejects by demonstrating Madonna's careful planning and control over her image and public identity. Madonna expressed power.

The New York Dolls in heels, Patti Smith, in white shirt and tie, and David Bowie, in jumpsuit and dyed hair are among the rock performers who have ventured to break with gender stereotypes, adopting androgynous images, weaving male/female. The comparative mythologist Mircea Eliade points to divine androgyny and says that this was often expressed in biological terms, including bisexuality. This expresses the coincidence of contraries. He writes: "We must simply note that the divinities of cosmic fertility are, for the most part, either hermaphrodites or male one year and female the next."[35] Eliade lists Attis, Adonis, Dionysus, Cybele the Great Mother, Purusa in the Rig Veda, and Siva Kali. He points out that the gods of Scandinavian mythology, Odin, Loki, Tuisco, Nerthus retain elements of androgyny. Some traditions hold that the primeval man was a hermaphrodite. Perhaps Janis Joplin at her grungiest may suggest this androgyny. But it is the members of Queen, or the New York Dolls, Alice Cooper, or Bowie in whom this androgyny is more apparent.

Gender has been involved in the arguments of some rock critics against "soft," "weak," "light" music. This has been identified by some critics as "feminine." These critics favor blues rock with a lack of adornment and critically reject "slick" production, or overproduction. That, on the face of it, may appear a reasonable distinction. However, a problem arises, notes Jones, when this becomes gendered into a simple dichotomy: hard rock is male, soft rock and pop is female. Viewed from this perspective Grace Slick seems to be caught within a cultural quandary. One would expect that critics of this disposition would favor the "authentic" blues and folk of the Jefferson Airplane and Hot Tuna to the commercial singles on Jefferson Starship's *Red Octopus* album. The Jefferson Airplane would be viewed as tougher and grittier and Jefferson Starship as lighter pop. Kambrew McLeod observes how rock critics have employed these terms within the discursive space of reviews and asserts that this "tells a story."[36] Such criticism associates tougher and grittier blues rock with masculinity and positions the feminine with the non-progressive, McLeod says. This is the rock critic's sense of the serious, authentic, raw elements of rock versus what the critics consider formulaic fluff.

Some feminist critics of rock have pointed to the masculine posturing of heavy metal bands. Deena Weinstein, among others, rejects the claim that the mythical stance of some heavy metal bands is all that misogynistic. In contrast, Deborah Harding and Emily Nett (1984) have called rock blatantly misogynistic. Joanne Gottlieb and Gayle Wald have viewed rock as deeply masculine. Norma Coates has written of "a constant process of reiteration and the performance of masculinity." Mimi Schippers has argued that "rock culture has relied upon and reproduced quite mainstream ideas about gender and sexuality and in these terms it does not live up to its rebellious countercultural image." Schippers points out that songs have often presented stories of the exploitation of women. Coates concludes that some rock songs create an "ultimately fictive masculinity." A stereotypical masculinity is "in play discursively and psychically," Coates says. Deena Weinstein observes that heavy metal celebrates masculinity and Robert Walser notes how it inscribes femininity. Heavy metal masculinity embraces the heroic image, as in the stance of Iron Maiden's Bruce Dickinson and his mythological narratives about heroism and valiant fighting.[37]

However, the goddess figure, the female rock performer—often a vocalist—voices another dimension that is powerful. Grace Slick is one of the forerunners who evoked this power. Grace Slick performed at the 1967 Monterey Pop Festival wearing a flowing white tunic. Psychedelic rock gave attention to visual performance. They sought new worlds and sang songs with themes of alienation, culture crisis, dissent relationships, social, racial, and sexual alienation. They called in "Volunteers," a song written by Balin and Kantner, for a revolution that would be peaceful. Whether Grace Slick, Paul Kantner, and the crew were able to create change with their call to revolutionize America is open to question. They became Starship and were successful on the pop music charts with their album *Red Octopus*, which featured the hit single "Miracles." Today, perhaps in search of the miraculous, Grace Slick spends time painting in her studio in Malibu. She recalls rock as "a young expression."[38] That "young expression" carries imaginative fire that Mary Shelley once brought to *Frankenstein*. It carries the poetic spirit by which Patti Smith infused her band's album *Horses*. It is the passionate guitars of Lita Ford and Joan Jett, the gutsy blues of Janis Joplin. It is an edgy rock voice, a female voice of determination that insists upon being heard.[39]

If women choose to extend their rock and roll vision, they might draw strength from Mary Shelley's Gothic fiction. For Shelley's story questioned the social order and gave attention to the marginalized who require nurture and care. Like her Romantic contemporaries Charlotte Smith, who wrote "Beachy Head," and Anna Barbauld, who wrote the dystopian *Eighteen Hundred and Eleven*—poems of time travel fantasy critiquing declining British civilization—Shelley's proto-science fiction tale drew upon her mother Mary Wollstonecraft's ardent feminism and upon the romantic affirmation of imagination. The dystopian fiction provides a tool for social critique of imperial or patriarchal power. The Romantic visionary mode offers an alternative. Perhaps the female perspective will also contribute a further "ethics of care" to the business of rock music.

That future will also add more women to the rolls of the Rock and Roll Hall of Fame. The women who have been inducted into the Rock and Roll Hall of Fame include female vocalists who are central to popular music R&B and Motown: Aretha Franklin, Diana Ross and The Supremes (Florence Ballard, Mary Wilson), Tina Turner, Martha and the Vandellas (Martha Reeves, Rosalind Ashford, Annette Beard, Betty Kelly, Lois Reeves), Gladys Knight (and the Pips), The Shirelles, The Ronettes, The Staple Singers, Ruth Brown, Etta James, Cynthia Robinson and Rosie Stone of Sly and the Family Stone. Other female inductees to the Rock and Roll Hall of Fame are: Janis Joplin, Dusty Springfield, Brenda Lee, Mama Cass and Michelle Phillips of the Mamas and the Papas, Christine McVie and Stevie Nicks of Fleetwood Mac, Ann Wilson and Nancy Wilson of Heart, Joni Mitchell, Patti Smith, Debbie Harry of Blondie, Anni-Frid Lyngstad and Agnetha Faltskog of Abba, Madonna, Darlene Love, Laura Nyro, Linda Ronstadt, Bonnie Raitt, Joan Jett and the Blackhearts, Nina Simone. The wide breadth of popular music is represented, as the Rock and Roll Hall of Fame defines rock broadly, including influential figures from the folksinger Joan Baez to the disco queen Donna Summer. In 2019, Chaka Kahn and Rufus, Janet Jackson, and Stevie Nicks in her solo career were among the nominees. Within the category of "influences" the Rock Hall of Fame has cited Mahalia Jackson, Dinah Washington, Bessie Smith, Billie Holiday, Wanda Jackson, Ma Rainey, and Sister Rosetta Tharpe.

U2: MUSIC FOR THE WORLD

"She Moves in Mysterious Ways," sings U2's Bono, enlisting a figure that is anima, female spirit and grace, Muse, and inspiration. For a *Boston Globe* writer this was a love song that was "rapturous." An *All Music* writer decided that it was structured like a religious chant.[40] It was the funk riff that started in Adam Clayton's bass that caught several listeners' attention. Of course, this lyric could describe a specific woman. But she just might be the spirit that moves through the world.

When U2 performed at Madison Square Garden on the rainy evening of a post-9/11 bomb scare, after performing "Bloody Sunday," Bono placed a kerchief on his head marked with the symbols of Jewish, Muslim, and Christian worlds. Then, as he unfurled the American flag, a chant went up from the top rim of the Garden: "USA!" It was strange how an Irish band stirred US nationalism shortly after its internationalist appeal for relief of famine in Africa. In the concert setting the rock tribe joined the chorus chant. U2 gestured toward an international community of compassion and concern. Yet, this tier of the New York crowd responded with jingoistic chants. Performers and writers are not in control of reception—the way their songs will be heard and interpreted. Certainly, Americans in New York City have every right to affirm their patriotism in a chant. However, the crowd's response raises some questions about how we respond and interpret the rock music message. Bruce Springsteen's "Born in the USA" was regarded by President Reagan and others as a proud anthem. It had more to do with the bitter and forgotten soldiers of Vietnam. In concert, Bono clearly wanted to gather people together in unity and to overcome division. Bono's symbolic expression appeared to reject religious and nationalistic division, almost in the same manner as John Lennon's "Imagine."

"Sunday Bloody Sunday" is the opening track of U2's *War* album. The song recalls the events of January 30, 1972, when thirteen Irish citizens were shot in Northern Ireland. Bono's lyric moves toward a sense of resurrection on Easter Sunday. The song was performed live in Glasgow at Tiffany's on December 1, 1982. This was the first date of the tour that previewed the *War* album. It also marked the tenth anniversary of the event. The song appeared as a live track on *Under a Blood Red Sky*. This was recorded in Germany at the Lorelei Ampitheatre on August 20, 1983. The song later was on the *Rattle and Hum* video, recorded in Denver at the McNichols Arena, Sunday, November 8, 1987. U2 had just learned of the Enniskillen, North Ireland bomb that took the lives of thirteen people. That night Bono verbally denounced Irish Americans who support the violence of the "revolution" in North Ireland. U2 has never taken sides. They never praise the IRA or Unionists or anyone else utilizing violent methods. They can be rebellious, nonconforming, and they assert human rights and social justice. But they are also entrepreneurs—witness Larry Mullen caring about selling merchandise and their shift of their accounts to avoid Irish taxation. They make a lot of money and they want to hold onto it.

From the opening notes of "I Will Follow" to the chords on "Beautiful Day," the Edge (Dave Evans) is central to U2's sound. The riffs are brief. The work is mostly rhythmic. The sound is unmistakable. The chord patterns and playing on "Sunday Bloody Sunday" speaks an aggression. His backing vocals are also important. The rhythm section of Larry Mullen (drummer) and Adam Clayton (bass guitar) are central to the band's energy and sound. Meanwhile, their vision is turned outward to the needs of the world.

U2 became a force in rock music in the 1980s. U2's debut album *Boy* appeared in November 1980. On December 6, 1980, U2 played their first New York City concert at the Ritz. On February 19, 1981, James Henke wrote of U2 in "Here Comes the Next Big Thing" in *Rolling Stone*. He called U2 "special" and "amazing." He remarked on the "power and passion." From their beginnings, U2 appears to have sought to project hope. In *Melody Maker* Paulo Hewitt asserted that U2 was about "integrity." U2 is rock but "transcends all genres" wrote Tim Sommer in *Trouser Press* (July 1, 1981). He refers to the emotion on their first album. Bono told him that they sought "a cinema sound." The lyrics were more image than story, he said. Hewitt added a comment on Bono's "romanticized vision, another trait of his rich Irish heritage."[41]

U2's single "Gloria" was released on October 5, 1981. The *October* album followed days later, on October 12, 1981. In November to December 1981 U2 was involved with a US tour. They started to record War on August 8, 1982. Scott Isler wrote in the *Trouser Press* (July 1, 1983) about the *War* album and a forty-two-day US tour. "Sunday, Bloody Sunday" opens the album. *Under the Blood Red Sky* followed on November 21, 1983. *The Unforgettable Fire* with producers Brian Eno and Daniel Lanois. "Pride (In the Name of Love)" was a hit single. *Rolling Stone* in March 1985 featured U2 in "Our Choice: Band of the 80s." Bono became involved with "Do They Know It's Christmas" and Live Aid, July 13, 1985. Bono went to Ethiopia September 1985 and in October joined Artists Against Apartheid. *Joshua Tree* burst out on March 4, 1987, and lifted U2 to further global attention. The singles "I Still Haven't Found What I'm Looking For" (May 1987) and "Where the Streets Have No Name" (August 1987). Bono spoke in the interview about the revolution that begins "at home in the heart" and the stimulation of the concert as "release." The band was involved in Conspiracy of Hope and Amnesty International benefits, June 4. He went to Central America in July. *Rattle and Hum* was released October 10–11, 1988 and went to number one.

The decade of the 1980s made clear what James Henke had written early in 1981. The band was one of the next greatest things. Bono could "break down the barrier between the stage and the audience."[42] That performance skill offered a connection, an interaction, a bridge to community. Of course, rock itself has developed as having potential for creating that bridge. Recordings distributed across a range of media bring us common references points. Most listeners will probably never know each other but they share these performances in common. The circulation of ideas in U2 songs and performances that support reflection on peace is valuable. Of course, to call this a global community is a stretch. This is a temporary in-concert collective. It is a widespread array of individuals who listen to the same songs. Even so, Visnja Cogan sees that U2 has reached across male and female and across generations and socioeconomic backgrounds. Rachel Seiler writes of the unity at U2 concerts as "a model for unity in daily life."[43]

An interviewer once asked Bono: "What's your definition of community?" He said, "This is the question that hangs in the sky over our heads at the moment. Through media, we have some strange faces in our backyard whom we weren't calling family until very recently, and we still don't really want to. But if you're going to enjoy your sneakers and your jeans made by developing countries you are already involved with those people. You cannot therefore just ignore some of the problems they're negotiating. They're living on your street. . . . Now that street goes around the globe."[44] And so U2 support activism. They are advocates of peace and reconciliation throughout the world. In "Pride (In the Name of Love)" and MLK we hear about Martin Luther King, Bishop Desmond Tutu, and antiapartheid in South Africa. U2 has allied with Amnesty International and highlighted the plight of prisoners like Aung San Suu Kyi, a female Burmese activist under house arrest. "New Years' Day" was inspired by the Polish Solidarity movement.

U2 AND THE CHRISTIAN IMAGINATION

U2 is charismatic, evangelical, and their lyrics can be read as sacred or secular. That is, Biblical allusions can be located throughout their songs, alongside an ambiguity that maintains openness to a secular reading as well. U2 appears to be available to the idea of divine inspiration and to spontaneous creation. Three of the band's four members (Bono/Paul Hewson, Edge/David Evans, Larry Mullen) have been involved with the Christian faith, although they dislike institutional church practices. U2 songs can be appreciated without any reference to Christian thought per se. However, some listeners have suggested that to have still not found what one is looking for is a spiritual search, as well as part of a life's journey. "She Moves in Mysterious Ways" could describe a person who is female and mysterious, or the Holy Spirit as anima mundi: God as a female dancer moving mysteriously through the world. Listeners can point to several U2 songs in this way: "40" is derived from Psalm 40 (How long must we sing this song?). "Gloria" takes three psalms: In you Lord (Psalm 31), O Lord have mercy (Psalm 51) and the exultate or rejoice of Psalm 33. "The Fly" draws upon Luke 10:18, with a star falling from the sky and the falsetto in the chorus suggesting the fall of Satan. This use of allegory, or double meaning, appears to be part of the U2's lyrical strategy, as some commentators have pointed out.[45]

U2 never wished to be identified as a Christian band. They did not fit that category. However, they let their faith infuse their work. They created from a concern for re-sacralization and re-enchantment of the world. They would be subtle in their suggestion of their spiritual inclinations and Gnostic in their approach and expression of Christianity. Music was the vehicle. The ambiguity of their lyrics would allow for broad appeal to a variety of audiences.[46]

In U2 faith turns toward social justice and toward the prophetic voice. In this sense, U2 is different from the American Christian evangelical right whose focus is on salvation. U2 focuses on the call for justice on earth more than personal salvation and heaven. Their radical Christianity, as Angela Pancella observes, is one that embraces the figure of Jesus in the temple throwing out the money-changers.[47]

The Troubles of Northern Ireland are brought into stark relief on "Sunday, Bloody Sunday." We hear the heartache in U2's recollection of the thirteen civil rights marchers massacred in Derry on January 30, 1972, in music that is driven by a relentless bass pulse. The conflict is interlaced with a sense of spiritual battle. Edge sings over the mention of Jesus, as if the Christ figure is covered over by voices from this world. The "victory" won by Jesus is obscured, covered by the Edge's crescendo on the chorus. This seems to be another suggestion of the hiddenness of "the Word." The faith holds that the hidden incarnate would arise and cast out the violent. Something fierce and apocalyptic seems to move through the song.[48]

The dialogical interplay between the religious and secular continues through U2's catalog. Galbraith suggests that the part of the rock audience that is secular and anti-Christian would presumably not be Biblically literate enough a group to grasp all of U2's allusions.[49] Yet, U2 would persist with their "between the lines" message. Galbraith points out that U2 will not hold their listeners to any specific message.

"Magnificent" is based on Luke 1. The Magnificat could be praise of art and life or the prayer of the Virgin Mary. It may be a love song, or a call to vocation as an artist, Galbraith suggests.[50] For Camille Paglia, the evangelical phrase is concerned with praise, a recognition of the divine presence in the world. It is a love song and "a manifesto of artistic mission." Paglia also suggests that to be born to be with you in this place and time must be about a God who works beyond space and time.[51] This song, as Galbraith points out, presents not only a Platonic conception of God. In Christian theology, God may be considered as not only as beyond space and time but also as immanent, as an incarnational God, a sacred "kingdom within."

U2: A VOICE FOR OUR COLLECTIVE FUTURE

Craig Delancey asks: "Why Listen to U2?"[52] Why be concerned with African debt, with Irish troubles, or with the other things that U2 is addressing? We might ask, are they visionary? Is Bono's and commitment prophetic? Is there an authenticity of concern? How are we to reconcile this with their global platform and their earnings and the corporate business goals that promote them? The answer is that these things are not mutually incompatible. U2 creates conscious, thoughtful rock.[53] As Rachel Seiler points out U2 concerts are rituals. Seiler says that U2 offers "an egalitarian model for relationships." And U2 encourages people to think for themselves.[54] "U2 matters" Scott Calhoun affirms. Rock history will show that. Craig Delancey sees in U2 "a vision of compassion and hope." He writes: "We must share with people a vision, even a utopian vision of a better world" and try to motivate them to "help us make it real."[55]

If we ask the ethical question whether we have a responsibility to future generations, Bono would likely answer this in the affirmative. Are we obliged to give to the needy to mitigate their suffering? How far does any responsibility of this kind extend? Beyond family and neighborhood to a distant place? What is the appropriate response? With our media, satellite communications and computers, we see more of that impoverished world. Bono appears to be on a mission to use his platform as fully as possible to provide relief and transform perspectives.

Immediately following the 1985 "We Are the World" Live Aid efforts, Bono and his wife traveled to Ethiopia. They stayed for several months, witnessing the conditions there. He continued his humanitarian activities throughout the 1990s. In 1999, Bono became a participant in Jubilee 2000 efforts to begin to eliminate African debt and appeal to the IMF and World Bank. In 2002, he engaged with Debt Aid Trade for Africa. The One campaign for the Development Relief Fund appeared in 2004. In 2006 Bono participated in Red relief efforts to relieve AIDS. He persists with Africa relief efforts.[56]

We can see that today we live in a world aching with human need. The United Nations Millennium Development Report of 2014 points at global hunger. It indicates that 1.2 billion people worldwide live in poverty. There 18,000 child deaths annually from preventable causes, 842 million people dealing with hunger, and 748 million living in conditions with unsafe water. (Child hunger and unsafe water conditions exist in US locations also.) Ethicist Peter Singer asserts that we should sacrifice to assist the poor of the world. If we have the ability to do this, we ought to. The libertarian rejects this view and contends that we have no moral obligation. When Bono puts his voice and personal action on the line it is likely not because he feels obliged; it is because he feels engaged, committed, and beckoned to do this.

WHERE DO WE GO FROM HERE?

Classic rock is alive not only as nostalgia but as a resource: a reference point for new creativity. The human imagination is infused by song, by literature, by creative art that is not timebound. In the song "Rock On," a one hit wonder from British rocker David Essex in 1973, the singer asked where we might "go from here" and if there was a way that was clear. The song itself has faded away like the blue jean queen he refers to but the rock music spirit has not. New generations will seize upon the sounds of the past and revise and redirect them. They will draw from the treasure chest of the past and will be inventive, creating rock that is fresh and new. All that is necessary is that the industry and audiences are supportive of this and "imagine" possibilities.

Here's an example: Ben arrived in the Freshman composition classroom everyday wearing a new rock band shirt. The band logos on those shirts ranged from those of The Doors and The Beatles to those of Pink Floyd and the Rolling Stones. They were all "classic rock" bands—not Imagine Dragons, Disturbed, or Shinedown. Not even the Foo Fighters. A similar encounter with eighteen-year-olds at a college raised a question for psychologist Ronald Riggio, who wrote "Why Do Young People Listen to Old Rock Music?"[57] He heard Led Zeppelin, The Beatles, The Rolling Stones, and other bands being played out the window of a dormitory. Riggio conjectured that some reasons for this might be more involved parenting and the "cultural enshrinement" of the sixties and seventies, or the fact that some musicians of the 1960s and 1970s were truly talented. We might also ask: Isn't there something in the rock music of the late 1960s and 1970s that is worth liking and appreciating? Or, is it a matter of hegemony: that baby boomers control the media these days? Might the lack of mainstream rock airplay—a top forty in the first months of 2019 that does not include a single rock song—send listeners off into their own spaces of listening?

The *Billboard* rock song chart for the first months of 2019 included singles by bands like Muse, Five Finger Death Punch, Disturbed, Ghost, Fall Out Boy, Greta van Fleet, Bring Me the Horizon. The gifted, perennial songwriter-performer Paul McCartney's video-songs "I Don't Know" and "Come on to Me" jumped onto the charts, preceding his album. Weezer, Jack White, Marilyn Manson, Smashing Pumpkins, Def Leppard, and Megadeth all showed up in the top fifty or so spots. With so much activity at festivals, in arenas, and in clubs throughout the world it is wrong to suggest that rock has faded to the margins. Rock bands continue to fill auditoriums. In 2018, Metallica broke attendance records in the Spokane Arena. System of a Down and Incubus drew 45,000 people to a concert in California. If a 2018 Guns N' Roses reunion tour grossed millions of dollars, was that merely nostalgia looking back in the rear-view mirror? Isn't it all cyclical? Rock history is moving in phases. Greta van Fleet comes to us sounding a bit like Led

Zeppelin, hair long, shirts flowing, looking like Percy Bysshe Shelley, or like they've stepped out of circa 1970. Band reunions are coming around again. The composition has a coda, a repeat sign. Styles are shifting, combining, weaving together into a new hybrid.

In 1979, Neil Young sang that rock can never die. In 2008 he declared that the days when rock might change the world had passed.[58] However, there are many fine younger artists with ideals and vision. Rock remains a force for change, a source for inspiration, and a platform for social concern. As David Crosby pointed out in *Stand and Be Counted* (2000): "Nobody kids themselves that they believe that he can solve the world's problems. We just want to make a difference."[59] Farm Aid, anti-apartheid concerts, African famine relief emerged in the 1980s. The impulse to launch big benefit concerts waned in the 1990s. The 9/11 tragedy brought back rock's voice of concern. In the new century, there have been concerts to assist with Haitian post-hurricane concerns, special needs like autism, and initiatives for African debt relief. There will be others and there will be new music. Where there is determination and vision, there is always the potential for change. The chords will change. Maybe the tune, amid the tensions of the times, will modulate to a new key. There will be those who seize the moment and play that tune. There will be those who listen, those who feel the rhythm, cheer, and hold onto the promise of rock and roll—with rock music imagination.

NOTES

1. Stephen Holden, "Rock and Roll Nostalgia: Look Back With Longing," *New York Times* (December 24, 1981). The emergence Holden addresses is the work of creativity and constructive imagination. Michael Polyani describes our knowledge of reality as "a vision" and recognizes that intuition and imagination are generally not regarded as a "rational way of making discoveries" ("The Creative Imagination," [pp. 147–63] *The Idea of Creativity*. Ed. Michael Krausz, Denis Duton, and Karen Bardsley. Leiden: Brill, 2009, p. 147). For Arthur Koestler art and science and "comic inspiration" may express emergent creativity: in both "a-ha" discovery and "ha-ha" laughter (pp. 271, 278). Arthur Koestler, *The Art of Creation*. New York: Macmillan, 1964.

2. Esther B. Fein, "Live Aid Concert is Aiming for the Sky," *New York Times* (July 12, 1985): C5.

3. Samuel G. Freedman, "Live Aid and the Woodstock Nation," *New York Times* (July 18, 1985): C19.

4. Freedman, C19. Greil Marcus is quoted by Freedman.

5. James F. Clarity and Warren Weaver, "Briefing: Live Aid," *New York Times* (November 1985). A30.

6. There was a satiric edge to this kind of questioning. Noel Gallagher of the band Oasis asked if any of the G8 leaders was really going to drop everything and change the African debt situation after listening to "Sweet Dreams" sung by Annie Lennox.

7. Net Aid, supervised by the United Nations Development Program, was modeled on the Live Aid concert. There was a request to forgive $371 billion in debt. A concert at Giants Stadium in the New Jersey Meadowlands went on for about eight hours with pop music acts like Puff Daddy, Sting, Jewel, Mary J. Blige, Sheryl Crow, and video clips of David Bowie, the Eurythmics, Bryan Adams, and others from Wembley Stadium near London. See Reebee

Garafalo, "Understanding Mega Events," *Peace Review* Vol. 5, No. 2 (1992): 189–98. Garafalo looks at Live Aid (1985), which raised $300 million for famine relief.

8. Midge Ure was a band member of Ultravox who later formed Visage with Billy Currie, Rusty Egan, and Steve Strange.

9. Jonathan D. Cohen, "Can Music Save Your Mortal Soul? A Bibliographical Survey of Rock as Religion," *Intermountain West Journal of Religious Studies* Vol. 7, Is. 1 (Fall 2010): 46–86, p. 12.

10. John Strausbough, *Rock Till You Drop: The Decline from Rebellion to Nostalgia*. London: Verso, 2001, p. 9.

11. The Who stopped performing a good while ago, after the passing of John Entwistle. The Who's Pete Townshend has moved on to other creative projects and Roger Daltrey has written his memoir, *Thanks A Lot Mr. Kibbelwhite: My Story*. New York: Henry Holt, 2018.

12. Lane Crothers, *Globalization and American Popular Culture*. Lanham: Rowman and Littlefield, 2013, p. 76.

13. Critics who see "world music," as a marketing strategy include: Timothy Brennan, "World Music Does Not Exist," *Discourse* Vol. 23, No. 1 (Winter 2001): 44–62; David Byrne, "Music: Crossing Music's Borders in Search of Identity, 'I Hate World Music.'" *The New York Times* (October 3, 1999); and Fred Goodman, *Voice* (August 6, 1990), cited in Robert Burnett, *The Global Jukebox: The International Music Industry*. London: Routledge, 2002. Critics who view world music as having some potential for global transformation include: Veit Erlmann 1996. Michael Chanan discusses international commerce and its impact on the recording industry. See Michael Chanan, *Repeated Takes: A Short History of Recording and Its Effects on Music*. London: Verso, 1995. Dana Da Silva explores the topic of whether music can change the world in "Music Can Change the World," *Africa Renewal* (December 2013), United Nations. Christina Nunez, "Music That Has Changed the World" *Global Citizen* (July 27, 2013) www.globalcitizen.org. Also see www.one.org/international.

14. This comment appears in the Introduction to *Music in the Post 9/11 World*. Ed. Jonathan Ritter and J. Martin Daughtry. New York: Routledge, 2007.

15. Kip Pegley and Susan Fast, "'America: A Tribute to Heroes': Music, Mourning and the Unified American Community," *Music in the Post 9/11 World*, 33–55.

16. Reebee Garafalo, "Pop Goes to War," *Music in the Post 9/11 World*, 1–32. September 11, 2001, was the scheduled release date for Bob Dylan's "Love and Theft" and Jay Z's *The Blueprint*. Aerosmith cancelled their shows. On September 21 a telethon raised $150 million for United Way with a concert that included Bruce Springsteen, U2, Stevie Wonder, Alicia Keys, Bon Jovi, and the Dixie Chicks. On October 20 the Madison Square Garden show included Paul McCartney, Elton John, Billy Joel, The Who (Townshend and Daltrey), David Bowie, and others. The next day Michael Jackson did a tribute at RFK Stadium in Washington, D.C. However, pop music buying declined some 15 percent in the New York City area and 5 percent overall according to Nielsen Sound Scan. Notoriously, Clear Channel censored songs.

17. Ibid.

18. Ibid.

19. Dave Marsh, "Bruce Springsteen Raises Cain," *Rolling Stone* (August 24, 1978).

20. John Steinbeck, *The Grapes of Wrath*. New York: Viking, 1939, pp. 362–63.

21. Dave Marsh, *Bruce Springsteen, Two Hearts*. New York: Routledge, 2004, p. 258.

22. Ronald D. Lankford, Jr. *Woman Singer-Songwriters in Rock: A Populist Rebellion in the 1990s*. Lanham: Scarecrow Press, 2010. Ronald D. Lankford, Jr. suggested that the singer-songwriter genre tended to be one that "lacked the rebellious nature of its rock pedigree" (xi). (This is arguable. Jackson Browne and Crosby and Stills, for example, were not lacking in this respect.) Lankford refers to singer-songwriters who were prominent in the 1970s, such as Joni Mitchell, Carole King, Carly Simon. In the mid to late 1980s emerged Suzanne Vega, Tracy Chapman, Melissa Etheridge. There was a re-emergence of female singer-songwriters between 1986 and 1988. He writes concerning Tori Amos, Sarah McLachlan, Sheryl Crow, Courtney Love, Liz Phair, P.J. Harvey. Helen Reddington, *The Lost Women of Rock Music: Female Musicians of the Punk Era*. London: Ashgate-Routledge, 2016. Judy Berman, "In the Age of Feminism Women Still Have to Scratch Their Names into the Musical Record," *The Village Voice* (July 22, 2016).

23. Susan McClary, "Women and Music on the Verge of a New Millennium," *Signs: Journal of Women in Culture and Society* Vol. 25, No. 4 (2000): 1283. McClary is cited by Kristin Lieb. Marian Meade, "Does Rock Degrade Women?" *New York Times* (March 14, 1971). Meade attacks The Rolling Stones' *Let It Bleed* album, "Under My Thumb," "Bitch," "Honky Tonk Woman," and Bob Dylan's "Just Like a Woman" for misogyny.

24. Kristin Lieb, *Gender, Branding and the Modern Music Industry*. New York and London: Routledge, 2013, pp. 20–23.

25. Jenny Garber, "Girls and Subcultures," *The Lost Women of Rock Music: Female Musicians in the Punk Era*. Ed. Helen Reddington. Aldershot: Ashgate, 2007, p. 3. Helen Davies, "All Rock is Homosocial: The Representation of Women in the British Music Press," *Popular Music* Vol. 20, Is. 3 (October 2001): 301–19.

26. Susan McClary, "Women and Music on the Verge of a New Millennium," *Signs: Journal of Women in Culture and Society* Vol. 25, No. 4 (January 2000): 1283–86.

27. Norma Coates, "Revolution Now: Rock and the Political Potential of Gender," (pp. 50–64) *Sexing the Groove: Popular Music and Gender*. Ed. Sheila Whiteley. London: Routledge, 1997.

28. Lieb, Introduction; Mavis Bayton, "How Women Became Rock Musicians," *Ethos*, University of Warwick (1989).

29. "Even as A Child I Felt Like an Alien," Patti Smith Interview, *The Guardian* (May 22, 2005).

30. Ibid.

31. For Theodor Adorno, the rise of mass culture included the capitalist ideological forces that pacified the proletariat, so they no longer knew their own real interests, were given trinkets, and forgot their revolutionary purpose. See Theodor Adorno, *Essays on Music*. Ed. Richard Leppert, trans. Susan H. Gillespie. University of California Press, 2002.

32. Garber, p. 3.

33. Joanne Gottlieb and Gayle Wald, "Smells Like Teen Spirit: Grrrl Riot, Revolution and Women in Independent Rock." *Microphone Fiends: Youth Music and Youth Culture*. Ed. Andrew Rose and Tricia Rose. New York: Routledge, 1994, p. 252.

34. Susan McClary, *Feminine Endings: Music Gender and Sexuality*. University of Minnesota Press, 1991, p. 149. There is patriarchal violence in rock, McClary concludes. Females are associated with desire (as in classical music with Salome, Carmen, Isolde). Madonna played upon this, Judith Butler contends that gender is performed. Norma Coates' interrogated masculine hegemony in rock as socially constructed. She recognized problems for women in rock and feeling alienation. "Revolution Now? Rock and the Political Potential of Gender," *Sexing the Groove, Popular Music and Gender*.

35. Mircea Eliade, *Myth and Reality*. Trans. Willard Trask. New York: Harper Torchbooks, 1968.

36. Kambrew McLeod, "Between Rock and a Hard Place: Gender and Rock Criticism," *Pop Music Press*. Ed. Steve Jones. Philadelphia: Temple University Press, 2002, p. 108–9. See Ken McLead, "Space Oddities: Aliens, Futurism, and Meaning in Popular Music," *Popular Music* Vol. 22, No. 3 (2003): 337–55.

37. Deborah Harding and Emily Nett, "Women in Rock Music," *Atlantis* 14 (Spring 1984): 72–80. Joanne Gottlieb and Gayle Wald, "Smells Like Teen Spirit: Grrrl Riot, Revolution and Women in Independent Rock," *Microphone Fiends: Youth Music and Youth Culture*. Ed. Andrew Rose and Tricia Rose. New York: Routledge, 1994, p. 252. Norma Coates (52–53) "Revolution Now? Rock and the Political Potential of Gender," *Sexing the Groove, Popular Music and Gender*. Mimi Schippers, *Rockin' Out of the Box: Gender Maneuvering in Alternative Hard Rock*. New Brunswick: Rutgers University Press, 2002, p. 23. Deena Weinstein, *Heavy Metal Music and Culture*. New York: Da Capo, 2000.

38. *Variety* interview with Steve Baltin, "As the Sun Sets on the Summer of Love's 50th Anniversary Jefferson Airplane's Grace Slick Gets Candid," *Variety* (September 1, 2017).

39. Orianthi is 34. Alanis Morrissette and Jewell have crossed the age of forty. P. J. Harvey has turned fifty and Liz Phair and Sheryl Crow have waved farewell to fifty. Alabama Shakes is fronted by female bassist Brittany Howard. Indeed, as rock has crossed the globe in the twenty-first century its voice is carried forth by more songstresses and that is a very good thing. We've

heard from Lita Ford, Siouxe and the Banshees, Gwen Stefani of No Doubt, Amy Lee of Evanescence, and bid farewell to Dolores O'Riordan of the Cranberries. John Harris suggests more interesting approaches appear to be coming from female musicians and more females are learning to play guitar than ever before. See John Harris, "For Rock to Survive It Will Have to Cut Down on the Testosterone," *The Guardian* (October 23, 2018).

40. Steve Morse, "U-2 Bounces Back," *Boston Globe* (November 1991). Denise Sullivan, "Song Review Mysterious Ways," AllMusic (1991). After 9/11/2001: U2 played at Madison Square Garden, New York on October 24, 25, 27, 2001. This was the "Elevation" tour. They also played at Super Bowl XXXVI (36): "Beautiful Day," "MLK," "Where the Streets Have No Name."

41. The Paulo Hewitt article in *Melody Maker* appears in *The U2 Reader: A Quarter Century of Commentary, Criticism, and Reviews*. Ed. Hank Borodwitz. Milwaukee: Hal Leonard, 2003, p. 7. The Tim Sommer article in Trouser Press (July 1, 1981) also appears in this book. James Henke, "Here Comes the Next Big Thing," *Rolling Stone* (February 19, 1981).

42. James Henke, "U2: Here Comes the Next Big Thing," *Rolling Stone* (February 19, 1981).

43. See Visnja Cogan, *An Irish Phenomenon*. London: Collins, 2006, rpt. New York: Pegasus, 2008. Benedict Anderson associated imagined community with nation and the circulation of print in *Imagined Communities: Reflections on the Origins and Spread of Nationalism*. New York: Verso, 2006. The notion of U2 community appears in Cogan 2008, p. 18. Rachel Seiler speaks of U2 "generating a sense of community" and "building cross-cultural bridges" ("Potent Crossroads: Where U2 and Progressive Meet," *Exploring U2*, p. 47).

44. Michka Assayas, *Bono on Bono*. New York: Riverhead. 2005, p. 219.

45. U2's relationship to Christian theology appears in several books. Steve Stockman, *Walk On: The Spiritual Journey of U2* (2001) was the first of these. Others followed: Robert Vagacs, *Political Fanatics: U2 in Theological Perspective*. Eugene, OR: Cascade Books, 2005; Christian Schoren, *One Step Closer: Why U2 Matters to Those Seeking God*. Ada, MI: Brazos Press, 2006; Stephen Catanzorite, *U2s Achtung Baby*. New York: Bloomsbury, 2007; and Greg Garrett, *We Get to Carry Each Other: The Gospel According to U2*. Louisville, KY: Westminster/John Knox Press, 2007.

46. See the extended analysis of U2's Biblical allusions and their lyrical strategy. Angela Pancella, "Biblical References in U2's Lyrics: Drawing Their Fish in the Sand Secret Biblical Allusions in the Music of U2," http://www.u2.com/lyrics/biblerefs.html. If one listens to October (October 1981) one can hear U2's various levels of meaning and their multivalent language makes use of Biblical symbols. Deane Galbraith, *Biblical Interpretation* Vol. 19 (2011): 181–222.

47. See Chris Heath's interview with Bono, "Once Upon a Time," in *Star Hits* (January 1987) which appears in Hank Bordowitz, *The U2 Reader*, p. 31.

48. See Deane Galbraith, "Drawing the Fish in the Sand: Secret Biblical Allusions in the Music of U2," *Biblical Interpretation* Vol. 19, No. 2 (2011): 181–222. The fish is a Christian symbol which was used by early Christian communities during times of political and social oppression.

49. Galbraith, "Drawing the Fish," p. 212.

50. Ibid.

51. Camille Paglia, *Salon* (July 2009). See also her remarks on U2 in "Obama's Hit and Big Miss," *Salon* (June 10, 2019).

52. Craig Delancey, "Why Listen to U2?" *U2 and Philosophy: How to Decipher an Atomic Bomb*. Ed. Mark A. Wrothall. Chicago: Open Court, 2006, pp. 123–34.

53. See Deena Weinstein, *Heavy Metal: The Music and Its Culture*. New York: Da Capo, 2000. Rachel E. Seiler, "Potent Crossroads: Where U2 and Progressive Meet," *Exploring U2: Is This Rock n' Roll? Essays on the Music, Work, and Influences of U2*. Ed. Scott Calhoun, Lanham: Scarecrow, 2012, p. 40.

54. Seiler, p. 49.

55. Scott Calhoun, *Exploring U2, Is This Rock and Roll: Essays on the Music, Work and Influence of U2*. Lanham: Scarecrow, 2011, p. xxvii. Craig Delancey, "Why Listen to U2?" (pp. 123–34) *U2 and Philosophy: How to Dismantle an Atomic Bomb*. Chicago: Open Court,

2006, p. 133. Scott Calhoun observes that academic papers about U2 began in the 1990s. He notes Bono turned to "humanitarian and philanthropic issues" (xxiv) in *Exploring U2*. They have "redefined the role of rock star" (xxvii).

56. The heart and soul of Geldof's and Bono's humanitarianism may be in their DNA, their Irish ancestral heritage: a historical awareness of the famine and a secularized call to mission. The Irish have long exemplified both the soul of the saints and the fierce commitment of the rebel, the poet's mystical romanticism and the loquacious talker's gift of the blarney. Bono has engaged with efforts for One, DATA for African debt relief, combatting AIDS, and Make Poverty History campaigns.

57. Ronald Riggio, "Why Do Young People Listen to Old Rock Music?" *Psychology Today* (August 2018).

58. Geir Moulson, "Music Can't Change the World," *Huffington Post*. Neil Young was interviewed by Geir Moulson, Associated Press. February 8, 2008.

59. David Crosby and David Bender, *Stand and Be Counted: A Revealing History of Our Times Through the Eyes of the Artists Who Helped Change Our World*. New York: Harper, 2000.

Selected Bibliography

Abbate, Carolyn. "What the Sorcerer Said." *Nineteenth Century Music* Vol. 12, Is. 3 (Spring 1989): 221–30.
Abbey, Eric. *Garage Rock and Its Roots: Musical Rebels and the Drive for Individuality.* Jefferson, NC: McFarland, 2006.
Abbey, Eric and Colin Helb, *Hardcore Punk, Punk, and Other Junk.* Lanham: Lexington, 2014.
Adorno, Theodor. *Essays on Music.* Ed. Richard Leppert, trans. Susan H. Gillespie. University of California Press, 2002.
Akkerman, Gregg. *Experiencing Led Zeppelin: A Listener's Companion.* Lanham: Rowman & Littlefield Publishers, 2014.
Assayas, Michka. *Bono on Bono.* New York: Riverhead, 2005.
Astor, Pete. *Richard Hell and the Voidoids Blank Generation*, 33 1/3. New York: Bloomsbury, 2014.
Attali, Jacques. *Noise: The Political Economy of Music.* Trans. B. Massumi. Minneapolis: University of Minnesota Press, 1985.
Attias, Bernardo Alexander. "Authenticity and Artifice in Rock and Roll: And I Guess That I Just Don't Care." *Rock Music Studies* Vol. 3, Is. 2 (2016): 131–47.
Auslander, Philip. *Performing Glam Rock and Theatricality in Popular Music.* Ann Arbor: University of Michigan Press, 2006.
———. *Liveness: Performance in a Mediatized Culture.* New York: Routledge, 1999, rpt. 2008.
Baker, Houston. *Blues, Ideology, and Afro-American Literature: A Vernacular Theory.* Chicago: University of Chicago Press, 1984.
Bakhtin, Mikhail. *The Dialogical Imagination: Four Essays.* Trans. Carol Emerson and Michael Holquist. Austin: University of Texas Press, 1981.
Baldwin, James. *The Price of the Ticket: Collected Non-Fiction.* New York: St. Martin's Press, 1985.
Bangs, Lester. *Psychotic Reactors and Carburetor Dung.* New York: Alfred A. Knopf, 1988.
Barthes, Roland. *Mythologies.* Trans, A Lavers. London: Paladin, 1973.
———. *Image, Music, Text.* Trans. S. Heath. London: Fontana, 1977.
Bayton, Mavis. *Frock Rock: Women, Performing Popular Music.* Oxford: Oxford University Press, 1998.
Beeber, Steven Lee. *Heebie Jeebies at CBGBs: A Secret History of Jewish Punk.* Chicago: Chicago Review Press, 2006.
Bennett, Andy. *Remembering Woodstock.* Aldershot: Ashgate, 2017.
———. "Heritage Rock: Rock Music Representation and Heritage Discourse." *Poetics* Vol. 37 (2009): 474–89.

Berger, Harris M. *Metal, Rock, and Jazz: Perceptions and the Phenomenology of Musical Experience*. Middletown: Wesleyan University Press, 1999.

Berger, Harris M., and M. T. Carroll, *Global Pop, Local Language*. Jackson: University Press of Mississippi, 2003.

Blythe, Will. "To Their Own Beat." *New York Times* (July 8, 2010).

Booker, Hugh and Yural Taylor. *Faking It: The Quest for Authenticity in Popular Music*. New York: W.W. Norton & Company, 2007.

Booth, Stanley. *The True Adventures of The Rolling Stones*. Chicago: Chicago Review Books, 1984, rpt. 2014.

Borodwitz, Hank. *The U2 Reader: A Quarter Century of Commentary, Criticism and Reviews*. Milwaukee: Hal Leonard, 2003.

Bottomley, Andrew J. "Play It Again: Rock Music Reissues and the Production of the Past for the Present," *Popular Music and Society* Vol. 39, No. 2 (2016): 151–74.

Bowden, Betsey. *Performed Literature: Words and Music of Bob Dylan* (1982). Lanham: University Press of America, 2001.

Bowman, Durrell. *Experiencing Rush: A Listener's Companion*. Lanham: Rowman and Littlefield, 2014.

Bowman, Durrell and Jim Burti. *Rush and Philosophy: Heart and Mind United*. Chicago: Open Court, 2011.

Boyd, Jenny and Holly George Warren. *Musicians in Tune: 75 Contemporary Musicians Discuss the Creative Process*. New York: Fireside, 1992.

Briggs, Jonathyne. *Globalization, Cultural Communities and Pop Music in France, 1958–1980*. New York and Oxford: Oxford University Press, 2015.

Burroway, Janet. "Books, Toxic Dreams." *New York Times* (April 27, 1997).

Burns, Gary. "Refab Four: Beatles for Sale in the Age of Music Video." *The Beatles Popular Music and Society*. Ed. Ian Inglis. New York: St. Martin's Press, 2000.

Burns, Lori, and Melisse Lafranse. *Disrupting Divas: Feminism, Identity and Popular Music*. London and New York: Routledge, 2001.

Byrne, David. *How Music Works*. London: Cannongate, 2012.

Calhoun, Scott. *U-2 Above, Across, Beyond: Interdisciplinary Assessments*. Lexington, 2014.

———. *Exploring U-2: Is This Rock and Roll: Essays on the Music, Work and Influence of U-2*. Lanham: Scarecrow Press, 2011.

Carroll, Rachel, and Adam Hansen, eds. *Lit Pop: Writing and Popular Music*. Farnham: Ashgate, 2014.

Carson, Mina, Tisa Lewis, and Susan M. Shaw. *Girls Rock! Fifty Years of Women Making Music*. Lexington: University Press of Kentucky, 2004.

Cateforis, Theo. *Are We Not New Wave?* Ann Arbor: University of Michigan Press, 2011.

Christgau, Robert. *Any Old Way You Choose It: Rock and Other Pop Music, 1967–1973*. New York: Penguin, 1973.

Christian, Elizabeth Barfoot. *Rock Brands: Selling Sounds in a Media Saturated Culture*. Lanham: Lexington, 2011.

Clarity, James F., and Warren Weaver, Jr. "Briefing: Live Aid." *New York Times* (November 12, 1985): A30.

Coates, Norma. "Revolution Now? Rock and the Political Potential of Gender." *Sexing the Groove: Popular Music and Gender*. Ed. Sheila Whiteley. London and New York: Routledge, 1997.

Cohen, Jonathan D. "Can Music Save Your Mortal Soul? A Bibliographic Survey of Rock as Religion." *Intermountain West Journal of Religion Studies* Vol. 7, Is. 1 (Fall 2010): 46–86.

Cohen, Sara. "Men Making a Scene: Rock Music and the Production of Gender." *Sexing the Groove: Popular Music and Gender*. Ed. Sheila Whitely. London: Routledge, 1997.

Copland, Aaron. *Music and Imagination*. Cambridge: Harvard University Press, 1952.

Covach, John C. *What's That Sound: An Introduction to Rock and Its History*. New York: W.W. Norton, 2006.

Covach, John C., and Graeme M. Boone. *Understanding Rock: Essays in Music Analysis*. New York and Oxford: Oxford University Press, 1997.

Cowart, David. "Don De Lillo: The Physics of *Great Jones Street*." *Pharmaceutical Philomela: Great Jones Street*. Athens: University of Georgia Press, 2002.

Coxkill, Gordon. Interview with David Bowie. *Bowie on Bowie: Encounters with David Bowie*. Ed. Sean Egan. Chicago Review Press, 2015.

Crafton, Lisa. "Tangle Matter and Ghost: U2, Leonard Cohen and Blakean Romanticism." *Rock and Romanticism: Blake, Wordsworth and Romanticism from Dylan to U2*. Ed. James Rovira. Lanham: Lexington Books, 2018.

Crazy Horse, Kandia. ed. *Rip It Up: The Black Experience in Rock n'Roll*. New York: Palgrave Macmillan, 2004.

Crosby, David, and David Bender. *Stand and Be Counted: A Revealing History of Our Times Through the Eyes of the Artists Who Helped Change Our World*. New York: Harper, 2000.

Crothers, Lane. *Globalization and American Popular Culture*. Lanham: Rowman and Littlefield, 2013.

Curtis, Jim. *Rock Eras: Interpretations of Music and Society, 1954–1984*. Bowling Green: Bowling Green State University Press, 1987.

Cusick, Suzanne. "Gender, Musicology and Feminism." *Rethinking Music*. Ed. Nicholas Cook and Mark Everist. Oxford: Oxford University Press, 1999.

Dalton, David. *Mr. Mojo Risin': Jim Morrison, The Last Holy Fool*. New York: St. Martin's Press, 1991.

Davies, Helen. "All Rock and Roll is Homosocial: The Representation of Women in the British Rock Press." *Popular Music* Vol. 20, Is. 3 (October 2001): 301–20.

Davies, Hunter. "Perfect Storm: The Further We Get from The Beatles the More Important They Become." *New Statesman* (August 22, 2014).

Davis, Fred. "Nostalgia, Identity, and the Current Nostalgia Wave." *Journal of Popular Culture* Vol. 11, Is. 2 (1977): 414–24.

De Curtis, Anthony. "Matters of Fact and Fiction: Interview with Don De Lillo." *Rolling Stone*. (November 17, 1988).

DeKoven, Marianne. *Utopia Limited: The Sixties and the Emergence of the Postmodern*. Durham: Duke University Press, 2004.

Delancey, Craig. "Why Listen to U2?" *U2 and Philosophy: How to Dismantle an Atomic Bomb*. Chicago: Open Court, 2006.

De Lillo, Don. *Great Jones Street*. Boston and New York: Houghton Mifflin, 1973.

Demsey, David. *John Coltrane Plays Giant Steps*. Milwaukee: Hal Leonard, 1996.

Dettmar, Kevin J.H., and William Richey. *Reading Rock and Roll: Authenticity, Appropriation, Aesthetic*. New York: Columbia University Press, 1999.

DiBlasi, Alex, and Victoria Willis. *Geek Rock*. Lanham: Lexington Books, 2014.

Dore, Florence. *Novel Sounds: Southern Fiction in the Age of Rock and Roll*. New York: Columbia University Press, 2018.

Downes, Julia. "Riot Grrrl: The Legacy and Contemporary Landscape of DIY Feminist Cultural Activism." *Riot Grrrl Revolution and Girl Style*. Ed. Nadine Monem. London: Black Dog, 2007.

Doyle, Roddy. *The Commitments*. New York: Vintage, 1987.

Du Bois, W.E.B. *The Souls of the Black Folk*. New York: Dover, 1994.

Easley, David. "Riff Schemes: Form and the Genre of Early American Hardcore Punk." *MTO: A Journal of the Society for Music Theory* Vol. 28, No. 1 (March 2015): 1–2.

Eastman, Jason T. *Southern Rock Revival*. Lanham: Lexington, 2017.

Egan, Jennifer. *A Visit to the Goon Squad*. New York: Alfred A. Knopf, 2010.

Egan, Sean ed. *Bowie on Bowie: Interviews and Encounters with David Bowie*. Chicago: Chicago Review Press, 2015.

Eliade, Mircea. *Myth and Reality*. Trans, Willard Trask. New York: Harper, 1968.

Elkins, James. *Six Stories from the End of Representation*. Palo Alto: Stanford University Press, 2008.

Ellison, Ralph. *Invisible Man*. New York: Random House, 1952.

———. *Shadow and Act*. New York: Vintage, Random House, 1964.

———. *Living with Music: Ralph Ellison's Jazz Writings*. Ed. Robert O'Meally. New York: Penguin/ Random House, 2000.

Encarnaceo, John. "Musical Structure as Narrative in Rock." *Portal: Journal of Multidisciplinary International Studies* Vol. 8, No. 1 (January 2011).
Everett, Walter. *Reading The Beatles: Cultural Studies and the Fab Four*. Albany: State University of New York Press, 2006.
———. *The Foundations of Rock: From Blue Suede Shoes to Suite: Judy Blue Eyes*. Oxford and New York: Oxford University Press, 2008.
———. *Expressions in Pop-Rock Music: Analytical and Critical Essays*. London and New York: Routledge, 2007.
———. "Swallowed by a Song: Paul Simon's Crisis of Chromaticism." *Understanding Rock, Essays in Music Analysis*. Ed. John C. Covach and Graeme Boone. New York and Oxford: Oxford University Press, 1997.
Faulk, Barry J. "Love and Lists in Nick Hornsby's *High Fidelity*." *Cultural Critique* Vol. 66 (2007): 153–76.
Fein, Esther B. "Live Aid Concert is Aiming for the Sky." *New York Times* (July 12, 1985): C5.
Field, Steven. "A Sweet Lullaby for World Music." *Public Culture* Vol. 12, No. 1 (2000): 145–71.
Firchow, Peter. *Huxley's Brave New World*. Ed. David Garrett Izzo. Jefferson, NC: McFarland, 2008.
Fowlie, Wallace. *Rimbaud and Jim Morrison: A Memoir*. Durham: Duke University Press, 1993.
Freedman, Samuel G. "Live Aid and the Woodstock Nation." *New York Times* (July 18, 1985): C19.
Frith, Simon. *Performing Rites: On the Value of Popular Music*. Cambridge: Harvard University Press, 1996.
Gaiman, Neil. Foreword. Samuel R. Delany, *Einstein Intersection*. Middletown: Wesleyan University Press, 1998. vii.
Galbraith, Deane. "Drawing the Fish in the Sand: Secret Allusions in the Music of U2." *Biblical Interpretation* Vol. 19, No. 2. (2011): 191–222.
Garber, Jenny. "Girls and Subcultures." *The Lost Women of Rock. Female Musicians in the Punk Era*. Aldershot: Ashgate, 2007.
Garcia, Jerry, Charles Reich and Jann Wenner. "Garcia: Signpost to New Space." *Rolling Stone* (1972).
Gates, David. "A Fan's Notes, The Boomer Files." *Newsweek* Vol. 148, Is. 3 (July 17, 2006).
Gates, Henry Louis. *The Signifying Monkey*. New York and Oxford: Oxford University Press, 1988.
Gennaro, Rocco and Casey Harison, *The Who and Philosophy*. Lanham: Lexington, 2016.
Gill, Andy. *Classic Bob Dylan, 1962–1969, My Back Pages*. London: Carlton, 1998.
Gilroy, Paul. "Bold as Love: Jimi's Afrocyberdelia. And the Challenge of the Not-Yet." *Critical Quarterly* (December 2004).
Gioia, Ted. *Delta Blues: The Life and Times of the Mississippi Masters Who Revolutionized American Music*. New York: W.W. Norton, 2008.
Godbey, Matt. "Gentrification, Authenticity and White Middle-Class in Jonathan Lethem's Fortress of Solitude." *Arizona Quarterly* Vol. 64, Is. 1 (2008).
Gordon, Robert. *Can't Be Satisfied: The Life and Times of Muddy Waters*. New York and Boston: Little Brown, 2002.
Gracyk, Theodore. *Rhythm and Noise: An Aesthetics of Rock*. Durham: Duke University Press, 1996.
Grimm, Boca. "Flashback: David Bowie's Failed Attempt to Adapt George Orwell's *1984*." *Rolling Stone* (June 23, 2017).
Guralnick, Peter. *Feel Like Going Home: Portraits in Blues and Rock n' Roll*. New York: Perrenial, 1971.
———. *Searching for Robert Johnson*. New York: E.P. Dutton, 1989.
———. *Careless Love: The Unmaking of Elvis Presley*. New York: Little Brown, 1999.
Hamelman, Steven. *But Is It Garbage? On Rock and Trash*. Athens: University of Georgia Press, 2004.
Hamilton, Jack. *Just Around Midnight*. Cambridge: Harvard University Press, 2016.

Harding, Deborah, and Emily Nett, "Women in Rock Music." *Atlantis* Vol. 14 (Spring 1984): 72–80.
Hargreaves, David, Dorothy Miell, and Raymond McDonald. *Musical Imaginations: Multidisciplinary Perspectives on Creativity.* Oxford: Oxford University Press, 2012.
Harman, Willis and Howard Rheingold. *Higher Creativity.* New York: Tarcher Perigree, 1984.
Hart, Mickey. *Drumming at the Edge of Magic: A Journey into the Spirit of Percussion.* Novato, CA: Grateful Dead Books, 1990.
Headlam, David. "Blues Transformations of the Music of Cream." *Understanding Rock: Essays in Music Analysis.* Ed. John C. Covach and Graeme Boone. Oxford and New York: Oxford University Press, 1997.
Hell, Richard. *I Dreamed I Was a Very Clean Tramp: An Autobiography.* New York: HarperCollins, 2013.
Henke, James. "U2: Here Comes the Next Big Thing." *Rolling Stone* (February 19, 1981).
Hilburn, Robert. "Some Glory Days Revisited." *Los Angeles Times* (November 8, 1998).
Hillman. James. *A Blue Fire.* Ed. Thomas Moore. New York: Harper, 1997
Holden, Stephen. "Rock and Roll Nostalgia: Looking Back with Longing." *Rolling Stone* (December 24, 1981).
Holinghaaus, Wade. *Philosophizing Rock: Dylan, Hendrix, Bowie.* Lanham: Scarecrow, 2013.
Holm-Hudson, Kevin, ed. *Progressive Rock Reconsidered.* New York and London, Routledge, 2002.
Holmes, John Clellan. *The Horn.* New York: Random House, 1958.
Hogsette, David S., "Swimming Against the Stream: Rush's Romantic Critique of Their Modern Age." *Rock and Romanticism: Blake, Wordsworth and Romanticism from Dylan to U2.* Ed. James Rovira. Lanham: Lexington Books, 2018.
Hubbs, Nadine. "The Imagination of Pop-Rock Criticism." *Expression in Pop-Rock Music: A Collection of Critical and Analytical Essays.* London and New York: Routledge, 2007.
Hughes, Bryn. "Harmonic Expectation in 12 Bar Blues Progressions." Florida State University, dissertation, 2011.
Hughes, Evan. *Literary Brooklyn: The Writers of Brooklyn and the Story of American City Life.* New York: Henry Holt, 2011.
Hughes, Langston. *The Big Sea.* New York: Alfred A. Knopf, 1940.
Huxley, Aldous. *Brave New World* (1932). New York: Harper Perennial, 2006.
———. *The Letters of Aldous Huxley.* Ed. Grover Smith. New York: Harper and Row, 1969.
———. *The Perennial Philosophy.* New York: Harper, 1945.
Inglis, Ian. *Performance and Popular Music.* Aldershot: Ashgate, 2006.
Irwin. William, ed. *Black Sabbath and Philosophy: Mastering Reality.* UK: Wiley-Blackwell, 2013.
Izzo, David Garret. *Huxley's Brave New World.* Jefferson: McFarland, 2008.
James, William. *Varieties of Religious Experience.* (1902) Cambridge: Harvard University Press, 1985.
———. "Great Men, Great Thoughts and the Environment." *Atlantic Monthly* Vol. 46 (October 1880): 441–59.
Jefferson, Margo. "Ripping off Black Music." *Harper's.* (January 1973).
Jones, James T. *Post-Jungian Criticism.* Ed. James S. Baumlin et.al. Albany: State University of New York Press, 2004.
Jones, Leroi (Amiri Baraka), *Blues People: Black Music in White America* (1963). rpt. New York: HarperCollins, 1999.
Jones, Steve. *Pop Music and the Press.* Philadelphia: Temple University Press, 2003.
Kearney, Mary Celeste. *Gender and Rock.* Oxford: Oxford University Press, 2017.
Kerouac, Jack. *On the Road* in *Road Novels 1957–1960.* New York: Library of America, 2007.
Kitts. Thomas. *John Fogerty: An American Son.* New York and London: Routledge, 2016.
———. ed. *"Finding Fogerty" Interdisciplinary Readings of John Fogerty and Creedence Clearwater Revival.* Lanham: Lexington, 2013.
———. *Ray Davies: Not Like Everybody Else.* New York and London: Routledge, 2008.
Kotarba, Joseph. *Baby Boomer Rock n' Roll Fans.* Lanham: Scarecrow, 2013.

Kramer, Lawrence. *Musical Meaning: Toward a Critical History*. Berkeley: University of California Press, 2002.

———. *Music and Poetry: The Nineteenth Century and After*. Berkeley: University of California Press, 1984.

———. "Dangerous Liaisons: The Literary Text in Musical Criticism." *Nineteenth Century Music* Vol. 13, Is. 2 (1989): 159–67.

———. "Musical Narratology: A Theoretical Outline." *Indiana Theory Review* Vol. 12 (1991): 141–62.

Kramer, Michael. *The Republic of Rock: Music Citizenship and the Sixties Counterculture*. New York and Oxford, 2013.

Kristiansen, Lars and Blaney, et. al. *Screaming for a Change: Articulating a Unifying Philosophy of Punk Rock*. Lanham: Lexington, 2010.

Lankford, Ronald D. *Women Singer-Songwriters in Rock: A Populist Rebellion in the 1990s*. Lanham: Scarecrow Press, 2010.

Leonard. Marion. *Gender and the Music Industry: Rock Discourse and Girl Power*. Aldershot: Ashgate, 2007.

Lethem, Jonathan. *The Fortress of Solitude*. Garden City: Doubleday, 2003.

———. *You Don't Love Me*. New York: Vintage, 2007.

Levine, Robert. "Music Labels Look to DVD's as Sales of CDs Decline." *New York Times* (December 27, 2004): C4.

Levi-Strauss, Claude. *The Savage Mind*. Trans. George Wedenfeld. Chicago: University of Chicago Press, 1966.

Lieb, Kristin J. *Gender, Branding, and the Modern Music Industry*. London and New York: Routledge, 2013.

Lloyd, Richard. *Everything is Combustible: CBGBs and Five Decades of Rock and Roll: The Memories of an Alchemical Guitarist*. Mount Desert, ME: Beech Hill Publishing, 2017.

Lodato, Suzanne M., and David Francis Urrows, eds. *Word and Music Studies: Essays on Music and the Spoken Word and on Surveying the Field*. Amsterdam and New York: Rodopi, 2005.

Lomax, Alan. *The Land Where the Blues Began*. New York: Pantheon, 1993.

Lorenz, Konrad. *Aggression*. London: Methuen, 1963.

Lott, Eric, *Love and Theft: Blackface Minstrelsy and the American Working Class* (1993). Oxford and New York: Oxford University Press, 2013.

Luter, Matthew. *Understanding Jonathan Lethem*. Columbia: University of South Carolina Press. 2015.

Macan, Edward. *Rocking the Classics*. Oxford: Oxford University Press, 1997.

———. *Endless Enigma: A Biography of Emerson, Lake and Palmer*. Chicago: Open Court, 2006.

———. "Reply to Chris Matthew Sciabbara." *Journal of Ayn Rand Studies* Vol. 5, No. 1 (2003): 173–88.

Malvinni, David. *Experiencing the Rolling Stones: A Listener's Companion*. Lanham: Rowman and Littlefield, 2016.

———. *The Grateful Dead and the Art of Rock Improvisation*. Lanham: Scarecrow Press, 2013.

Marcus, Greil. *Mystery Train: Images of America in Rock n' Roll Music*. New York: E.P. Dutton, 1975. rpt. New York: Plume, 2008.

Marcuse, Herbert. *Marxism, Revolution, and Utopia: The Collected Papers of Herbert Marcuse*. Ed. Douglas Kellner and Clayton Pierce. London and New York: Routledge, 2014.

Marsh, Dave. *Bruce Springsteen: Two Hearts*. New York and London: Routledge, 2004.

Marshall, Lee. *Bootlegging: Romanticism and Copyright in the Music Industry*. London Sage Productions, 2005.

Martin, Bill. *Listening to the Future: The Time of Progressive Rock, 1968–1978*. Chicago: Open Court, 1998.

———. *Music of Yes: Structure and Vision in Progressive Rock*. Chicago: Open Court, 1997.

McClary, Susan. *Feminine Endings: Music, Gender, and Sexuality*. Minneapolis: University of Minnesota Press, 1991.

———. *Conventional Wisdom: The Content of Musical Form*. Berkeley: University of California Press, 2000.

———. "Women and Music on the Verge of a New Millennium." *Signs: Journal of Women in Culture and Society* Vol. 25, Is. 4 (2000): 1283–86.

McClary, Susan and Robert Walser, "Start Making Sense! Musicology Wrestles with Rock." *On the Record: Pop, Rock, and the Written Word*. Ed. Simon Frith and Andrew Goodwin. New York: Pantheon, 1990.

McDonald, Chris. "Open Secrets, Individualism and Middle-Class Identity in the Songs of Rush." *Popular Music and Society* Vol. 31 (2008): 313–28.

McLeod, Kebrew. "1/2 a Critique of Rock Criticism in North America." *Popular Music* Vol. 20, Is. 1 (January 2011): 47–60.

McNally, Dennis. *Desolate Angel: Jack Kerouac, The Beat Generation and America*. Cambridge: Da Capo Press, 2003.

———. *On Highway 61: Music, Race and the Evolution of Cultural Freedom*. Berkeley and New York: Counterpoint, 2014.

Meisel, Perry. *The Myth of Popular Culture: From Dante to Dylan*. New York: John Wiley and Sons, 2009.

———. *The Cowboy and the Dandy: Crossing Over from Romanticism to Rock and Roll*. Oxford: Oxford University Press, 1999.

Milward, John. *Crossroads: How the Blues Shaped Rock n' Roll*. Boston: Northeastern Press, 2013.

Moist, Kevin M. "Introduction—Global Psychedelia in Counterculture." *Rock Music Studies* Vol. 5, No. 3 (2018): 197–204.

Moody, Rick. *Garden State*. New York: Pushcart Press, 1992.

Moore, Allan F. "Jethro Tull and the Case for Modernism in Mass Culture." *Analyzing Popular Music*. Ed. Allan F. Moore. Cambridge: Cambridge University Press, 2003.

Moore, Allan F., and Remy Martin. *Rock: The Primary Text: Developing a Musicology of Rock*. London: Ashgate, Routledge 2018.

Morrison, Jim. *The Lords and the New Creatures*. London: Omnibus, 1985.

———. *The American Night*. New York: Villard, Random House, 1991.

———. *The Writings of Jim Morrison, Vol. II*. New York: Vintage, Random House, 1990.

Murray, Albert. *Stomping the Blues*. Minneapolis: University of Minnesota Press, 1976.

———. *The Hero and the Blues* (1973). rpt. New York: Penguin, 1996.

Myers, Paul. *A Wizard, True Star: Todd Rundgren in the Studio*. London: Jawbone Press, 2010

Nisenson, Eric. *Ascension: John Coltrane and His Quest*. New York: Da Capo, 1995.

Nora, Pierre. *Realms of Memory*. New York: Columbia University Press, 1996–1998.

O'Connor, Michael, Hyun-Ah Kim, and Christina Labriola. *Music, Theology and Justice*. Lanham: Lexington, 2017.

O'Dair, Barbara, ed. *Trouble Girls: The Rolling Stone Book of Women in Rock*. New York: Random House, 1997.

Orwell, George. "The Scientists Take Over." *Manchester Review* (August 16, 1945).

Palmer, Robert. *Deep Blues: A Musical and Cultural History of the Mississippi Delta*. New York: Penguin, 1992.

Pareles, Jon. "The Stars Give a Party for a Global Web Site." *New York Times* (October 11, 1999): C1.

Pattison, Robert. *The Triumph of Vulgarity*. Oxford and New York: Oxford University Press, 1987.

Peacock, James. *Jonathan Lethem*. Manchester: Manchester University Press, 2012.

Peart, Neil. *Far and Near: Days Like These*. Toronto: ECW Press, 2014.

Peck, Dale. "Rick Moody is the Worst Writer of His Generation." *New Republic* (July 1, 2002).

Pegg, Nicholas. *The Complete David Bowie*. London: Titan, 2011.

Peterson, Richard A. "Why 1955? Explaining the Advent of Rock Music." *Popular Music* Vol. 9, Is. 1 (January 1990): 97–116.

Pollack, Bruce. *By the Time We Get to Woodstock: The Great Rock and Roll Revolution of 1969*. Milwaukee and New York: Backbeat Books, 2009.

Poster, Mark. *The Mode of Information: Poststructuralism and the Social Context*. Cambridge: Polity, 1990.
Phillipou, Michelle. *Death Metal and Music Criticism*. Lanham: Lexington, 2012.
Powers, Devon. "Rock Criticism's Public Intellectuals." *Popular Music and Society* (August 2010): 533–48.
Rabaka, Reiland. *Civil Rights Music: Soundtrack of the Civil Rights Movement*. Lanham: Lexington, 2016.
Rand, Ayn. *The Romantic Manifesto* (1969). New York: New American Library, Signet, 1971.
Rega, Moti. *Pop Rock Music: Aesthetic Cosmopolitanism in Late Modernity*. Malden, MA: Polity, 2013.
Reist, Nancy. "Clinging to the Edge of Magic: The Shamanic Aspects of The Grateful Dead." *Perspectives on the Grateful Dead: Critical Writings*. Ed. Robert G. Weiner. Westport, CT: Greenwood, 1999.
Remnick, David. Interview with Philip Roth. *The New Yorker* (May 8, 2000): 76–89.
Reynolds, Simon and Joy Press. *The Sex Revolts: Gender Rebellion and Rock n' Roll*. Cambridge: Harvard University Press, 1995.
Rhodes, Carl. "Outside the Gates of Eden: Utopia and Work in Rock Music." *Group and Organization Management* Vol 32, No. 1 (February 2007): 22–49.
Ricks, Christopher. *Dylan's Vision of Sin*. New York: Echo/HarperCollins, 2005.
Riggio, Ronald. "Why Do Young People Listen to Old Music?" *Psychology Today* (August 2018).
Rimbaud, Arthur. *Arthur Rimbaud Complete Works*. Trans. Paul Schmidt. New York: Harper Colophone, 1975.
Riordan, James. *Break on Through: The Life and Death of Jim Morrison*. New York: William Morrow, 1992.
Rodden, John. *George Orwell: The Politics of Literary Reputation*. New York and Oxford: Oxford University Press, 1989.
Root, Douglas T. "William Blake: The Romantic Alternative." *Rock and Romanticism: Blake, Wordsworth and Rock from Dylan to U2*. Ed. James Rovira. Lanham: Lexington Books, 2018.
Roszak, Theodore. *The Making of the Counterculture*. London: Faber and Faber, 1970.
Rouget, Gilbert. *Music and Trance: A Theory of the Relations Between Music and Possession*. Chicago: University of Chicago Press, 1985.
Rovira, James, ed. *Rock and Romanticism: Blake, Wordsworth and Rock from Dylan to U2*. Lanham: Lexington Books, 2018.
Sanjek, David. "The Bloody Heart of Rock n' Roll: Images of Popular Music in Contemporary Speculative Fiction." *Journal of Popular Culture* Vol. 28, No. 1 (1995): 179–209.
Sannaeh, Kalefah. "The Persistence of Progressive Rock." *New Yorker* (June 19, 2017).
Sartre, Jean Paul. "Existentialism is a Humanism." *Existentialism from Dostoevsky to Sartre*. Ed. Walter Kaufmann. New York: Meridian, 1956.
Scanlan, John. *Easy Riders: Rolling Stones On the Road in America, From Delta Blues to 70s Rock*. London: Reaktion Books, 2015.
Schaffer, R. Murray. *The Soundscape: Our Sonic Environment and the Turning of the World*. Rochester, VT: Destiny, 1994.
Scher, Stephen Paul. "Interrelations of Music and Literature." Modern Language Association, 1982.
Sheinbaum, John J. *Good Music: What It Is and Who Gets to Decide*. Chicago: University of Chicago Press, 2019.
Sciabarra, Chris Matthew. "Rand, Rush, and Rock." *The Journal of Ayn Rand Studies* Vol. 4, No. 1 (2003): 161–85.
Segrest, James. *Moaning at Midnight: The Life and Times of Howlin' Wolf*. New York: Da Capo, 2005.
Seiler, Rachel E. "Potent Crossroads: Where U2 and Progressive Meet." *Exploring U2: Is This Rock and Roll, Essays on the Music, Work and Influence of U2*. Ed. Scott Calhoun. Lanham: Scarecrow Press, 2012.

Shaw, Russell. "Sorry, Neil Young. Music Could Never Change the World." *Huffington Post* (December 2017).
Shepherd, John. *Tin Pan Alley*. London and New York: Routledge, Kegan Paul, 1982.
Shepherd, John. "Musicology and Popular Music Studies." *Music as Social Text*. Cambridge: Blackwell, 1991.
Shumway, David. "Rock and Roll as a Cultural Practice." *South Atlantic Quarterly* Vol. 90, No. 4 (Fall 1991): 753–69.
Shumway, David R. "Rock n' Roll Soundtracks and the Production of Nostalgia." *Cinema Journal* Vol. 38, No. 2 (1999): 36–51.
Simonelli, David. *Working Class Heroes: Rock Music and British Society in the 1960s and 1970s*. Lanham: Lexington Books, 2013.
Smith, Eric D. *Globalization, Utopia and Postcolonial Science Fiction*. New York: Palgrave Macmillan, 2012.
Smith, Patti. "Todd's Electric Exploration: Rock and Roll for the Skull." *Creem* (April 1973): 56–57.
Smyth, Gerry. *Music in Contemporary British Fiction: Listening to the Novel*. Palgrave Macmillan, 2008.
Spector, Stanley J. "The Grateful Dead and Friedrich Nietzsche: Transformation in Music and Consciousness." *Countercultures and Popular Music*, Ed. Sheila Whiteley and Jedediah Sklaver. Farnham: Ashgate, 2014.
Staubmann, Helmut, ed. *The Rolling Stones: Sociological Perspectives*. Lanham: Lexington Books, 2013.
Steinbeck, John. *The Grapes of Wrath* (1939). New York: Penguin, 1985.
Stephenson, Ken. *What to Listen for in Rock: A Stylistic Analysis*. New Haven: Yale University Press, 2002.
Strausbough, John. *Rock 'Till You Drop: The Decline from Rebellion to Nostalgia*. London: Verso, 2001.
Strunk, Oliver. *Source Readings in Music History*. Vol. 6. Ed. Ruth Solie and Leo Treitler. New York: W.W. Norton, 1997.
Stump, Paul. *The Music's All That Matters: A History of Progressive Rock*. London: Quartet, 1997, rpt. Whitstable, Kent: Harbour Books, 2010.
Sylvan, Robin. *Traces of the Spirit: The Religious Dimensions of Popular Music*. New York: New York University Press, 2002.
Tagg, Philip. "Analyzing Popular Music: Theory, Method and Practice." *Popular Music* Vol. 2 (1987): 35–65.
Tandy, Gary. "When the Light That's Lost Within Us Reaches the Sky: Jackson Browne's Romantic Vision." *Rock and Romanticism: Blake, Wordsworth and Romanticism from Dylan to U2*. Ed. James Rovira. Lanham: Lexington Books, 2018.
Tart, Charles. *Transpersonal Psychologies*. Garden City: Doubleday, 1975.
Temperley, David. *The Musical Language of Rock*. New York and Oxford: Oxford University Press, 2018.
Thompson, Dave. *Turn It on Again: Peter Gabriel, Phil Collins and Genesis*. San Francisco: Backbeat Books, 2005.
———. *True Adventure on the Front Lines of Punk, 1976–1977*. Chicago: Chicago Review Press, 2009.
Tracy, Steven C. "The Blues Novel." *Cambridge Companion to the African American Novel*. Ed. Maryemma Graham. Cambridge: Cambridge University Press, 2004.
———. ed. *Write Me a Few of Your Lines*. Amherst: University of Massachusetts Press, 1999.
Trynka, Paul. *Brian Wilson, The Making of the Rolling Stones*. New York: Plume, 2014.
Usmani, Basmin. "Because Punk Still Rocks." *New York Times* (September 17, 2016).
Van Gelder, Lawrence. "Arts, Briefly." *New York Times* (June 1, 2005): 2.
Varrale, Simone. *Globalization, Music, and Cultures of Distinction: The Rise of Pop Music Criticism in Italy*. New York: Palgrave Macmillan, 2016.
Veggian, Henry. *Understanding Don De Lillo*. Columbia: University of South Carolina Press, 2015.

Wald, Gayle. "Just a Girl? Rock Music, Feminism, and the Cultural Construction of Female Youth." *Signs: Journal of Women in Culture and Society* Vol. 23, No. 3 (Spring 1998): 585–610.

Walker, Luke. "Tangled Up in Blake: The Triangular Relationship among Dylan, Blake, and the Beats." *Rock and Romanticism: Blake, Wordsworth and Romanticism from Dylan to U2*. Ed. James Rovira. Lanham: Lexington Books, 2018.

Walser, Robert. *Running with the Devil: Power, Gender, and Madness in Heavy Metal Music*. Middletown: Wesleyan University Press, 1993.

Washburne, Christopher J., and Maiken Derno. *Bad Music: The Music We Love to Hate*. London and New York: Routledge, 2004.

Watt, Ian. *The Rise of the Novel*. London: Chatto and Windus, 1957.

Weber, Erin Torkelson. *The Beatles and the Historians: An Analysis of Writings About the Fab Four*. Jefferson: McFarland, 2016.

Weinman, Jaime. "The Demise of Rock and Roll Nostalgia." *Macleans* (October 1, 2016).

Weinstein, Deena. "The Globalization of Metal." *Heavy Metal Rules the Globe. Heavy Metal Music Around the World*. Eds. Harris Berger and Jeremy Wallach. Durham: Duke University Press, 2011.

———. *Heavy Metal: The Music and Its Culture*. Boston: Da Capo Press, 2000.

Weiskopf, Walt, and Ramon Rider. *Coltrane, A Player's Guide to His Harmony*. New Albany, IN: J. Aebersaid, 1991.

White, Bob W., ed. *Music and Globalization: Critical Encounters*. Bloomington: Indiana University Press, 2012.

Whiteley, Sheila. *The Space Between the Notes*. London and New York: Routledge, 1992.

———. ed. *Sexing the Groove: Popular Music and Gender*. London and New York: Routledge, 1997.

———. *Progressive Rock and the Psychedelic Coding in the Music of Jimi Hendrix*. Cambridge: Cambridge University Press, 1990.

Wicke, Peter. *Rock Music: Culture, Aesthetics and Sociology*. Cambridge: Cambridge University Press, 1990.

Willis, Ellen. *The Essential Ellen Willis: Out of the Vinyl Deeps*. Ed. Nona Willis Aronowitz. Minneapolis: University of Minnesota Press, 2014.

———. *Beginning to See the Light*. New York: Alfred A. Knopf, 1981.

Wolf, Werner. *The Musicalization of Fiction: A Study in the Theory and History of Intermediality*. Amsterdam: Rodopi, 1999.

Womack, Kenneth. "The Beatles as Modernists." *Music and Literary Modernism*. Ed. Robert McParland. Newcastle-on-Tyne: Cambridge Scholars Press, 2009.

Womack, Kenneth, and Kathryn B. Cox. *The Beatles' Sergeant Pepper and the Summer of Love*. Lanham: Lexington, 2017.

Wyman, Bill, and Richard Havers, *Bill Wyman's Blue Odyssey*. London and New York: DK Publishing, 2001.

Yagoda, Ben. *The B Side: The Death of Tin Pan Alley and the Rebirth of the Great American Song*. New York: Penguin, 2015.

Zak III, Albin. *The Poetics of Rock: Cutting Tracks, Making Records*. Berkeley: University of California Press, 2011.

Zollo, Paul. *Songwriters on Songwriting*. New York: Da Capo. 2003.

Index

2112 (Rush), 89, 104–105, 107, 110

Abba, 175
Abbate, Carolyn, 141
Abbey, Eric, 96
Abbey Road, 66, 71
Abrahams, Mick, 71
Abrahams, Peter, 152
Abrams, M. H., 127
Adorno, Theodor, 99, 184n31
African relief, 159, 161, 177, 180
Airto, 130
Alan Parsons Project, 142
alchemy, 110
alienation, 9, 92, 94, 103, 107, 115, 130
Alpert, Richard (Ram Dass), 45, 51
Altamont, 50
Alter Bridge, 65
alternate tuning, 2
"American Pie," 55–56
American Record Company, 23
Anderson, Ian, 71
Anderson, Jon, 67, 68–70
Anderson, Kevin J., 89, 109–110
The Animals, 21
Anthony, John, 72
Arendt, Hannah, 99
Armstrong, Louis, 18
Ashford, Rosalind, 175
Asia, 70
Atlantic Records, 30

authenticity, 4, 7, 20, 21, 63, 87, 94, 98, 116, 137, 139, 171, 173

Baba, Meher, 28
Bach, J. S., 64–65
Badfinger, 75, 80, 83
Baez, Joan, 175
Baker, Ginger, 29–30
Baker, Houston, 17
Bakhtin, Mikhail, 13n17, 146
Baldwin, James, 20
Balin, Marty, 47, 54, 174
Ballard, Florence, 175
The Band, 75, 123
Bangs, Lester, 11, 64, 66–67, 154
Banks, Tony, 71–72
Barbauld, Anna, 175
Barre, Martin, 71
Barron, Frank, 4
Bartok, Bela, 44, 64, 67
The Beach Boys, 47, 64, 76
Beard, Annette, 175
Beat Generation, 42–44, 121
The Beatles, 2, 10, 20, 22, 24–25, 27, 47, 56–57, 64, 66, 79, 138–139, 142, 154, 181
Beck, Jeff, 24, 83
The Bee Gees, 30, 72
Beethoven, Ludwig van, 127, 128
Bellamy, Edward, 41, 45
Benatar, Pat, 5, 170, 173

Benet, William Rose, 18
Benjamin, Walter, 88
Bennett, Andy, 56
Bennett, Tony, 66
Benzon, Bill, 131
Bergson, Henri, 5
Bernstein, Leonard, 131
Berry, Chuck, 16, 20, 22, 23, 27, 29, 65, 88
Big Brother and the Holding Company, 47
Billboard, 51, 77, 181
Bittan, Roy, 166, 167
Black, Cilla, 24
Black Flag, 96, 97
Black Sabbath, 89, 152
Blackwell, Otis, 17
Blair, Tony, 161
Blake, William, 67, 116, 117, 120, 132n1
Blakey, Art, 20
Bledsoe, Jules, 18
Blind Faith, 30
Blondie, 95, 97, 170
Bloom, Allan, 49
Bloomfield, Mike, 25, 38n21
Blue Oyster Cult, 96, 121
blues, 1–4, 7, 15–36, 48–50, 63, 66, 76, 88, 123, 173
Bolan, Marc, 91
Bon Jovi, 161, 164, 183n16
Bond, Graham, 29, 30
Bono (Paul Hewson), 5, 161, 175–178, 180, 185n55–186n56
Boone, Pat, 25
Boston (band), 54
The Boston Globe, 175
The Bowery, 44, 94
Bowie, David, 5, 9, 11, 66, 89, 90, 91–93, 103, 112n7–112n8, 112n14, 116, 138, 139, 173
Boyd, Jenny, 5, 130, 135n55
Boyd, Patti, 6
Bradbury, Ray, 9, 109
Brahms, Johannes, 64
Bramlett, Bonnie, 30
Brave New World: (novel), 98–103; (album), 98
Brill Building, 3, 27
Bring Me the Horizon, 181
Brecker, Michael, 80
Brecker, Randy, 80

Brown, Ruth, 175
Brown, Terry, 107
Browne, Jackson, 124, 125, 132n1, 138
Brownstein, Carrie, 172
Bruce, Jack, 30
Bruford, Bill, 66, 69
Brunswick Records, 18
Buchla, Donald, 68
Buckingham, Lindsey, 33
Bunker, Clive, 71
Burgess, Anthony, 6
Burns, Gary, 57
Burns, Robert, 125
Burroughs, Willliam S., 44, 90, 92
Bush, Kate, 6
The Byrds, 35, 46, 55, 123
Byrne, David, 66
Byron, Lord (George Gordon), 117, 125

Cage, John, 94
Cale, John, 31, 93, 95
Calhoun, Scott, 180, 185n55
Campbell, Joseph, 48, 62, 127
Canned Heat, 23
Capote, Truman, 11
Carlisle, Belinda, 170
Carroll, Lewis (Charles Dodgson), 11, 139
The Cars, 83, 97
Carson, Johnny, 124
Casady, Jack, 47, 50, 52
Cateforis, Theo, 97
Cavern Club, 24, 25
CBGBs, 44, 94, 147, 167
Celtic mysticism, 31
Chandler, Raymond, 26
Chapin, Harry, 140
Chapman, Ian, 92
Charles, Ray, 27
Charles, Ron, 151–152, 157n70
Cheever, John, 147
Chess, Leonard, 16
Chess, Phil, 16
Chess Records, 16, 24, 25
Chicago (band), 142
Chinmoy, Sri, 35
Chopin, Frederic, 64
Christgau, Robert, 11, 64, 66, 79
Churchill, Savannah, 17
civil rights, 50, 123

Clapton, Eric, 6, 20, 24, 29–30, 35
The Clash, 95–96, 148, 154
Clayton, Adam, 175, 176
Clemons, Clarence, 166
Coates, Norma, 171, 174, 184n34
Cobain, Kurt, 21, 116, 122
Cohen, Leonard, 119
Cold War, 87
Coleman, Leon, 18
Coleman, Ray, 25
Coleridge, Samuel Taylor, 6, 107, 115, 117–118, 127, 132n2, 140
Colgrove, Jim, 81–82
Colley, Dennis, 81
Collins, Albert, 20
Collins, Judy, 46
Collins, Phil, 72–73
Coltrane, John, 20, 34–36
Columbia Records, 18, 23, 123
Colvin, Douglas (Dee Dee Ramone), 95
Commerford, Tim, 111
concert for Bangladesh, 159
concert for New York City, 159
Conrad, Joseph Conrad, 110
Cooke, Sam, 20
Cooper, Alice (Vincent Furbay), 91, 173
Copland, Aaron, 65, 68, 117
Corey, Richard, 81
Cornell, Chris, 111
Cornick, Glenn, 71
Cornwell, Hugh, 95
Costello, Elvis (Declan Bailey), 51, 138
counterculture, 1, 41–42, 50–51, 52, 54, 62, 64, 87, 99, 106, 171
Covach, John, 70, 83n2, 142, 155n13
Covington, Joey, 52
Cowart, David, 143–144
Crawdaddy, 47
Cream, 3, 29–30, 39n44
creativity, 1, 5, 8, 49, 51, 66, 93, 115, 129–131, 139, 160, 170
Creedence Clearwater Revival, 49, 88
Creem (magazine), 51, 82
Croce, Jim, 140
Crosby, David, 2, 5, 36, 46, 52–53, 54, 182
Crosby, Stills and Nash, 3, 88, 161
Crosby, Stills, Nash, and Young, 46
Crow, Sheryl, 170, 184n39
Crowe, Cameron, 57

Culture Club, 97
culture texts (recordings as), 138
Cummings, John (Johnny Ramone), 95
Curtis, Ian, 89

Daltrey, Roger, 28
Danko, Rick, 123
Darnielle, John, 152
Daugherty, J. D., 95
Dave Clark Five, 24
Davies, Ray, 129–130, 138
Davis, Cyril, 29
Davis, Miles, 35
Davidson, Donald, 19
De Lillo, Don, 143–145, 156n27
De Nunzio, Keith (Keith Clayton), 147
De Nunzio, Vinny, 147
Deacon, John, 73–74
Dead Kennedys, 97, 154
Dean, James, 55
Dean, Roger, 66, 68
Debussy, Claude, 64
Decca Records, 71
Deep Purple, 2, 71, 97, 141
Def Jam Records, 98
Def Leppard, 181
DeKoven, Marianne, 45
Delancey, Craig, 179–180
Demeski, Stan, 147
demise of rock, 57
Depeche Mode, 64
Derek and the Dominos, 30
Derringer, Rick, 80
Di Bartola, Tiffanie, 152
Dick, Philip K., 109
Dickens, Charles, 43, 101–102
Dickinson, Bruce, 89, 98, 174
Dickinson, Emily, 6
The Dictators, 95
Diddley, Bo (Ellas McDaniel), 16
Didion, Joan, 11
Dio, Ronnie James, 98
Dionysian festival, 48
Dionysus, 49, 173
Dixon, Willie, 15–16, 24, 30, 31
Domino, Fats, 20
The Doors, 2, 50, 63, 88, 120, 156n27, 160, 181
Dore, Florence, 144

Dowd, Tom, 30
Downes, Geoffrey, 70
Doyle, Roddy, 145–146
dreams, 115, 129–131, 139, 160
Dreiser, Theodore, 18
drugs, 44, 45, 47, 48, 50, 51, 63, 77, 78, 144, 145, 147
Dryden, John, 125
Dryden, Spencer, 47
Du Bois, W. E. B., 17
Dudgeon, Gus, 32
Duran Duran, 97
DX7 keyboard, 64
Dylan, Bob, 2, 6–7, 37n10, 47, 51, 55, 66, 71, 89, 118–124, 139–140, 141, 148, 183n16
dystopia, 1, 8, 9, 62, 63, 87–90, 93, 95, 98, 110, 111

The Eagles, 24, 80, 88, 97, 140, 141
Eastern religions, 42, 51, 63, 70, 82
Eastman, Linda, 30, 66
ecology, 8, 11, 110
The Ed Sullivan Show, 25
Eddie and the Hot Rods, 95
The Edge (Dave Evans), 176, 179
Egan, Jennifer, 150–152
Electric Kool-Aid Acid Test (Wolfe), 44
Electric Light Orchestra (ELO), 23, 65
elegy, 125
Eliade, Mircea, 45, 47–48, 130, 173
Elkins, James, 4–5, 132
Ellison, Ralph, 19–20
Emerson, Keith, 63–64, 67–68, 83n2
Emerson, Lake, and Palmer, 49, 61, 63–64, 67–68
Encarnaceo, John, 138, 141
Eno, Brian, 66, 177
Entwistle, John, 28
Erdelyi, Tommy (Tommy Ramone), 95
Ertegun, Ahmet, 30
Essex, David, 181
E Street Band, 165
Etheridge, Melissa, 170, 171, 173
Evan, John, 71
Everett, Walter, 12n2, 142
Everly Brothers, 20, 25

Fairport Convention, 71

Fall Out Boy, 181
Faltskog, Agnetha, 175
Federici, Danny, 167
The Feelies, 147
Ferlinghetti, Lawrence, 43, 44, 59n23
Fier, Anton, 147
The Fillmore, 47
Fillmore East, 36, 71
Five Finger Death Punch, 181
Fleetwood, Mick, 32
Fleetwood Mac, 24, 29, 32–33, 71, 129, 162, 173
FM radio, 47
Fogelberg, Dan, 66
Fogerty, John, 88
folk, 1, 2, 3, 7, 19, 21, 24, 52
Foo Fighters, 181
Ford, Henry, 100, 102
Ford, Lita, 174
Foreigner, 97
Foster, Stephen, 44
Fowlie, Wallace, 120
Frampton, Peter, 4
Franklin, Aretha, 170
Freed, Allan, 16
Fresh, Doug E., 98
Freud, Sigmund, 96
Fricke, David, 94
Frieerg, David, 52
Frith, Simon, 20, 38n23, 41, 64, 118

Gabriel, Peter, 51, 71–73
Gaiman, Neil, 53
garage rock, 96
Garcia, Jerry, 35, 46, 47, 48, 52, 63
Garrett, Amos, 81
Gaye, Marvin, 153
Geldof, Bob, 160–162, 186n56
gender, 173–174
Genesis, 61, 63, 65, 69, 71–73
Gentle Giant, 61, 83n2
Gers, Janik, 98
Gershwin, George, 27, 35–36
Gershwin, Ira, 3
Ghost, 181
Giger, H. R., 65
Ginastera, Alberto, 65, 67
Ginsberg, Allen, 43, 44, 88–89, 121
Gitlin, Todd, 50

glam rock, 95
Gleason, Ralph, 49
Glitter, Gary, 95
globalization, 162
Goethe, Johann Wolfgang von, 5, 6
Goffin, Gerry, 27
Gordon, Kim, 66, 170, 172
Gothicism, 117, 118
Gouldman, Graham, 24
Gracyk, Theodore, 17, 138
Grainger, Porter, 19
Gramm, Phil, 97
Grand Funk, 75, 83
The Grateful Dead, 3, 8, 32, 35, 47–48, 49, 59n33, 63, 130
Green Day, 96
Green, Peter, 25, 32–33
Greenman, Ben, 153
Greenslade, Arthur, 71
Gress, Jessie, 83
Greta Van Fleet, 181–182
Guns n' Roses, 181
Guthrie, Woody, 37n10, 169
Guy, Buddy, 16

Hackett, Steve, 65, 72–73, 84n13
Haitian relief, 182
Hammerstein, Oscar, 3
Hamersveld, John Van, 66
Hammond organ, 61, 64, 72
Hardy, Dave, 66
Harris, Steve, 11, 98
Harrison, George, 24, 27, 51
Harry, Deborah, 170, 175
Hart, Lorenz, 3
Hart, Mickey, 47–48, 130
Hartz, Liam, 146
Harvey, P. J., 170
Haslam, Annie, 67
Hassan, Ihab, 87
Hawkes, Greg, 83
Hawkins, Coleman, 17
Hawkwind, 66
Hawthorne, Nathaniel, 89
Headon, Nicky, 96
Heart, 140, 170
heavy metal, 51, 117
Hegel, G. W. F., 106, 126, 127–128
Heider, Wally, 52

Heine, Heinrich, 6
Heinlein, Robert, 9, 52, 53–54, 69
Hell, Richard, 94, 147
Helm, Levon, 123
Hendrix, Jimi, 9, 16, 24, 33–34, 35, 47, 50, 63, 88, 160
Henke, James, 177
Hentschel, Dave, 72
Herman's Hermits, 24
hero's journey, 62
Hesse, Hermann, 6, 69
Hilburn, Robert, 167
Hill, Lauren, 161
Hillman, James, 129
hip hop/rap, 97
Hoffman, Abbie, 29
Hofmann, E. T. A., 116, 119, 128, 134n45
Holden, Stephen, 160, 182n1
Holderlin, Friedrich, 119
Holiday, Billie, 43
Holland-Dozier-Holland, 76
Hollander, John, 6
The Hollies, 20, 24
Holly, Buddy, 20, 29
Holmes, John Clellan, 43
Holst, Gustav, 65, 125
Home Box Office (HBO), 57
Hopkins, Lightnin', 49
Hopper, Hugh, 68
Horkheimer, Max, 99
Horn, Jim, 80, 82
Hornsby, Bruce, 142
Hot Tuna, 50, 52
Howe, Steve, 65, 67, 69, 70–71, 83n2
Howlin' Wolf, 15–16, 24, 29, 32
Hudson, Garth, 123
Hughes, Langston, 18, 19, 37n14, 38n17
human rights, 11
Hurston, Zora Neale, 16
Husker-Du, 4
Huxley, Aldous, 63, 89, 98–104, 147
Huxley, Julian, 99
Hyman, Jeffrey (Joey Ramone), 95
Hynde, Chriss, 170, 172, 173

Idol, Billy, 95
imagination, 1, 4–5, 8, 9, 11, 12, 61, 65, 111, 115, 116–117, 119, 129, 137, 138, 139, 159, 160

Incredible String Band, 71
Incubus, 181
Inglis, Ian, 17, 27, 45
Irish troubles, 179
Iron Butterfly, 3
Iron Maiden, 4, 5, 62, 89, 98, 118, 174

Jackson, Janet, 175
Jackson, Mahalia, 175
Jackson, Wanda, 175
Jagger, Mick, 25, 26, 38n36, 57, 126, 155
James, Elmore, 32–33
James, Etta, 16, 175
James, William, 5, 131, 139
Jameson, Frederic, 87
Janacek, Leos, 64
jazz, 1, 6, 17, 20, 34–36, 41, 43, 44, 139
Jefferson Airplane, 6, 8, 47–52, 54, 63, 142, 173
Jefferson Starship, 50–51, 52, 54, 173
Jerome, Judson, 45
Jethro Tull, 61, 65, 71, 89
Jett, Joan, 170, 171, 173–175
Joel, Billy, 4, 140
John, Elton, 4, 15, 139, 142, 161
Johnson, Robert, 23, 25, 29–32
Johnson, Samuel, 126
Jones, Brian, 25, 26–27
Jones, Mick, 96
Jones, Nemiah, 29
Joplin, Janis, 9, 66, 116, 170, 171, 173
Joyce, James, 6
Judas Priest, 4, 89, 98
Jung, C. G., 130, 135n56

Kael, Pauline, 44
Kahn, Chaka, 175
Kansas (band), 6
Kant, Immanuel, 126
Kantner, China, 52
Kantner, Paul, 47, 50, 52–54, 88
Kaukonen, Jorma, 47, 49, 50, 52, 54
Kaukonen, Peter, 52
Kaye, Lenny, 4, 95, 96, 112n18
Kaylan, Howard, 124
Keats, John, 6, 117, 122, 125, 127–129
Keeshan, Dave, 154
Keith, Ben, 81
Kellogg, Carolyn, 152

Kelly, Tara, 153
Kelson, John, 80, 82
Kennedy, Robert, 26
Kent State, 9
Kerouac, Jack, 6, 42, 43
Kesey, Ken, 44
Kuehnert, Stephanie, 152, 154
Kierkegaard, Soren, 128
King, Albert, 30
King, B. B., 20, 32
King, Carole, 27, 76
King, Freddie, 15, 32
King, Stephen, 11
King Crimson, 61, 65, 67, 69
The Kinks, 7, 21, 24, 28, 29
Kirwan, Danny, 32, 33
Kitts, Thomas, 129, 132n1, 135n50
Knight, Gladys, 175
Knopfler, Mark, 88
Koestler, Arthur, 89, 182n1
Kogale, Robbie, 80
Korner, Alex, 20
Kraftlub, 163
Kral, Ivan, 95
Kramer, Lawrence, 35–36, 39n64, 127, 141
Kreutzmann, Bill, 48
Kristal, Hilly, 95

Lady Gaga, 170, 173
Lake, Greg, 63, 64, 67–68
Landau, Jon, 30, 47
Lanois, Daniel, 177
Larsen, Nella, 16
Lauper, Cindi, 150, 170
Lead Belly, 17, 19, 21, 24, 37n10
League, Michael, 46
Lear, Edward, 139
Leary, Dennis, 57
Leary, Timothy, 44, 45, 50, 63
Led Zeppelin, 2, 3, 23, 29, 31–32, 65, 118, 181
Lee, Alvin, 3, 29
Lee, Geddy (Gary Weinreb), 103, 106–108, 110
Le Guin, Ursula, 9
Lennon, John, 5, 10, 12n2, 22, 24, 27, 47, 57, 66, 79, 125, 138–139, 159
Lesh, Phil, 48, 59n40

Lethem, Jonathan, 148–150
Lewis, C. S., 52, 90
Lewis, Jerry Lee, 20, 51
Lieb, Kristin, 171–172
Lifeson, Alex (Zivojinovich), 103, 106, 107
Lightfoot, Gordon, 140
Lindquist, Mark, 153
Liszt, Franz, 64, 117
Little Richard, 20, 27, 29, 51
Live Aid, 11, 159, 160–161
L.L. Cool J, 98
Lloyd, Richard, 147
Lomax, Alan, 17, 19, 37n10
Lomax, John, 19, 37n10
Lorenz, Konrad, 96–97
Los Angeles Times, 152
Lott, Eric, 17
Love, Courtney, 170
Love, Darlene, 175
Lovejoy, A. O., 116
Lowe, James, 78, 79
LSD, 44, 45, 50, 51, 63
Lukacs, Georg, 116
Lyngstad, Anni-Frid, 175
Lynott, Phil, 146

Macan, Edward, 62, 67, 84n13, 106
MacLuhan, Marshall, 160
Madonna, 153, 161, 170, 173, 175, 184n34
Mahavishnu Orchestra, 35
Mailer, Norman, 11
Mama Cass, 175
Manfred Mann, 29
Mann, Aimee, 170
Mann, Thomas, 6
Manuel, Richard, 123
Mapplethorpe, Robert, 66
Marcus, Greil, 1, 11, 26, 137, 161
Marcuse, Herbert, 45, 99
Marilyn Manson, 181
the Marquee Club, 71
Marsden, Gerry, 24
Marsh, Dave, 64, 66, 167, 168
Martha and the Vandellas, 76
Martin, Bill, 64
Marx, Karl, 99, 106
The Matrix, 111
Matthews, Dave, 161

Max, Peter, 66
Max's Kansas City, 147
May, Brian, 73–74, 84n18
Mayall, John, 29, 71
Mayfield, Curtis, 153
MC5, 96
McCartney, Paul, 12n2, 24, 27, 66, 139, 181
McClary, Susan, 141, 171, 184n34
McClure, Michael, 43
McCullers, Carson, 19
McDowell, Fred, 26
McGee, Celia, 152
McGuire, Barry, 89
McKernan, Ron, 48
McLaughlin, John, 35, 51
McLean, Don, 55–56
McTell, Blind Willie, 26
McVie, Christine, 33, 173, 175
McVie, John, 32
Meat Loaf, 83, 140
Megadeth, 181
Meisel, Perry, 10, 17, 24, 116, 122, 133n6
Mellencamp, John, 66, 140
Mellotron, 61, 68, 69, 72
Melnick, Monte, 95
Melody Maker, 91, 95, 112n7, 177
Meltzer, Richard, 47
Melville, Herman, 89
memory, 56–57
Mercer, Glenn, 147
Mercer, Johnny, 3
Mercury Records, 105
Mercury, Freddie, 66, 73–74
Metallica, 2, 11, 89, 98, 112n18, 113n31, 140, 181
Meyer, Leonard, 127
Miley, Bubba, 17
Million, Bill, 147
Minahan, John, 125, 127
minstrel shows, 16
Mitchell, Joni, 7, 46, 66, 125, 170, 175
Mitchell, Mitch, 34
modes, 142
mods, 28
Monterey Pop Festival, 34, 174
Moody, Rick, 147–148, 156n38
The Moody Blues, 2, 63–65, 129, 142
Moog, Robert, 68

Moon, Keith, 28, 162
Moorcock, Michael, 104
Moraz, Patrick, 70
Morello, Tom, 111
Morris, William, 90
Morrison, Jim, 119–120
Morrison, Sterling, 93
Morse code, 108
Motown, 16, 73, 170, 175
Mott the Hoople, 94
Mountain, 30
Mozart, W. A., 5, 128
MTV, 11
Mullen, Larry, 176, 178
Mundi, Billy, 81
Murray, Charles Shaar, 34, 95
Muse, 181
Musset, Alfred de, 116

Nabokov, Vladimir, 6, 130
narrative, 56, 57, 138–139, 141
Nash, Graham, 24, 46, 52, 66
National Health, 69
Neal, William, 65
new journalism, 11
New York Dolls, 67, 75, 83, 91, 94, 173
Nickelback, 140
Nicks, Stevie, 33, 173, 175
Nico (Crista Paffgen), 93, 95
Nietzsche, Friedrich, 6, 89, 106, 118
Nine Inch Nails, 89
Nirvana, 141, 142, 153
Nisenson, Eric, 34–36, 39n55
Nixon, Richard, 50
Nizami, Ganjavi, 6
No Doubt, 172
Nora, Pierre, 56
Norfleet, Cecelia, 81
nostalgia, 55, 56–57, 149
Novalis (Friedrich von Hardenberg), 118, 119
Numan, Gary, 63, 64, 110
Nyro, Laura, 170
The Naz, 75

Ochs, Phil, 118
O'Connor, Flannery, 19
O'Connor, Sinead, 170
odes, 125

One Flew Over the Cuckoo's Nest (Kesey), 44
Ono, Yoko, 66
Orr, David, 121
Orwell, George, 6, 89, 90–91, 100
Orwell, Sonia, 90
Osborne, Ozzy, 89

Page, Jimmy, 20, 31, 118
Palmer, Carl, 63, 67, 68
Papalardi, Felix, 30
Patti Smith Group, 95, 97, 121
Pattison, Robert, 49, 116, 118–119
Paul Butterfield Band, 81
payola, 16
Pearl Jam, 140, 151
Pearlman, Sandy, 96
Peart, Neil, 89, 103–110
Peck, Dale, 148, 157n40
Peckham, Morse, 116
Pennebaker, D. A., 123
Perrotta, Tom, 153, 154
Petty, Tom, 41
Phair, Liz, 170
Phillips, Anthony, 71
Phillips, Michelle, 175
Pink Floyd, 61, 63, 66, 71, 104, 127, 181
Plant, Robert, 31, 32, 139
Poe, Edgar Allan, 5–6, 89
poetry, 5, 7, 115, 121–122, 125–128
The Police, 6
Polygram Records, 105
Pop, Iggy, 91, 93, 95, 154
Pope, Alexander, 125
Porter, Cole, 3
post 9/11 music, 163–164
Poster, Mark, 109
Pound, Ezra, 6
Presley, Elvis, 20, 22, 27, 29, 51, 55
The Pretenders, 170
Pretty Things, 29
Prince, 89, 153
Prince, Prairie, 83
Procol Harum, 49, 61, 64
progressive rock, 49, 50, 61–67
Prophets of Rage, 111
Proust, Marcel, 6
psychedelia, 61–63, 65, 66, 174
Public Broadcasting System (PBS), 46

Index 205

punk/new wave, 4, 94–95, 97, 172

Quatro, Suzi, 170
Quicksilver Messenger Service, 47, 49, 52
Queen, 6, 73–75, 173

radio airplay, 16, 46, 67, 108, 148
Radiohead, 89
Rage against the Machine, 89, 111
Rakha, Alla, 48
Raitt, Bonnie, 170, 171, 175
The Ramones, 94–96, 97, 149, 154
Rand, Ayn, 105–107
Ratt, 4
Ravel, Maurice, 64
RCA Records, 47, 91
rebellion, 1, 2, 4, 7, 25, 28, 41, 115, 116, 127, 130, 132, 171, 176
The Record Plant, 80
records, 56
Redding, Noel, 33
Redding, Otis, 153
Reed, Lou, 6, 91, 93–95, 112n14
Reeves, Martha, 175
reggae, 96
Reich, Charles, 8, 48, 63
REM, 51, 97, 161
Renaissance, 67
REO Speedwagon, 4
The Replacements, 4
Rexroth, Kenneth, 43
Reynolds, Blind Joe, 29
Rice, Elmer, 19
Richards, Keith, 25, 26, 118, 126
Richman, Jonathan, 95
Ricks, Christopher, 121
Riggs, Derek, 98
Rimbaud, Arthur, 82, 119–122, 133n18, 172
Riot Grrrl, 171, 172
ritual, 140
Roach, Max, 20
Robertson, Robbie, 123
Robeson, Paul, 18
Robinson, Cynthia, 175
Robinson, Vicki Sue, 81
rock music in fiction, 10, 137–143
Rodden, John, 91
Rodgers, Richard, 3

Rolling Stone (magazine), 11, 30, 47, 48, 56, 63, 77, 78, 91, 111n1, 160, 167, 171, 177
The Rolling Stones, 23, 24–27, 29, 38n32, 58, 88, 93, 123, 126, 161, 184n23
Romanticism, 9, 12, 61, 111, 115–132
Romney, Hugh (Wavy Gravy), 44
rondo form, 64
The Ronettes, 175
Ronson, Mick, 91
Ronstadt, Linda, 175
Ross, Diana, 175
Roszak, Theodore, 8, 42, 50, 87, 130
Roth, Philip, 143
Rotten, Johnny, 95
Rouget, Gilbert, 131
Roxy Music, 94, 95
RSO Records, 30
Ruff, Hope, 81
Run D.M.C., 98
Rundgren, Todd, 75–83
Rush, 4, 6, 66, 89, 103–110
Rush, Otis, 16, 32
Rutherford, Mike, 71, 73

San Francisco, 42, 43, 47, 49, 51, 63
Sandburg, Carl, 17
Santana, 3, 24, 32, 63, 79, 132
Saturday Review, 18
Sauter, Brenda, 147
Scher, Stephen Paul, 6
Schippers, Mimi, 171, 174
Schoenberg, Arnold, 48
Schopenhauer, Arthur, 118
Schubert, Franz, 6
Schuckett, Ralph, 83
Schumann, Robert, 6, 131
science fiction, 8, 9, 52–54, 66, 67, 69, 74, 89–92, 104–105
Scorcese, Martin, 57
Scorpions, 4
Scott, Ken, 90
The Searchers, 24
Seeger, Pete, 7, 169
Seger, Bob, 140, 142
Seiler, Rachel, 178, 180
Serling, Rod, 9, 104
Sex Pistols, 95, 112n20
Shakespeare, William, 6, 100

shamanism, 48, 120, 130
Shankar, Ravi, 48
Shelley, Mary, 90, 174–175
Shelley, Percy Bysshe, 26, 116–119, 126, 128, 130, 182
Shepherd, John, 143
Shirley, Kevin, 98
The Shirelles, 175
Simon, Carly, 140, 172
Simon, Paul, 6, 96, 119, 125, 162
Simone, Nina, 175
Sincero, Jen, 152
skiffle, 24
Slayer, 98
Slick, Grace, 47, 50–53, 170, 173, 174
Sloan, P. J., 89
Sly and the Family Stone, 16, 153, 175
Smashing Pumpkins, 181
Smith, Adrian, 98
Smith, Bessie, 18–19, 24, 38n17, 175
Smith, Charlotte, 175
Smith, Patti, 66, 82, 95, 97, 119, 121, 154, 170–174
The Smiths, 97
Snyder, Gary, 43
social justice, 8, 46
Soft Machine, 63, 68
Sohl, Richard, 95
song cycle, 127
Sonic Youth, 66, 170
Sorrel, Rosalie, 52
Sparks, 75, 95
Spencer, Jeremy, 32
Spencer Davis Group, 24, 29, 71
Spiotta, Dana, 152
spirituals, 3
Springfield, Dusty, 175
Springsteen, Bruce, 6, 11, 41, 88, 89, 104, 118, 121, 138, 140, 164–170, 176
Squire, Chris, 67, 69
Squires, Constance, 152
The Staple Singers, 175
Stapledon, Olaf, 90
Starr, Ringo, 66, 139
Steely Dan, 97, 140
Stefani, Gwen, 170, 172
Stein, Chris, 95
Steinbeck, John, 5, 167, 168
Steinman, Jim, 83, 140

Stevens, Becca, 46
Stevens, Cat, 66
Stevens, Guy, 96
Stewart, Chris, 72
Stigwood, Robert, 30
Stills, Stephen, 2, 46, 54
Sting, 6, 88, 161
Stipe, Michael, 51
Stone, Steve, 98
The Stooges, 67, 95, 151
Stravinsky, Igor, 48, 125
Strickland, Bobby, 83
Strummer, Joe, 95–96, 113n23
Styron, William, 19
Sultan, Kasim, 83
Summer, Donna, 175
Summer of Love, 42
Supertramp, 129
surrealism, 62
Swift, Jonathan, 130
Sylvan, Robin, 45
Syme, Hugh, 66, 108, 110
synesthesia, 62
System of a Down, 181

Talese, Gay, 11
Talking Heads, 95, 97, 157n46
Tallent, Gary, 167
Tart, Charles, 5, 131
Taylor, Charles, 116
Taylor, James, 125
Taylor, Roger, 6, 73, 74
Tchaikovsky, Peter Illych, 65
Television, 95, 112n18, 167
The Temptations, 140, 141
Ten Years After, 3
Tharpe, Sister Rosetta, 175
Thin Lizzy, 146
Thompson, Hunter S., 11
Thornton, Big Mama, 27
Thunders, Johnny, 154
Tieck, Ludwig, 118
Tin Pan Alley, 3, 25
Tolkein, J. R. R., 6, 109
Tom Petty and the Heartbreakers, 41
Toomer, Jean, 16
Townshend, Pete, 2, 28–29, 51, 66, 94, 118, 138
Traffic, 63, 117

Index 207

trance, 47, 131
Trouser Press, 177
Trower, Robin, 79
Trump, Donald, 26
Tucker, Maureen, 93
Tuff Darts, 95
Turbeville, Dan, 81
Turner, Tina, 175
The Turtles, 83, 123
The Twilight Zone, 104
Tyler, Steven, 12

U2, 5, 161, 175–180, 185n40, 185n43, 185n46
Uggams, Leslie, 17
unconscious, 5, 92, 115, 129, 130, 131
United Nations, 180
utopia, 1, 8, 9, 41, 44–45, 62, 87, 100, 106, 159
Utopia (band), 75

Van Halen, 4
Van Halen, Eddie, 116
Van Vechten, Carl, 17–19
Vanilla Fudge, 71
Varese, Edgard, 125
Vaughan, Stevie Ray, 23
Veggian, Henry, 144
The Velvet Underground, 2, 66–67, 88, 93–94, 95, 112n15, 147
Verlaine, Paul, 119, 122
Vernon, Mike, 32
Vicious, Sid, 95
Vietnam, 44, 50, 152, 176
visual art, 65–66, 74
Vito, Rick, 82
Volman, Mark, 83, 124
Vonnegut, Kurt, 89

Wagner, Richard, 5, 118
Waits, Tom, 124
Wakeman, Rick, 65, 68–69, 70
Wallas, Graham, 131
Waller, Fats, 17
Walser, Robert, 31, 141, 143, 174
Warhol, Andy, 66, 94
Warren, Harry, 3
Warren, Robert Penn, 19
Washington, Dinah, 175

Watergate, 9, 50, 87
Waters, Muddy, 15–16, 20, 29
Waters, Roger, 66
Watt, Ian, 144
Watts, Alan, 51
Watts, Charlie, 25, 126
"We Are the World," 180
Webern, Anton, 48
Weckerman, Dave, 147
Weezer, 181
Weinberg, Max, 168
Weinstein, Deena, 45, 104, 174
Weir, Bob, 48
Welch, Bob, 33
Welleck, Rene, 116
Wells, H. G., 89, 99
Wells, Junior, 16
Wenner, Jann, 30, 47
West, Leslie, 30
West, Nathanael, 124
Whalen, Philip, 43
White, Jack, 181
Whitesnake, 4
Whitman, Walt, 6
The Who, 7, 24, 28–29, 117, 126, 138, 142, 151, 162, 164, 183n11
Williams, Larry, 27
Williams, Lucinda, 170
Williams, Paul, 47
Williams, Tony, 35
Williamson, Sonny Boy, 15, 29, 32
Willis, Ellen, 93–94, 112n20, 124
Willis, Michelle, 46
Wilson, Ann, 175
Wilson, Brian, 3
Wilson, Mary, 175
Wilson, Nancy, 175
Winehouse, Amy, 170
Winter, Johnny, 20
Winwood, Stevie, 24, 142
Wolfe, Tom, 11, 44
Wollstonecraft, Mary, 175
Womack, Kenneth, 57
women in rock, 159, 170
women's rights, 8, 11, 45
Wonder, Stevie, 125, 161
Wood, Ronnie, 38n32, 66
Woodstock, 8, 28, 34, 42, 46, 50, 57, 80, 81, 87, 161, 171

"Woodstock" (song), 46
Wordsworth, William, 116, 117, 119, 127, 128
Wright, Richard, 20

The Yardbirds, 7, 24, 29, 63, 117, 118
Yes, 49, 61, 63, 65, 66, 68–70, 83n2, 117
Yogananda, Swami Paramahansa, 70

Young, Neil, 1, 46, 51, 140, 182
The Youngbloods, 8

Zamyatin, Yvgeny, 9, 89, 104
Zappa, Frank, 3, 4, 35, 47, 124, 139, 141
Zevon, Warren, 124
The Zombies, 3

About the Author

Robert McParland is professor of English at Felician University and a member of the American Society of Composers, Authors and Publishers (ASCAP). His popular music writings include publications on The Beatles, The Who, U2, Bruce Springsteen, Paul Simon, and American lyricists. His books include *Beyond Gatsby: How Fitzgerald, Hemingway and the Writers of the 1920s Shaped American Culture*, *From Native Son to King's Men: The Literary Landscape of the 1940s*, *Citizen Steinbeck*, *Mark Twain's Audience*, and *Charles Dickens's Audience*.

www.ingramcontent.com/pod-product-compliance
Lightning Source LLC
Chambersburg PA
CBHW050905300426
44111CB00010B/1386